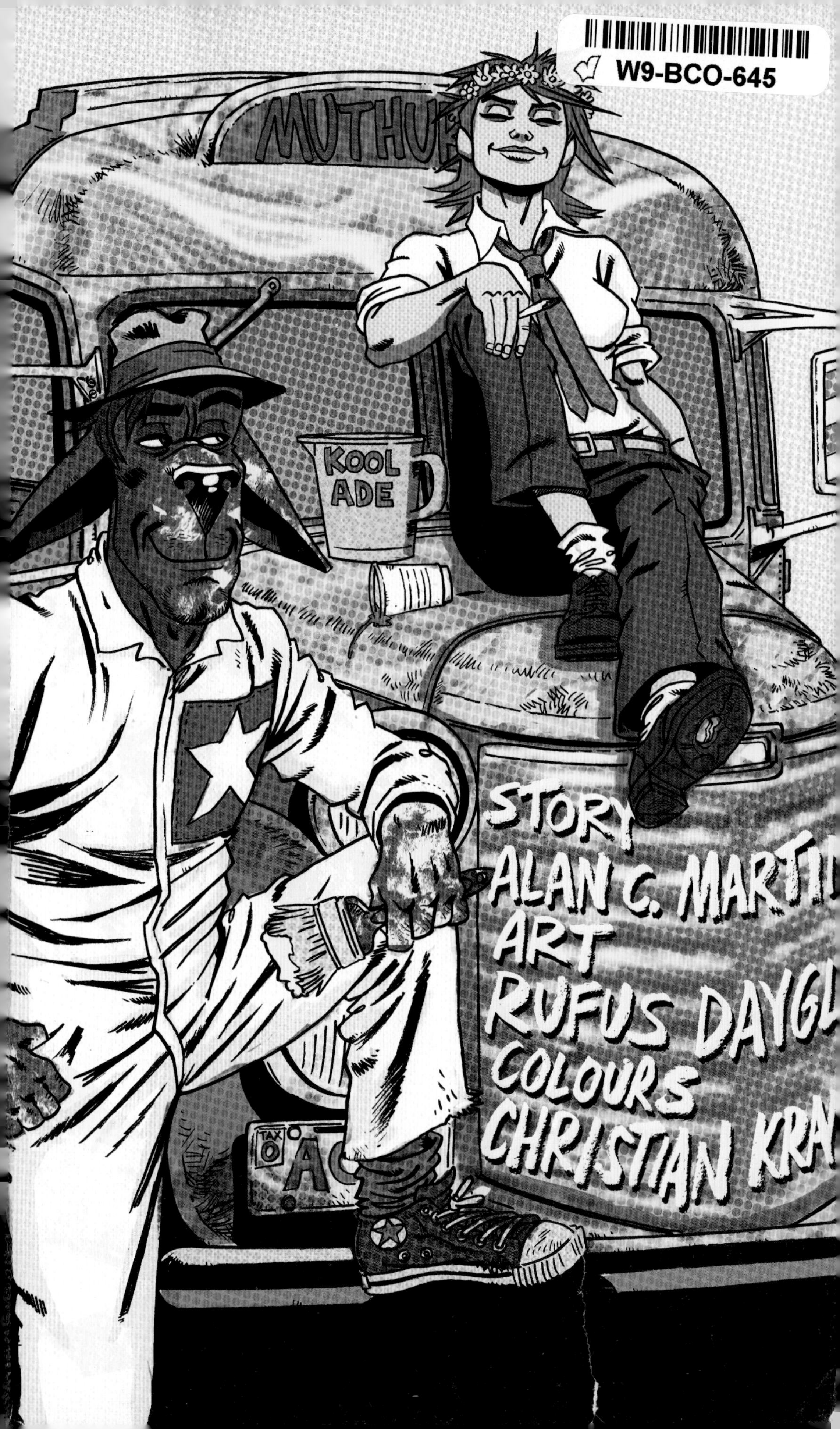

MUTHU
KOOL ADE
STORY
ALAN C. MARTI
ART
RUFUS DAYGL
COLOURS
CHRISTIAN KRA

Original Series Edits by CHRIS RYALL & TOM WALTZ • Letters by ROBBIE ROBBINS & CHRIS MOWRY
Collection Edits by MARIAH HUEHNER • Cover Artwork by ASHLEY WOOD

ISBN: 978-1-60010-280-6
11 10 09 08   1 2 3 4
www.IDWPUBLISHING.com

IDW PUBLISHING: OPERATIONS
Moshe Berger, Chairman / Ted Adams, President / Matthew Ruzicka, CPA, Controller / Alan Payne, VP of Sales / Lorelei Bunjes, Dir. of Digital Services / Marci Hubbard, Executive Assistant / Alonzo Simon, Shipping Manager

EDITORIAL
Chris Ryall, Publisher/Editor-in-Chief / Scott Dunbier, Editor, Special Projects / Andy Schmidt, Senior Editor / Justin Eisinger, Editor / Kris Oprisko, Editor/Foreign Lic. / Denton J. Tipton, Editor / Tom Waltz, Editor / Mariah Huehner, Assistant Editor

DESIGN
Robbie Robbins, EVP/Sr. Graphic Artist / Ben Templesmith, Artist/Designer / Neil Uyetake, Art Director / Chris Mowry, Graphic Artist / Amauri Osorio, Graphic Artist

STAND BY WHILE I PAD YOUR SKULL...

THE ORIGINAL INSPIRATION FOR *VISIONS OF BOOGA* CAME AFTER A VIEWING OF BILLY WILDER'S *SOME LIKE IT HOT*. I WANTED TO PITCH TANK GIRL AND BOOGA AGAINST THE WORLD WITHOUT A PENNY TO THEIR NAME (WHICH WAS ALWAYS MY FAVOURITE OPENING IN LAUREL AND HARDY'S FILMS), AND HAVE THEM TRAVEL ACROSS A CONTINENT TO ESCAPE THE CLUTCHES OF THE EVIL MOB. ONCE THEY WERE OUT ON THE ROAD, I COULDN'T HELP MY OLD PERENNIAL INSPIRATIONS OF THE BEAT GENERATION AND EARLY HIPPYDOM FILTERING INTO THE MIX, SO THINGS STARTED TO WARP A LITTLE FROM THERE ON IN.

ULTIMATELY THE VISIONS THAT BOOGA BRINGS ABOUT BY READING THE MYSTICAL OLD BEAT GENERATION BOOK OUT LOUD ARE NOTHING MORE THAN THE QUESTIONS THAT WERE ARISING IN MY MIND AS I WAS WRITING IT ("WHY AM I WRITING THIS?", " IS STOR JUST COMMENTARY OR IS IT LIFE CHANGING? WORLD CHANGING?", " OR IS MY JOB TO SUPPLY A CERTAIN SMALL SECTION OF SOCIETY WITH THE SATISFACTION THAT SOMEONE OUT THERE CAN RELATE TO THE STRANGE THOUGHTS IN THEIR HEADS?") WHEN I SHOULD HAVE BEEN FOCUSING ON THE PLOT, CHARACTERIZATION AND STORY TWISTS THAT WOULD HAVE DELIVERED ANSWERS TO ALL THE ABOVE.

THAT SAID, I THINK THE FINAL PIECE WORKS VERY WELL AS A WHOLE - FAR SLOWER AND MORE DOWNBEAT THAN TANK GIRL HAS EVER BEEN BEFORE, AND SOMEHOW DELIVERING INSIGHT AND PATHOS IN ITS OWN RIDICULOUS WAY.

RUFUS REALLY GOT HIS TEETH INTO THIS ONE, AT LAST GIVEN THE CHANCE TO EVOLVE HIS OWN TAKE ON TANK GIRL WITH BRILLIANT STYLE AND PANACHE, WITH FINAL FLOURISHES FROM WUNDERKIND COLOURIST CHRISTIAN PUTTING A GREAT BIG CHERRY ON THE CAKE (I LOVE HOW THE STARK, COLD BLUENESS OF THE EAST COAST AT THE START OF THE STORY SLOWLY MORPHS INTO THE RICH SUN-DRENCHED SATURATION OF THE WEST COAST IN THE FINAL PAGES).

I HOPE YOU ENJOY *VISIONS OF BOOGA*, IT'S ALREADY ONE OF MY PERSONAL FAVOURITES.

PLANT YOU NOW, DIG YOU LATER.

ALAN C. MARTIN

THE RED SQUIRREL HIDE
PAXTON HOUSE
BERWICKSHIRE
AUGUST 2008

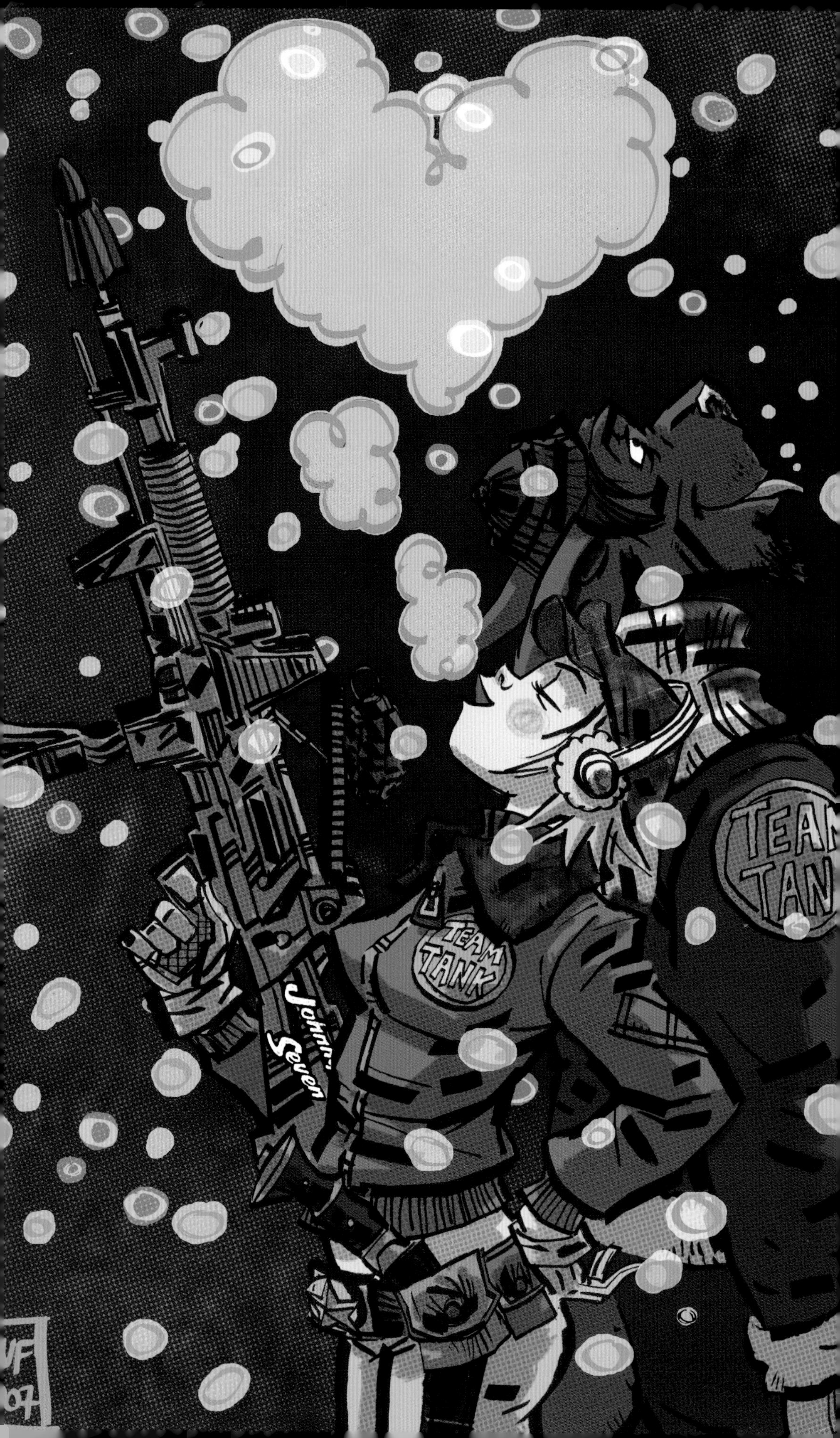
TEAM TANK
Johnny Seven

TANK GIRL

A FEISTY, SEXY, ANGRY, OVERLY FASHION CONSCIOUS, RENEGADE TANK-PILOT WITH A PARTICULARLY BENT SENSE OF HUMOUR. SHE LEFT THE ARMY SOME TIME AGO AND TOOK THEIR BEST TANK WITH HER.

FAVOURITE FILM: *GODZILLA VS MOTHRA.*

FAVOURITE LP: *THE ROLLING STONES – THEIR SATANIC MAJESTIES REQUEST.*

LIKES: KIDNEY BEANS.

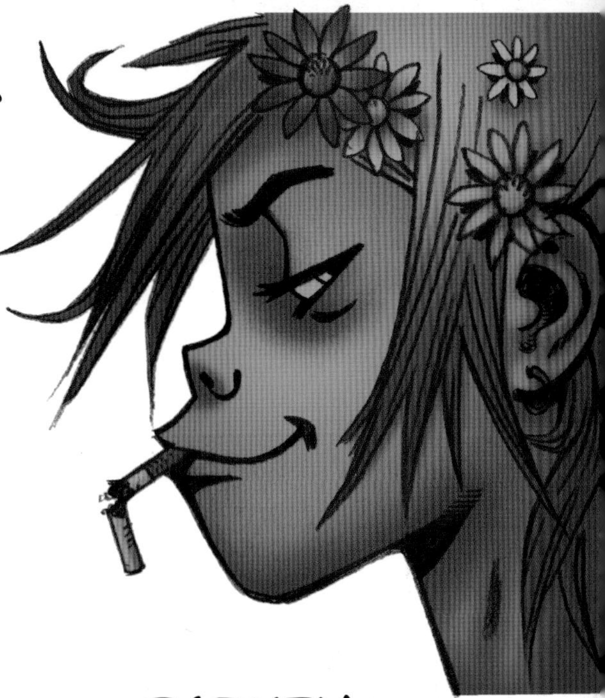

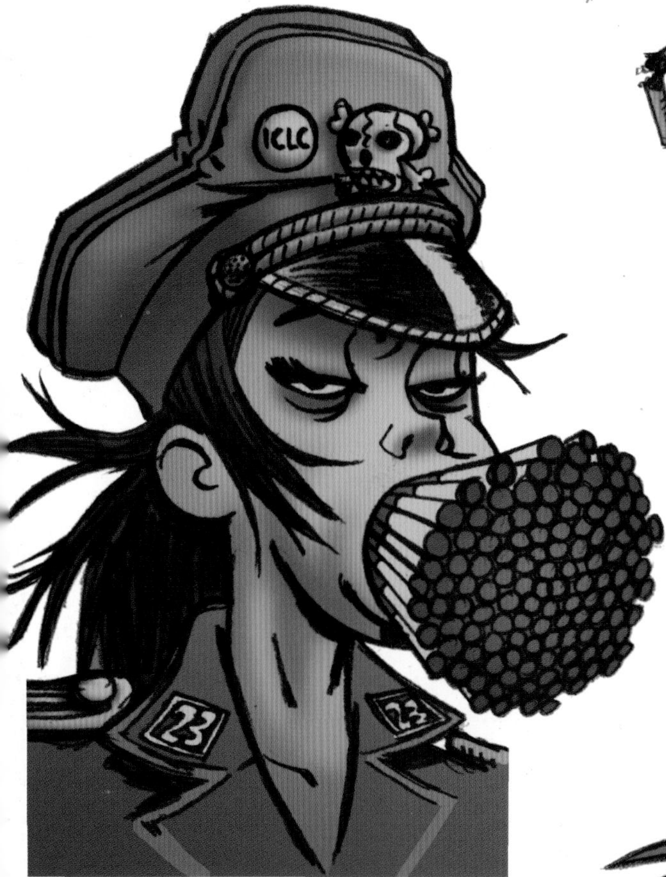
ICLC
23
23

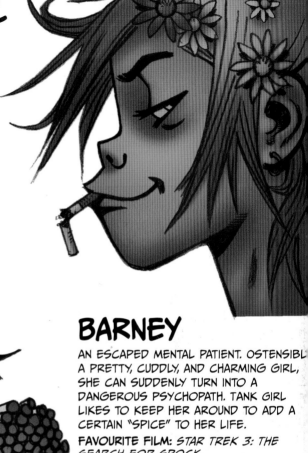

BARNEY

AN ESCAPED MENTAL PATIENT. OSTENSIBL A PRETTY, CUDDLY, AND CHARMING GIRL, SHE CAN SUDDENLY TURN INTO A DANGEROUS PSYCHOPATH. TANK GIRL LIKES TO KEEP HER AROUND TO ADD A CERTAIN "SPICE" TO HER LIFE.

FAVOURITE FILM: *STAR TREK 3: THE SEARCH FOR SPOCK.*

FAVOURITE LP: *MUD – MUD ROCK.*

LIKES: CLAMBAKES.

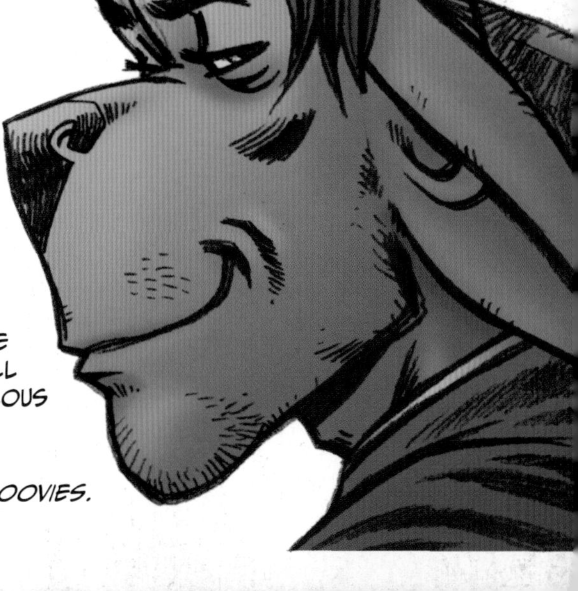

BOOGA

TANK GIRL'S DOPEY KANGAROO BOYFRIEND. MOVED INTO THE TANK ONE DAY WITHOUT BEING INVITED AND HAS STAYED EVER SINCE. OFTEN THE BUTT OF TANK GIRL'S JOKES, HE IS ALWAYS WELL MEANING AND EAGER TO JOIN IN ON ANY RIDICULOUS SCHEME THAT COMES HIS WAY.

FAVOURITE FILM: *SOME KIND OF WONDERFUL.*

FAVOURITE LP: *TEENAGE HEAD – THE FLAMIN' GROOVIES.*

LIKES: SOFT PYJAMAS.

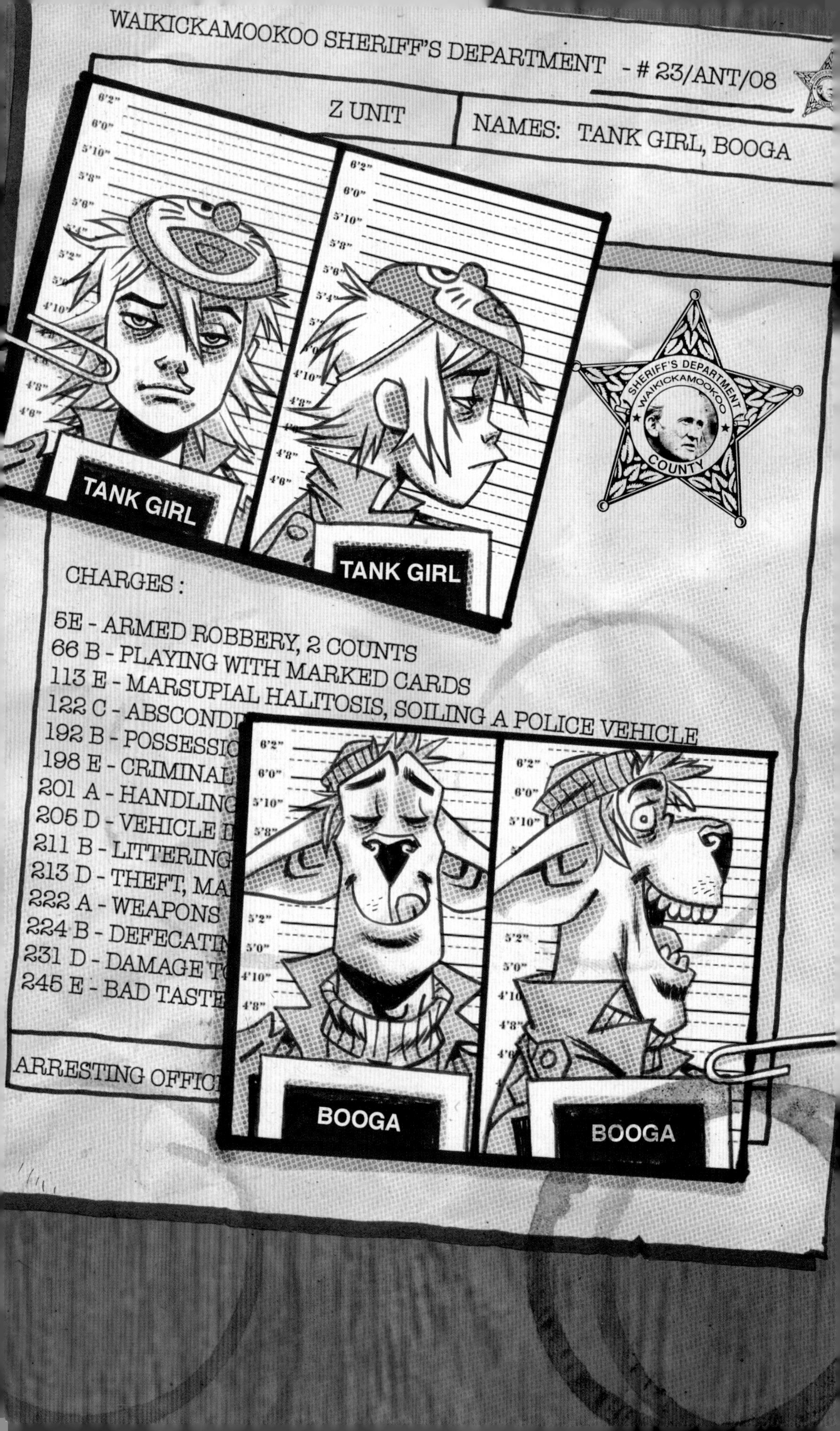
WAIKICKAMOOKOO SHERIFF'S DEPARTMENT - # 23/ANT/08
Z UNIT
NAMES: TANK GIRL, BOOGA
TANK GIRL
TANK GIRL
SHERIFF'S DEPARTMENT
WAIKICKAMOOKOO
COUNTY
CHARGES :
5E - ARMED ROBBERY, 2 COUNTS
66 B - PLAYING WITH MARKED CARDS
113 E - MARSUPIAL HALITOSIS, SOILING A POLICE VEHICLE
122 C - ABSCOND
192 B - POSSESSI
198 E - CRIMINAL
201 A - HANDLING
205 D - VEHICLE
211 B - LITTERING
213 D - THEFT, MA
222 A - WEAPONS
224 B - DEFECATI
231 D - DAMAGE T
245 E - BAD TASTE
ARRESTING OFFIC
BOOGA
BOOGA

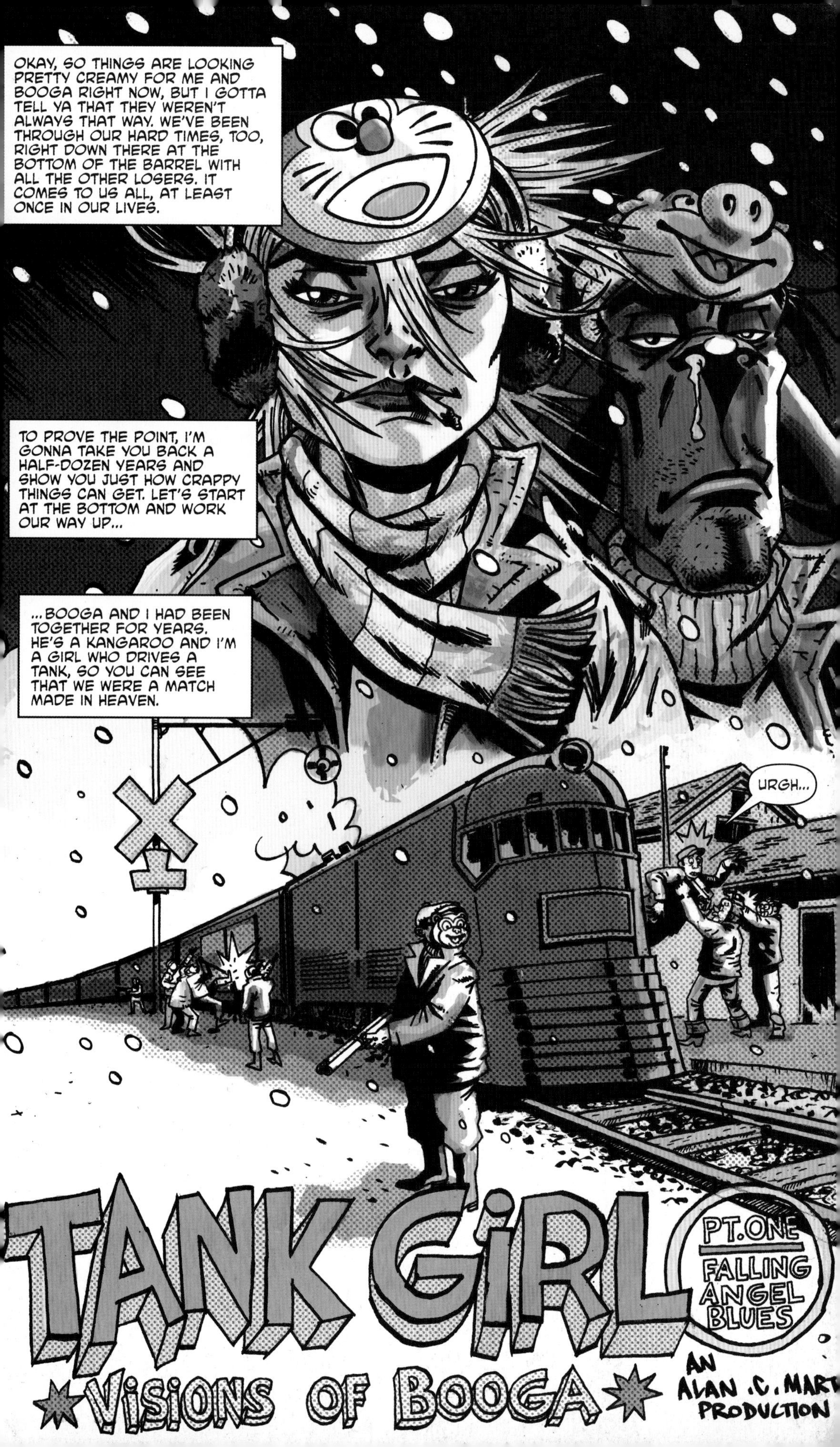
OKAY, SO THINGS ARE LOOKING PRETTY CREAMY FOR ME AND BOOGA RIGHT NOW, BUT I GOTTA TELL YA THAT THEY WEREN'T ALWAYS THAT WAY. WE'VE BEEN THROUGH OUR HARD TIMES, TOO, RIGHT DOWN THERE AT THE BOTTOM OF THE BARREL WITH ALL THE OTHER LOSERS. IT COMES TO US ALL, AT LEAST ONCE IN OUR LIVES.
TO PROVE THE POINT, I'M GONNA TAKE YOU BACK A HALF-DOZEN YEARS AND SHOW YOU JUST HOW CRAPPY THINGS CAN GET. LET'S START AT THE BOTTOM AND WORK OUR WAY UP...
...BOOGA AND I HAD BEEN TOGETHER FOR YEARS. HE'S A KANGAROO AND I'M A GIRL WHO DRIVES A TANK, SO YOU CAN SEE THAT WE WERE A MATCH MADE IN HEAVEN.
URGH...
TANK GIRL
PT. ONE
FALLING ANGEL BLUES
VISIONS OF BOOGA
AN ALAN .C. MART PRODUCTION

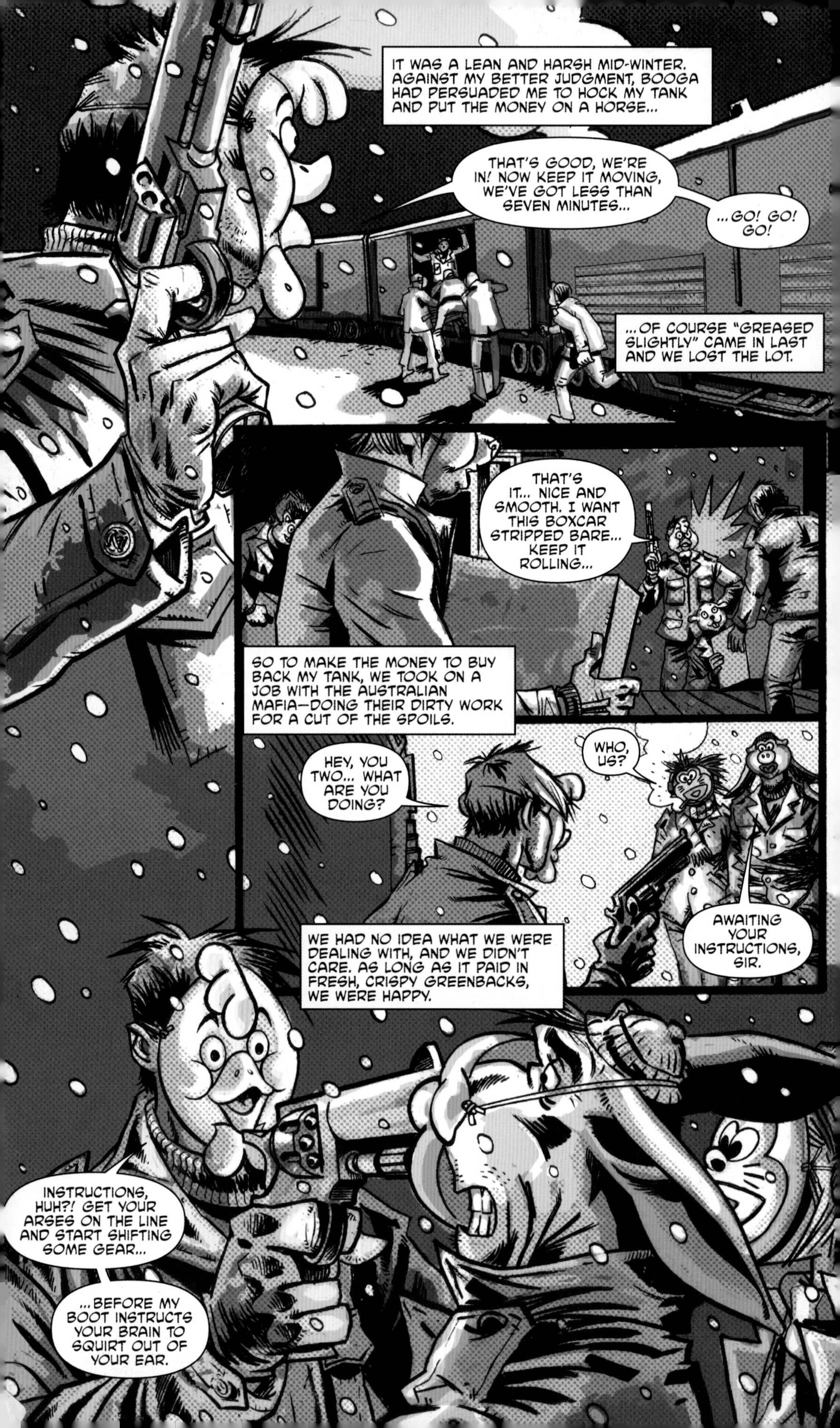
IT WAS A LEAN AND HARSH MID-WINTER. AGAINST MY BETTER JUDGMENT, BOOGA HAD PERSUADED ME TO HOCK MY TANK AND PUT THE MONEY ON A HORSE...
THAT'S GOOD, WE'RE IN! NOW KEEP IT MOVING, WE'VE GOT LESS THAN SEVEN MINUTES...
...GO! GO! GO!
...OF COURSE "GREASED SLIGHTLY" CAME IN LAST AND WE LOST THE LOT.
THAT'S IT... NICE AND SMOOTH. I WANT THIS BOXCAR STRIPPED BARE... KEEP IT ROLLING...
SO TO MAKE THE MONEY TO BUY BACK MY TANK, WE TOOK ON A JOB WITH THE AUSTRALIAN MAFIA--DOING THEIR DIRTY WORK FOR A CUT OF THE SPOILS.
HEY, YOU TWO... WHAT ARE YOU DOING?
WHO, US?
AWAITING YOUR INSTRUCTIONS, SIR.
WE HAD NO IDEA WHAT WE WERE DEALING WITH, AND WE DIDN'T CARE. AS LONG AS IT PAID IN FRESH, CRISPY GREENBACKS, WE WERE HAPPY.
INSTRUCTIONS, HUH?! GET YOUR ARSES ON THE LINE AND START SHIFTING SOME GEAR...
...BEFORE MY BOOT INSTRUCTS YOUR BRAIN TO SQUIRT OUT OF YOUR EAR.

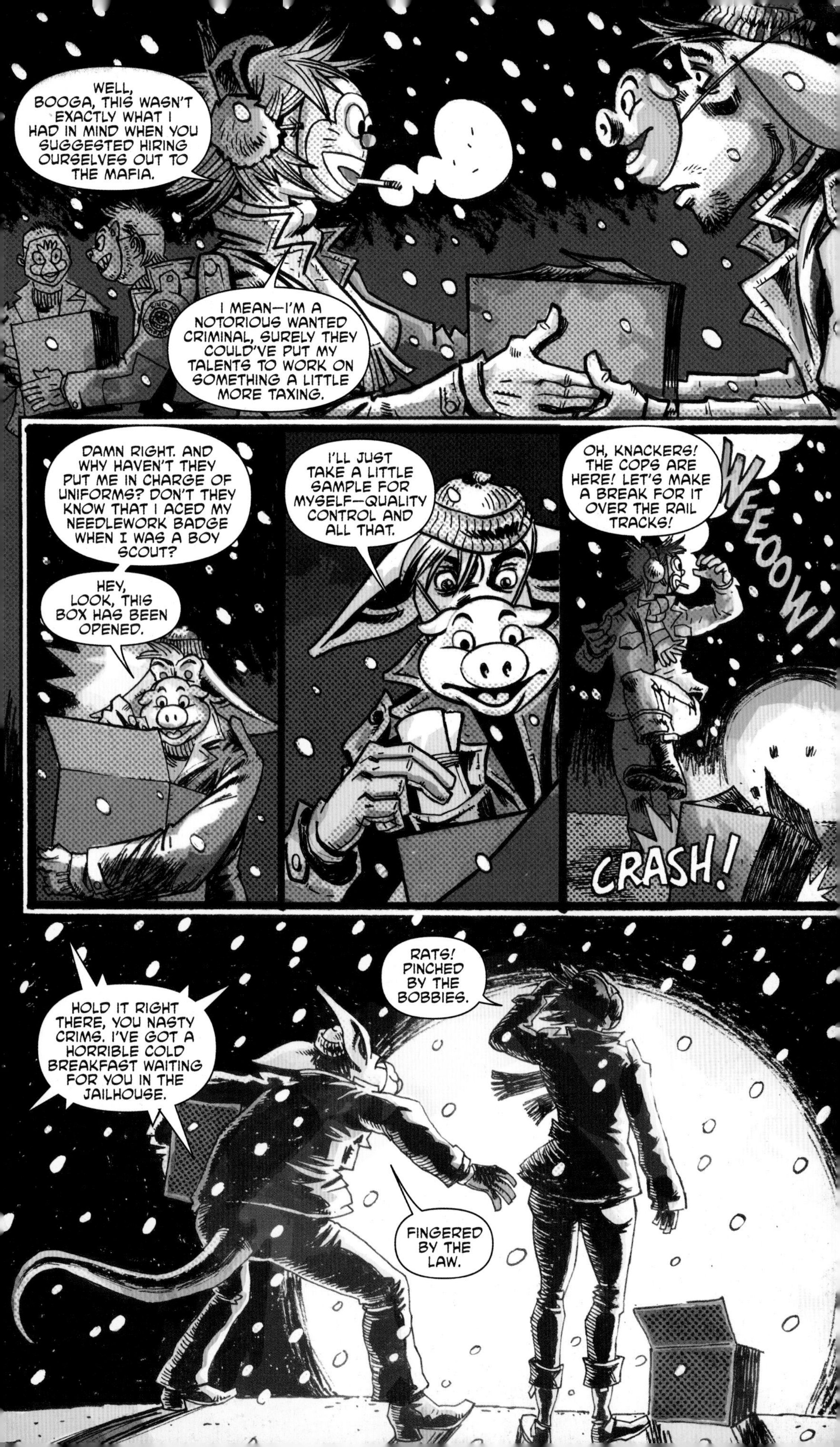
WELL, BOOGA, THIS WASN'T EXACTLY WHAT I HAD IN MIND WHEN YOU SUGGESTED HIRING OURSELVES OUT TO THE MAFIA.
I MEAN—I'M A NOTORIOUS WANTED CRIMINAL, SURELY THEY COULD'VE PUT MY TALENTS TO WORK ON SOMETHING A LITTLE MORE TAXING.
DAMN RIGHT. AND WHY HAVEN'T THEY PUT ME IN CHARGE OF UNIFORMS? DON'T THEY KNOW THAT I ACED MY NEEDLEWORK BADGE WHEN I WAS A BOY SCOUT?
HEY, LOOK, THIS BOX HAS BEEN OPENED.
I'LL JUST TAKE A LITTLE SAMPLE FOR MYSELF—QUALITY CONTROL AND ALL THAT.
OH, KNACKERS! THE COPS ARE HERE! LET'S MAKE A BREAK FOR IT OVER THE RAIL TRACKS!
WEEOOW!
CRASH!
HOLD IT RIGHT THERE, YOU NASTY CRIMS. I'VE GOT A HORRIBLE COLD BREAKFAST WAITING FOR YOU IN THE JAILHOUSE.
RATS! PINCHED BY THE BOBBIES.
FINGERED BY THE LAW.

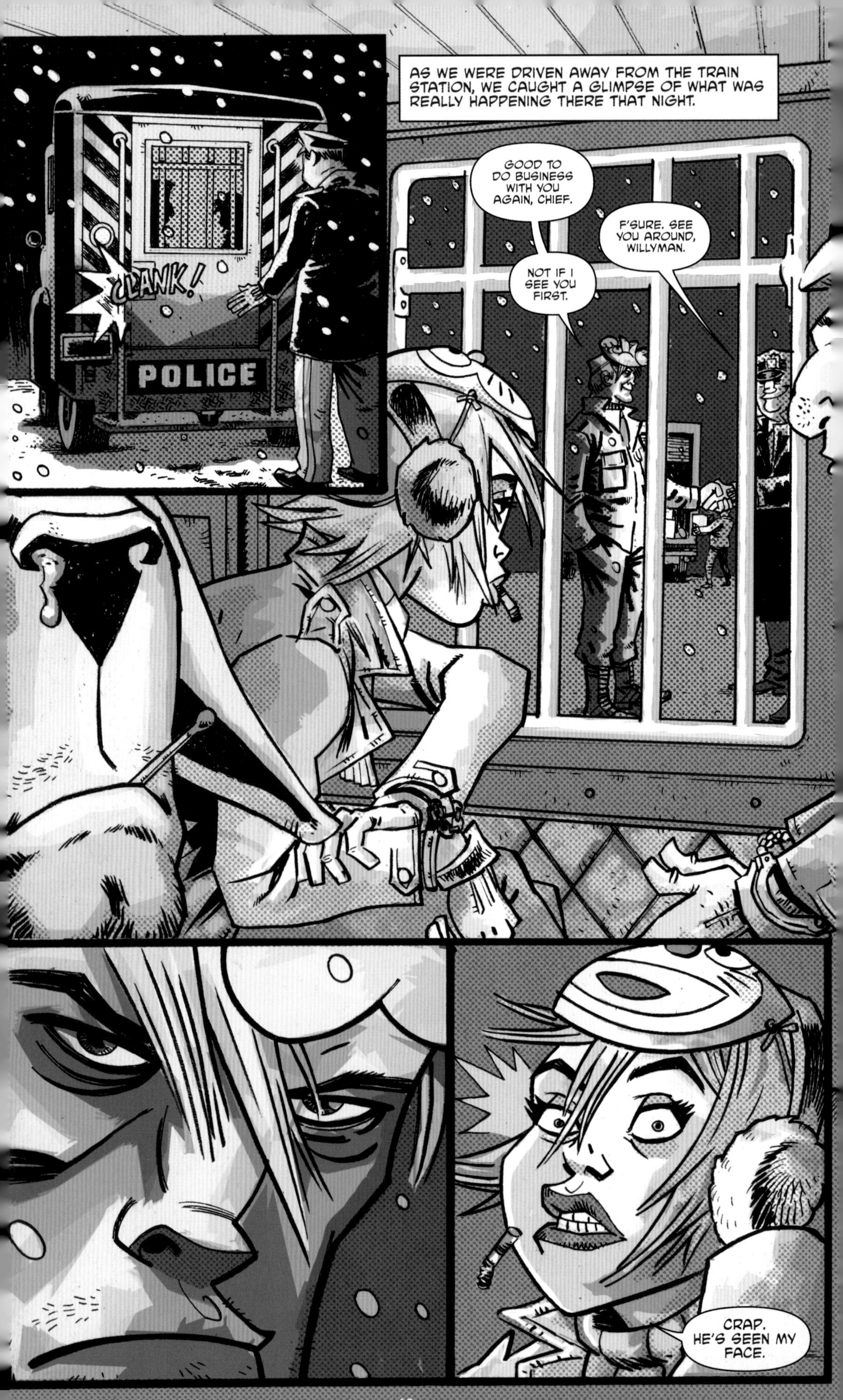

CLANK!
POLICE
AS WE WERE DRIVEN AWAY FROM THE TRAIN STATION, WE CAUGHT A GLIMPSE OF WHAT WAS REALLY HAPPENING THERE THAT NIGHT.
GOOD TO DO BUSINESS WITH YOU AGAIN, CHIEF.
F'SURE. SEE YOU AROUND, WILLYMAN.
NOT IF I SEE YOU FIRST.
CRAP. HE'S SEEN MY FACE.

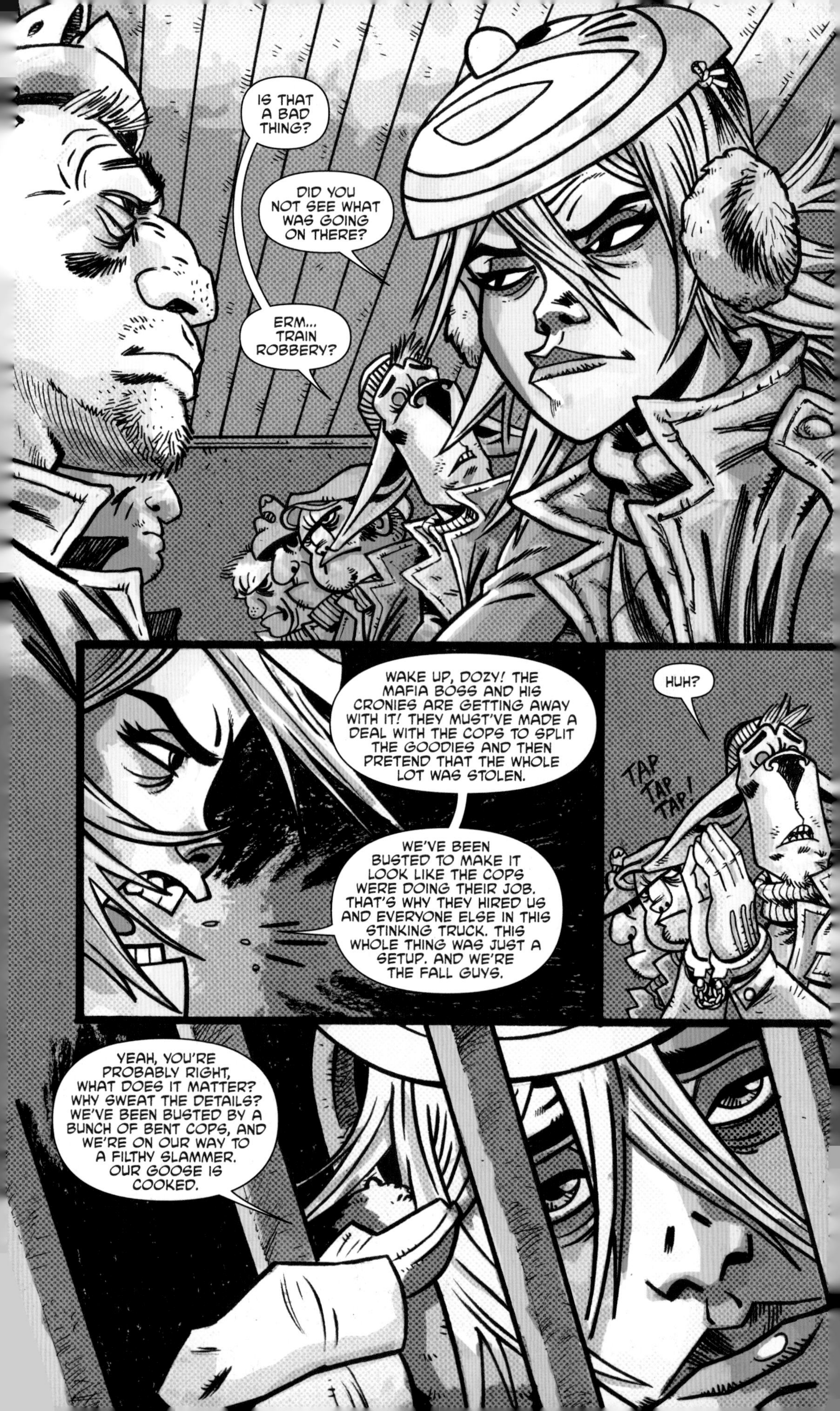

IS THAT A BAD THING?
DID YOU NOT SEE WHAT WAS GOING ON THERE?
ERM... TRAIN ROBBERY?
WAKE UP, DOZY! THE MAFIA BOSS AND HIS CRONIES ARE GETTING AWAY WITH IT! THEY MUST'VE MADE A DEAL WITH THE COPS TO SPLIT THE GOODIES AND THEN PRETEND THAT THE WHOLE LOT WAS STOLEN.
WE'VE BEEN BUSTED TO MAKE IT LOOK LIKE THE COPS WERE DOING THEIR JOB. THAT'S WHY THEY HIRED US AND EVERYONE ELSE IN THIS STINKING TRUCK. THIS WHOLE THING WAS JUST A SETUP. AND WE'RE THE FALL GUYS.
HUH?
TAP TAP TAP!
YEAH, YOU'RE PROBABLY RIGHT, WHAT DOES IT MATTER? WHY SWEAT THE DETAILS? WE'VE BEEN BUSTED BY A BUNCH OF BENT COPS, AND WE'RE ON OUR WAY TO A FILTHY SLAMMER. OUR GOOSE IS COOKED.

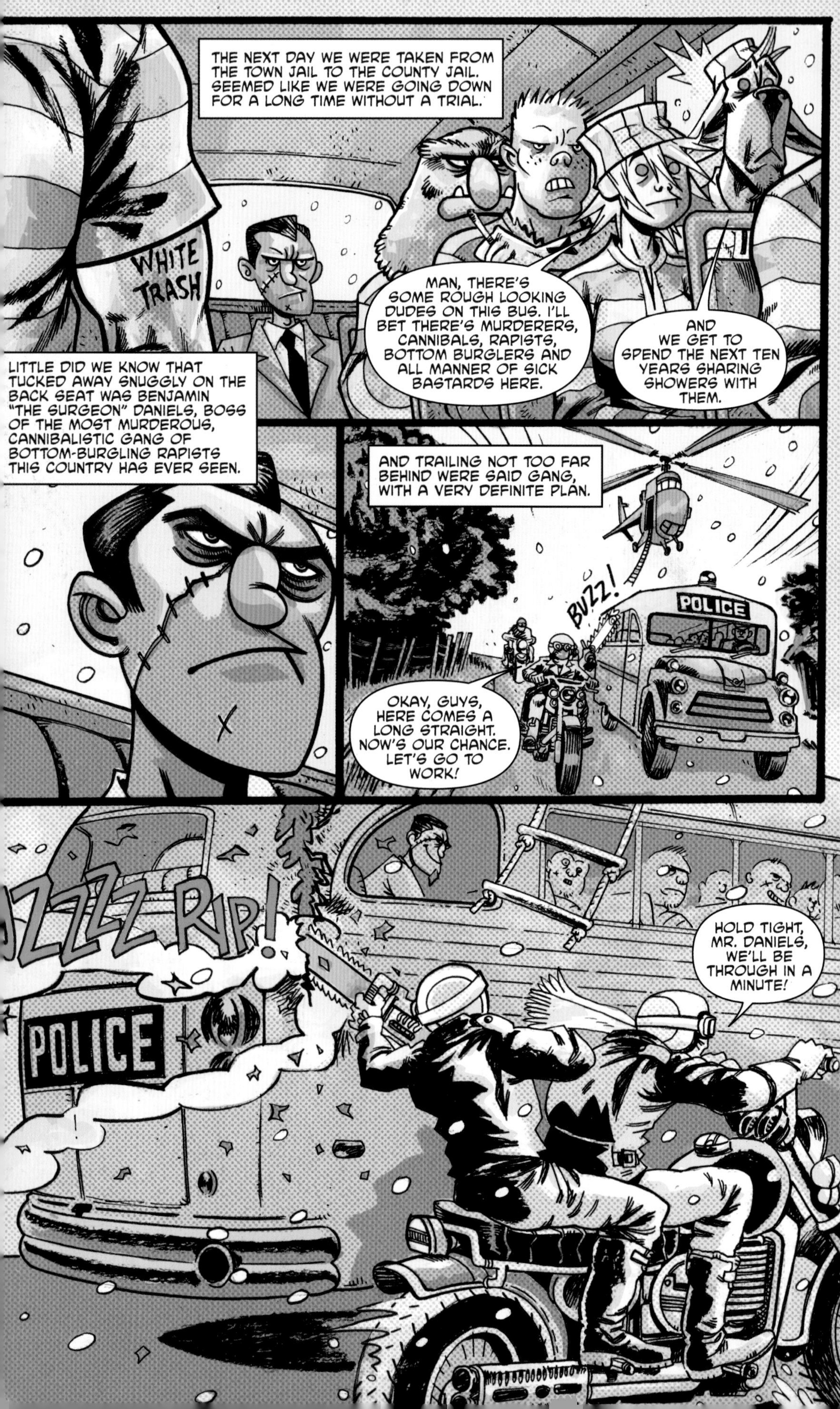
THE NEXT DAY WE WERE TAKEN FROM THE TOWN JAIL TO THE COUNTY JAIL. SEEMED LIKE WE WERE GOING DOWN FOR A LONG TIME WITHOUT A TRIAL.
WHITE TRASH
MAN, THERE'S SOME ROUGH LOOKING DUDES ON THIS BUS. I'LL BET THERE'S MURDERERS, CANNIBALS, RAPISTS, BOTTOM BURGLERS AND ALL MANNER OF SICK BASTARDS HERE.
AND WE GET TO SPEND THE NEXT TEN YEARS SHARING SHOWERS WITH THEM.
LITTLE DID WE KNOW THAT TUCKED AWAY SNUGGLY ON THE BACK SEAT WAS BENJAMIN "THE SURGEON" DANIELS, BOSS OF THE MOST MURDEROUS, CANNIBALISTIC GANG OF BOTTOM-BURGLING RAPISTS THIS COUNTRY HAS EVER SEEN.
AND TRAILING NOT TOO FAR BEHIND WERE SAID GANG, WITH A VERY DEFINITE PLAN.
BUZZ!
POLICE
OKAY, GUYS, HERE COMES A LONG STRAIGHT. NOW'S OUR CHANCE. LET'S GO TO WORK!
ZZZZ RIP!
POLICE
HOLD TIGHT, MR. DANIELS, WE'LL BE THROUGH IN A MINUTE!

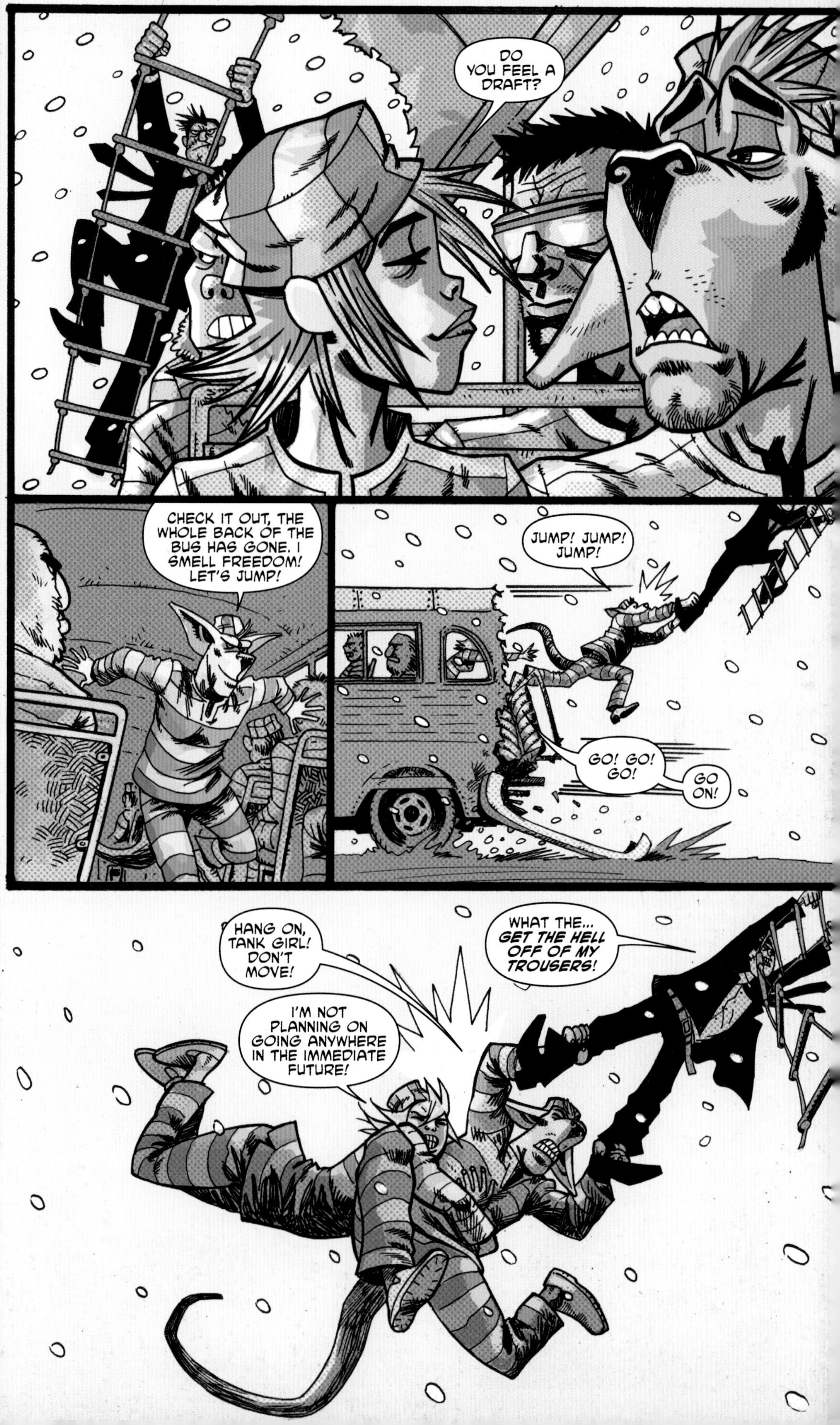
DO YOU FEEL A DRAFT?
CHECK IT OUT, THE WHOLE BACK OF THE BUS HAS GONE. I SMELL FREEDOM! LET'S JUMP!
JUMP! JUMP! JUMP!
GO! GO! GO!
GO ON!
HANG ON, TANK GIRL! DON'T MOVE!
WHAT THE... *GET THE HELL OFF OF MY TROUSERS!*
I'M NOT PLANNING ON GOING ANYWHERE IN THE IMMEDIATE FUTURE!

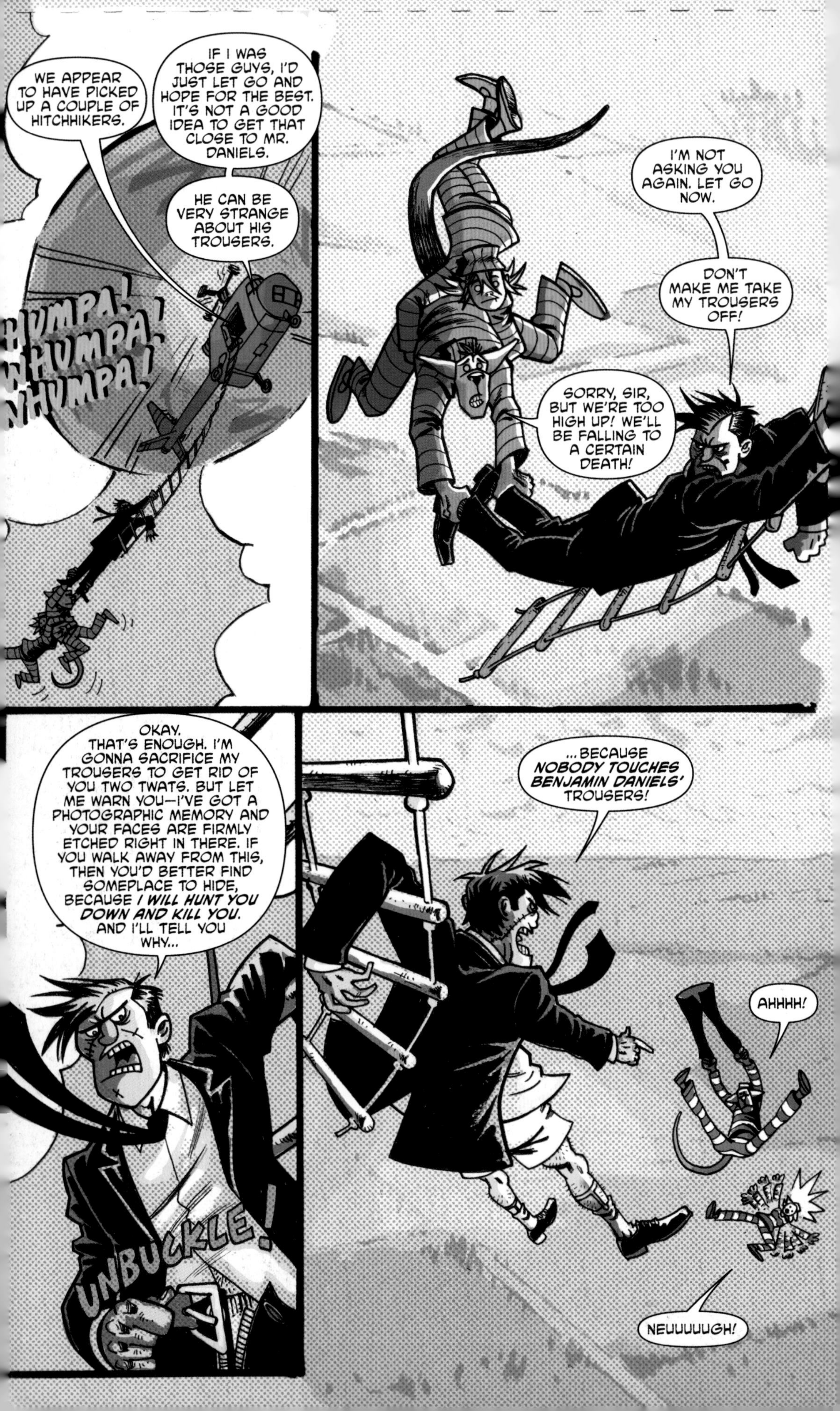

WE APPEAR TO HAVE PICKED UP A COUPLE OF HITCHHIKERS.
IF I WAS THOSE GUYS, I'D JUST LET GO AND HOPE FOR THE BEST. IT'S NOT A GOOD IDEA TO GET THAT CLOSE TO MR. DANIELS.
HE CAN BE VERY STRANGE ABOUT HIS TROUSERS.
WHUMPA! WHUMPA! WHUMPA!
I'M NOT ASKING YOU AGAIN. LET GO NOW.
DON'T MAKE ME TAKE MY TROUSERS OFF!
SORRY, SIR, BUT WE'RE TOO HIGH UP! WE'LL BE FALLING TO A CERTAIN DEATH!
OKAY. THAT'S ENOUGH. I'M GONNA SACRIFICE MY TROUSERS TO GET RID OF YOU TWO TWATS. BUT LET ME WARN YOU--I'VE GOT A PHOTOGRAPHIC MEMORY AND YOUR FACES ARE FIRMLY ETCHED RIGHT IN THERE. IF YOU WALK AWAY FROM THIS, THEN YOU'D BETTER FIND SOMEPLACE TO HIDE, BECAUSE *I WILL HUNT YOU DOWN AND KILL YOU*. AND I'LL TELL YOU WHY...
UNBUCKLE!
...BECAUSE *NOBODY TOUCHES BENJAMIN DANIELS'* TROUSERS!
AHHHH!
NEUUUUUGH!

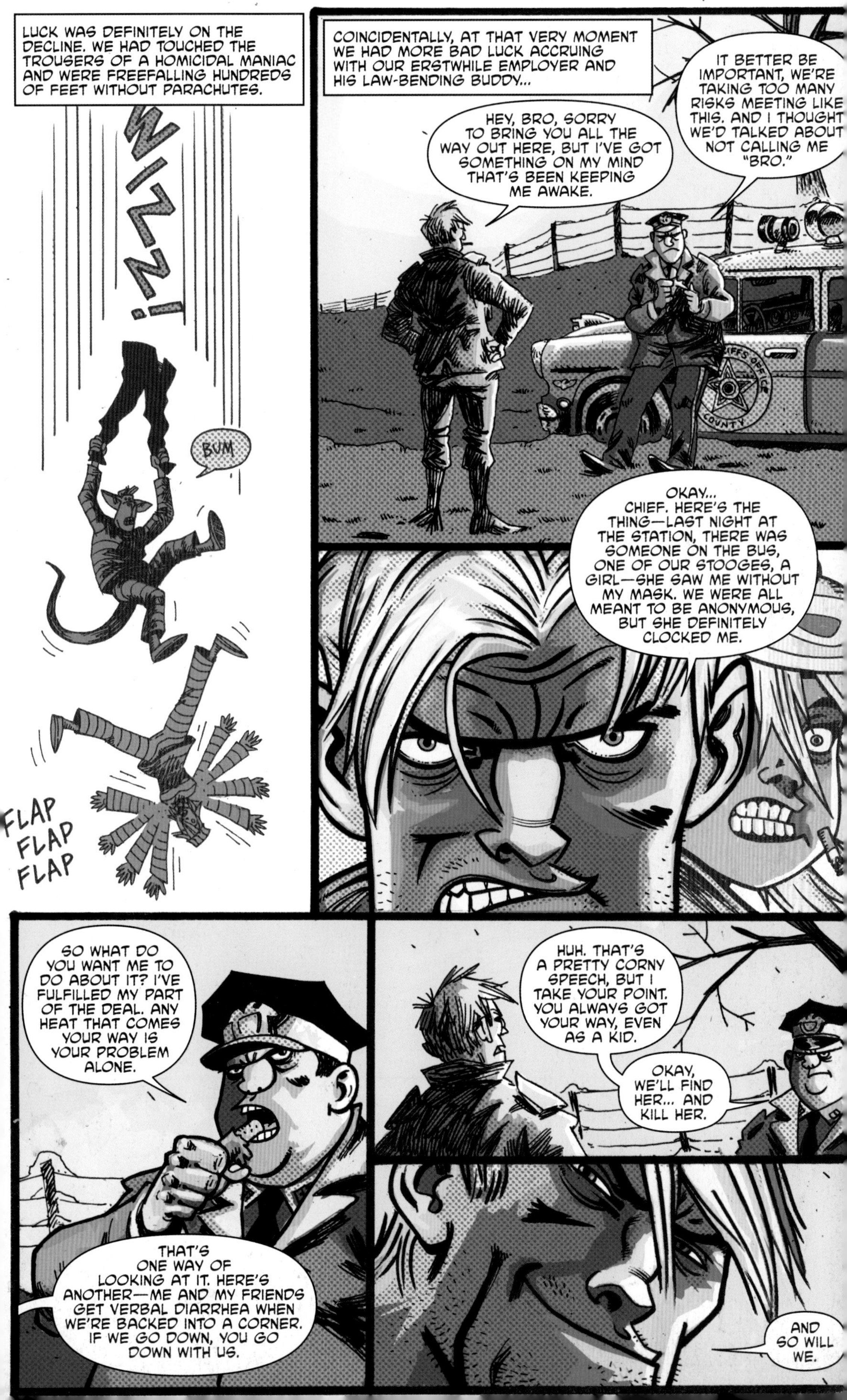

LUCK WAS DEFINITELY ON THE DECLINE. WE HAD TOUCHED THE TROUSERS OF A HOMICIDAL MANIAC AND WERE FREEFALLING HUNDREDS OF FEET WITHOUT PARACHUTES.
WIZZ!
BUM
FLAP FLAP FLAP
COINCIDENTALLY, AT THAT VERY MOMENT WE HAD MORE BAD LUCK ACCRUING WITH OUR ERSTWHILE EMPLOYER AND HIS LAW-BENDING BUDDY...
HEY, BRO, SORRY TO BRING YOU ALL THE WAY OUT HERE, BUT I'VE GOT SOMETHING ON MY MIND THAT'S BEEN KEEPING ME AWAKE.
IT BETTER BE IMPORTANT, WE'RE TAKING TOO MANY RISKS MEETING LIKE THIS. AND I THOUGHT WE'D TALKED ABOUT NOT CALLING ME "BRO."
COUNTY
OKAY... CHIEF. HERE'S THE THING—LAST NIGHT AT THE STATION, THERE WAS SOMEONE ON THE BUS, ONE OF OUR STOOGES, A GIRL—SHE SAW ME WITHOUT MY MASK. WE WERE ALL MEANT TO BE ANONYMOUS, BUT SHE DEFINITELY CLOCKED ME.
SO WHAT DO YOU WANT ME TO DO ABOUT IT? I'VE FULFILLED MY PART OF THE DEAL. ANY HEAT THAT COMES YOUR WAY IS YOUR PROBLEM ALONE.
THAT'S ONE WAY OF LOOKING AT IT. HERE'S ANOTHER—ME AND MY FRIENDS GET VERBAL DIARRHEA WHEN WE'RE BACKED INTO A CORNER. IF WE GO DOWN, YOU GO DOWN WITH US.
HUH. THAT'S A PRETTY CORNY SPEECH, BUT I TAKE YOUR POINT. YOU ALWAYS GOT YOUR WAY, EVEN AS A KID.
OKAY, WE'LL FIND HER... AND KILL HER.
AND SO WILL WE.

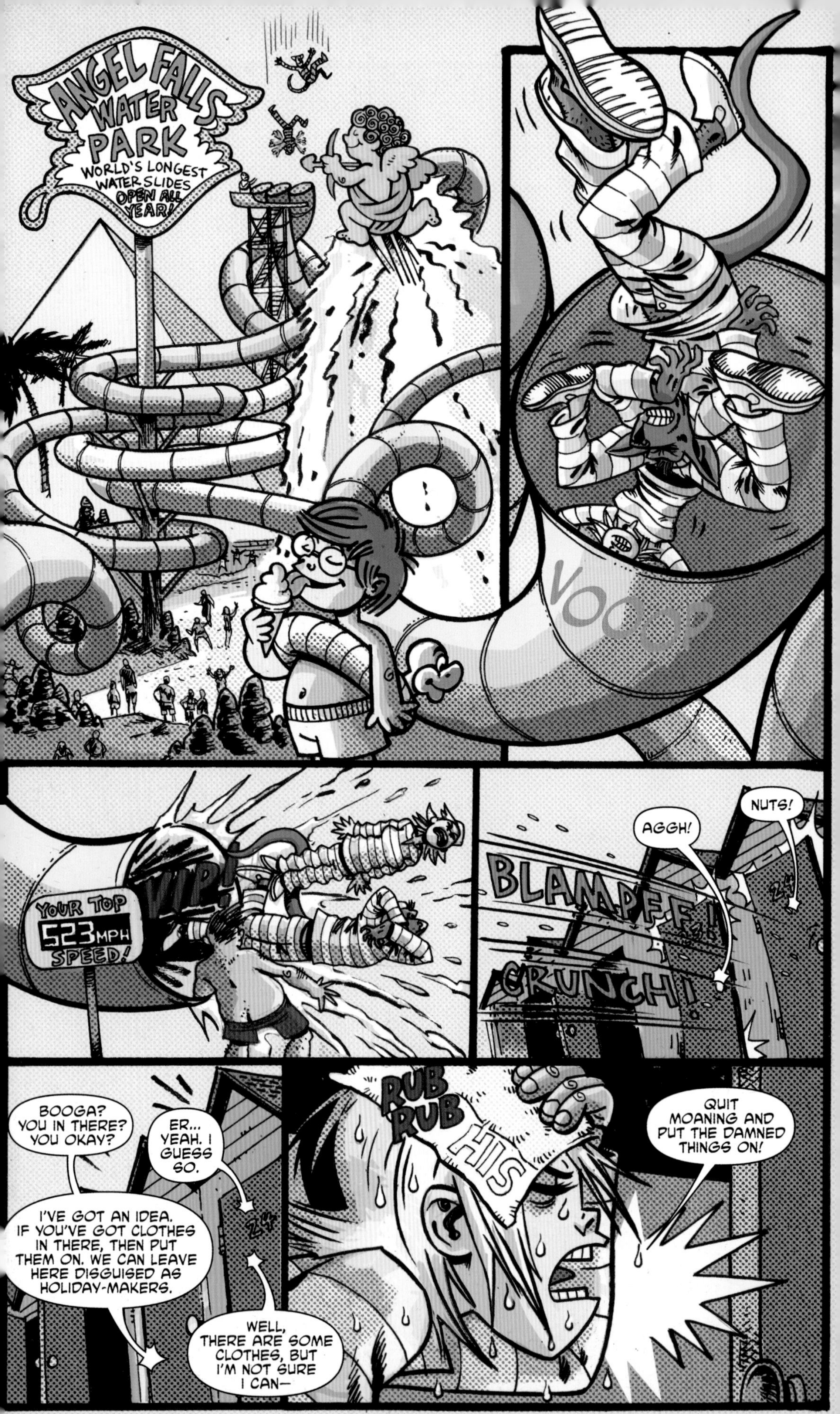

ANGEL FALLS WATER PARK
WORLD'S LONGEST WATER SLIDES OPEN ALL YEAR!
VOOOP
YOUR TOP 523 MPH SPEED!
VIP!
AGGH!
NUTS!
BLAMPFF!
CRUNCH!
BOOGA? YOU IN THERE? YOU OKAY?
ER... YEAH. I GUESS SO.
I'VE GOT AN IDEA. IF YOU'VE GOT CLOTHES IN THERE, THEN PUT THEM ON. WE CAN LEAVE HERE DISGUISED AS HOLIDAY-MAKERS.
WELL, THERE ARE SOME CLOTHES, BUT I'M NOT SURE I CAN—
RUB RUB
HIS
QUIT MOANING AND PUT THE DAMNED THINGS ON!

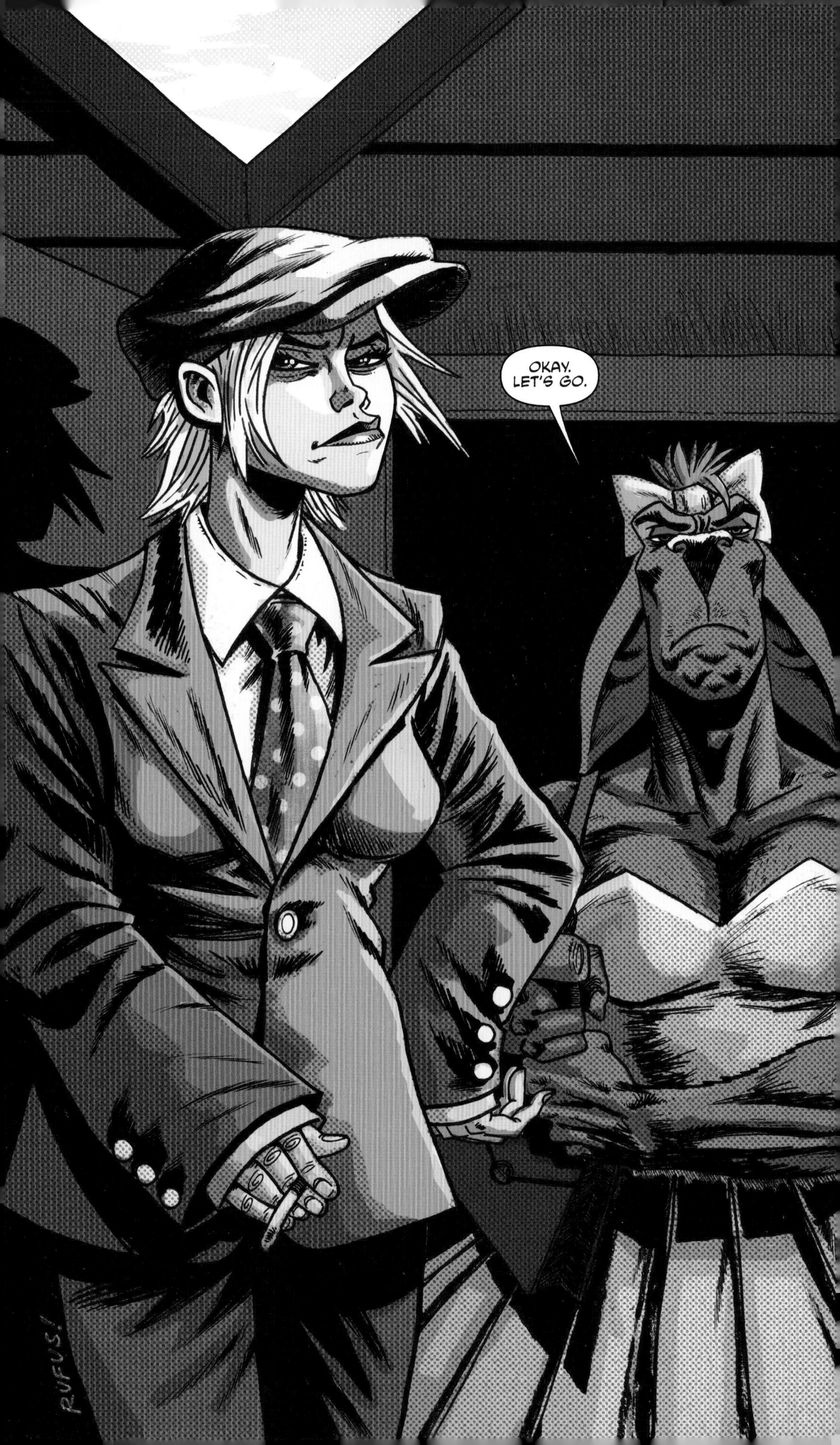
OKAY. LET'S GO.
RUFUS!

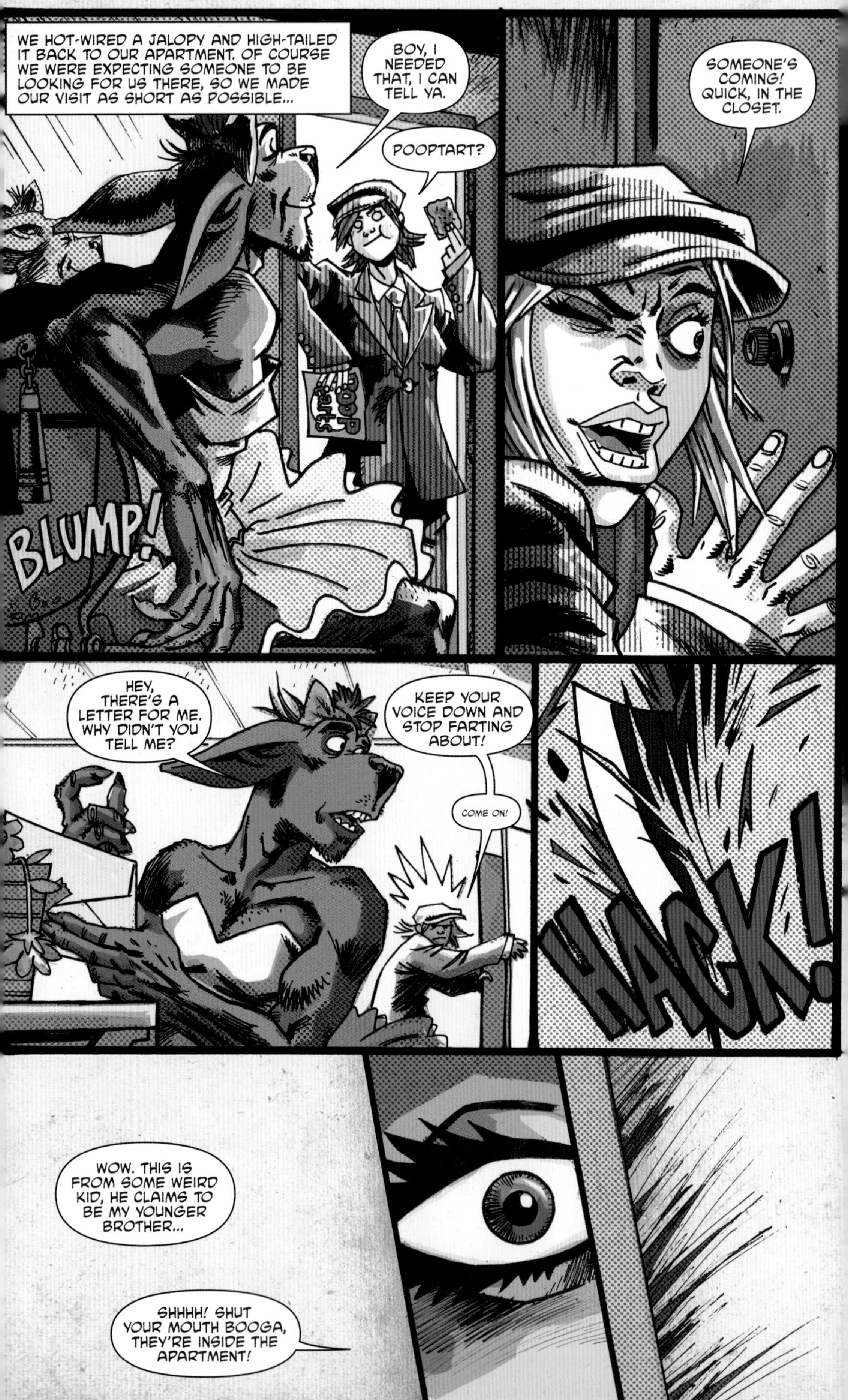

WE HOT-WIRED A JALOPY AND HIGH-TAILED IT BACK TO OUR APARTMENT. OF COURSE WE WERE EXPECTING SOMEONE TO BE LOOKING FOR US THERE, SO WE MADE OUR VISIT AS SHORT AS POSSIBLE...
BOY, I NEEDED THAT, I CAN TELL YA.
POOPTART?
BLUMP!
SOMEONE'S COMING! QUICK, IN THE CLOSET.
HEY, THERE'S A LETTER FOR ME. WHY DIDN'T YOU TELL ME?
KEEP YOUR VOICE DOWN AND STOP FARTING ABOUT!
COME ON!
HACK!
WOW. THIS IS FROM SOME WEIRD KID, HE CLAIMS TO BE MY YOUNGER BROTHER...
SHHHH! SHUT YOUR MOUTH BOOGA, THEY'RE INSIDE THE APARTMENT!

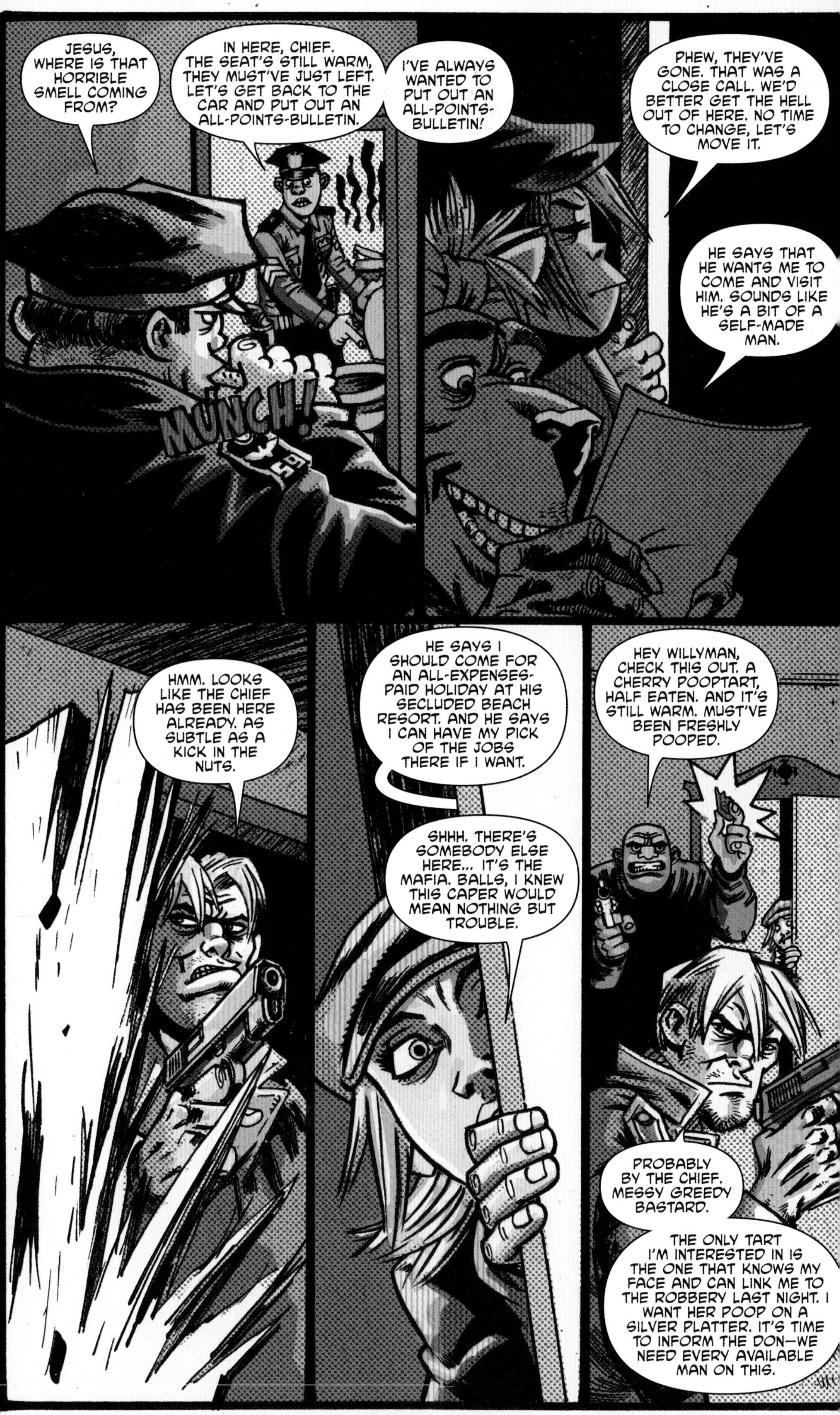

JESUS, WHERE IS THAT HORRIBLE SMELL COMING FROM?
IN HERE, CHIEF. THE SEAT'S STILL WARM, THEY MUST'VE JUST LEFT. LET'S GET BACK TO THE CAR AND PUT OUT AN ALL-POINTS-BULLETIN.
I'VE ALWAYS WANTED TO PUT OUT AN ALL-POINTS-BULLETIN!
MUNCH!
PHEW, THEY'VE GONE. THAT WAS A CLOSE CALL. WE'D BETTER GET THE HELL OUT OF HERE. NO TIME TO CHANGE, LET'S MOVE IT.
HE SAYS THAT HE WANTS ME TO COME AND VISIT HIM. SOUNDS LIKE HE'S A BIT OF A SELF-MADE MAN.
HMM. LOOKS LIKE THE CHIEF HAS BEEN HERE ALREADY. AS SUBTLE AS A KICK IN THE NUTS.
HE SAYS I SHOULD COME FOR AN ALL-EXPENSES-PAID HOLIDAY AT HIS SECLUDED BEACH RESORT. AND HE SAYS I CAN HAVE MY PICK OF THE JOBS THERE IF I WANT.
SHHH. THERE'S SOMEBODY ELSE HERE... IT'S THE MAFIA. BALLS, I KNEW THIS CAPER WOULD MEAN NOTHING BUT TROUBLE.
HEY WILLYMAN, CHECK THIS OUT. A CHERRY POOPTART, HALF EATEN. AND IT'S STILL WARM. MUST'VE BEEN FRESHLY POOPED.
PROBABLY BY THE CHIEF. MESSY GREEDY BASTARD.
THE ONLY TART I'M INTERESTED IN IS THE ONE THAT KNOWS MY FACE AND CAN LINK ME TO THE ROBBERY LAST NIGHT. I WANT HER POOP ON A SILVER PLATTER. IT'S TIME TO INFORM THE DON—WE NEED EVERY AVAILABLE MAN ON THIS.

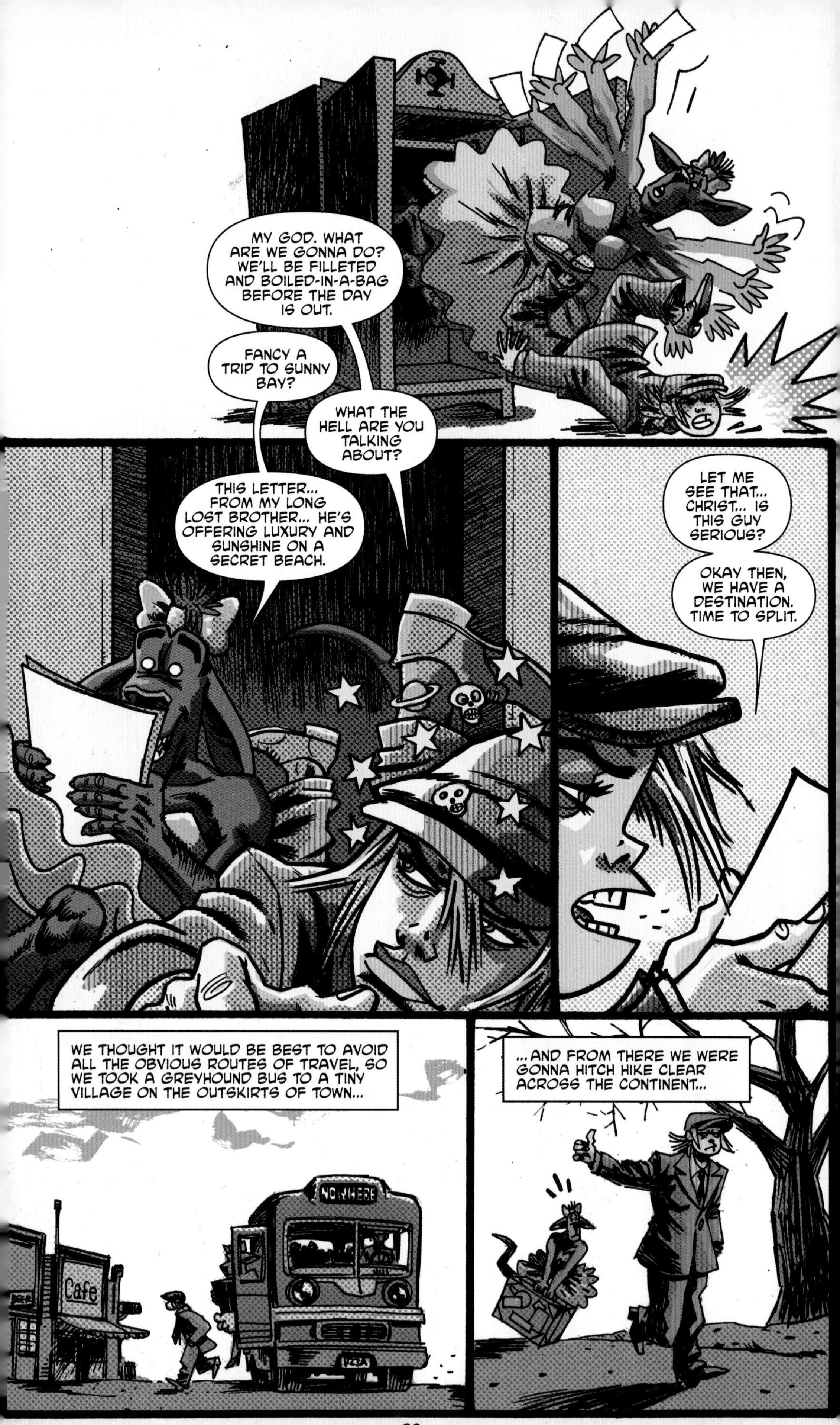
MY GOD. WHAT ARE WE GONNA DO? WE'LL BE FILLETED AND BOILED-IN-A-BAG BEFORE THE DAY IS OUT.
FANCY A TRIP TO SUNNY BAY?
WHAT THE HELL ARE YOU TALKING ABOUT?
THIS LETTER... FROM MY LONG LOST BROTHER... HE'S OFFERING LUXURY AND SUNSHINE ON A SECRET BEACH.
LET ME SEE THAT... CHRIST... IS THIS GUY SERIOUS?
OKAY THEN, WE HAVE A DESTINATION. TIME TO SPLIT.
WE THOUGHT IT WOULD BE BEST TO AVOID ALL THE OBVIOUS ROUTES OF TRAVEL, SO WE TOOK A GREYHOUND BUS TO A TINY VILLAGE ON THE OUTSKIRTS OF TOWN...
NO WHERE
Cafe
...AND FROM THERE WE WERE GONNA HITCH HIKE CLEAR ACROSS THE CONTINENT...

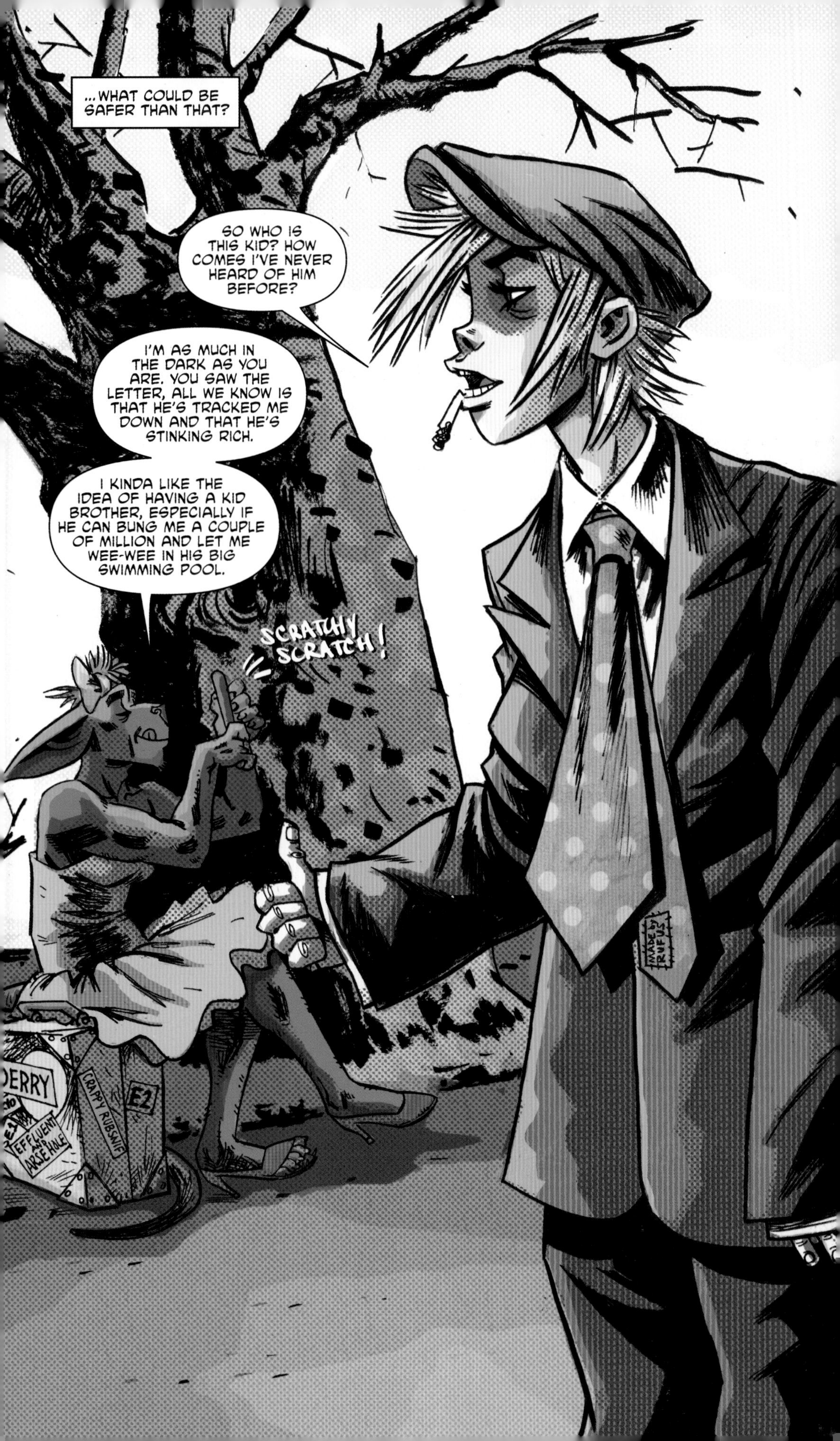
...WHAT COULD BE SAFER THAN THAT?
SO WHO IS THIS KID? HOW COMES I'VE NEVER HEARD OF HIM BEFORE?
I'M AS MUCH IN THE DARK AS YOU ARE. YOU SAW THE LETTER, ALL WE KNOW IS THAT HE'S TRACKED ME DOWN AND THAT HE'S STINKING RICH.
I KINDA LIKE THE IDEA OF HAVING A KID BROTHER, ESPECIALLY IF HE CAN BUNG ME A COUPLE OF MILLION AND LET ME WEE-WEE IN HIS BIG SWIMMING POOL.
SCRATCHY SCRATCH!
MADE by RUFUS
DERRY
CRAPPY RUBSNIF
E2
EFFLUENT AND ARSEHOLE

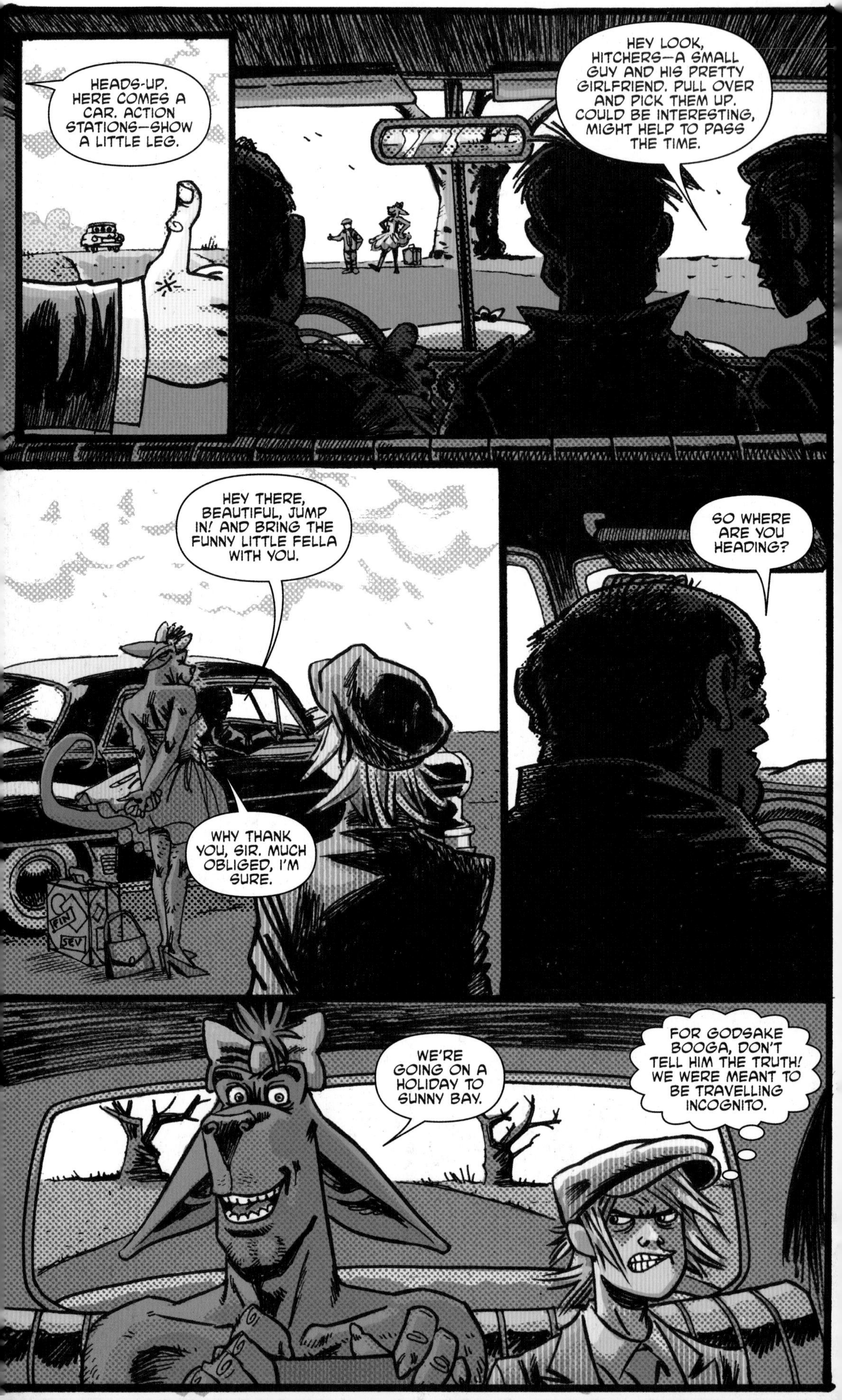
HEADS-UP. HERE COMES A CAR. ACTION STATIONS—SHOW A LITTLE LEG.
HEY LOOK, HITCHERS—A SMALL GUY AND HIS PRETTY GIRLFRIEND. PULL OVER AND PICK THEM UP. COULD BE INTERESTING, MIGHT HELP TO PASS THE TIME.
HEY THERE, BEAUTIFUL, JUMP IN! AND BRING THE FUNNY LITTLE FELLA WITH YOU.
WHY THANK YOU, SIR. MUCH OBLIGED, I'M SURE.
FIN
SEV
SO WHERE ARE YOU HEADING?
WE'RE GOING ON A HOLIDAY TO SUNNY BAY.
FOR GODSAKE BOOGA, DON'T TELL HIM THE TRUTH! WE WERE MEANT TO BE TRAVELLING INCOGNITO.

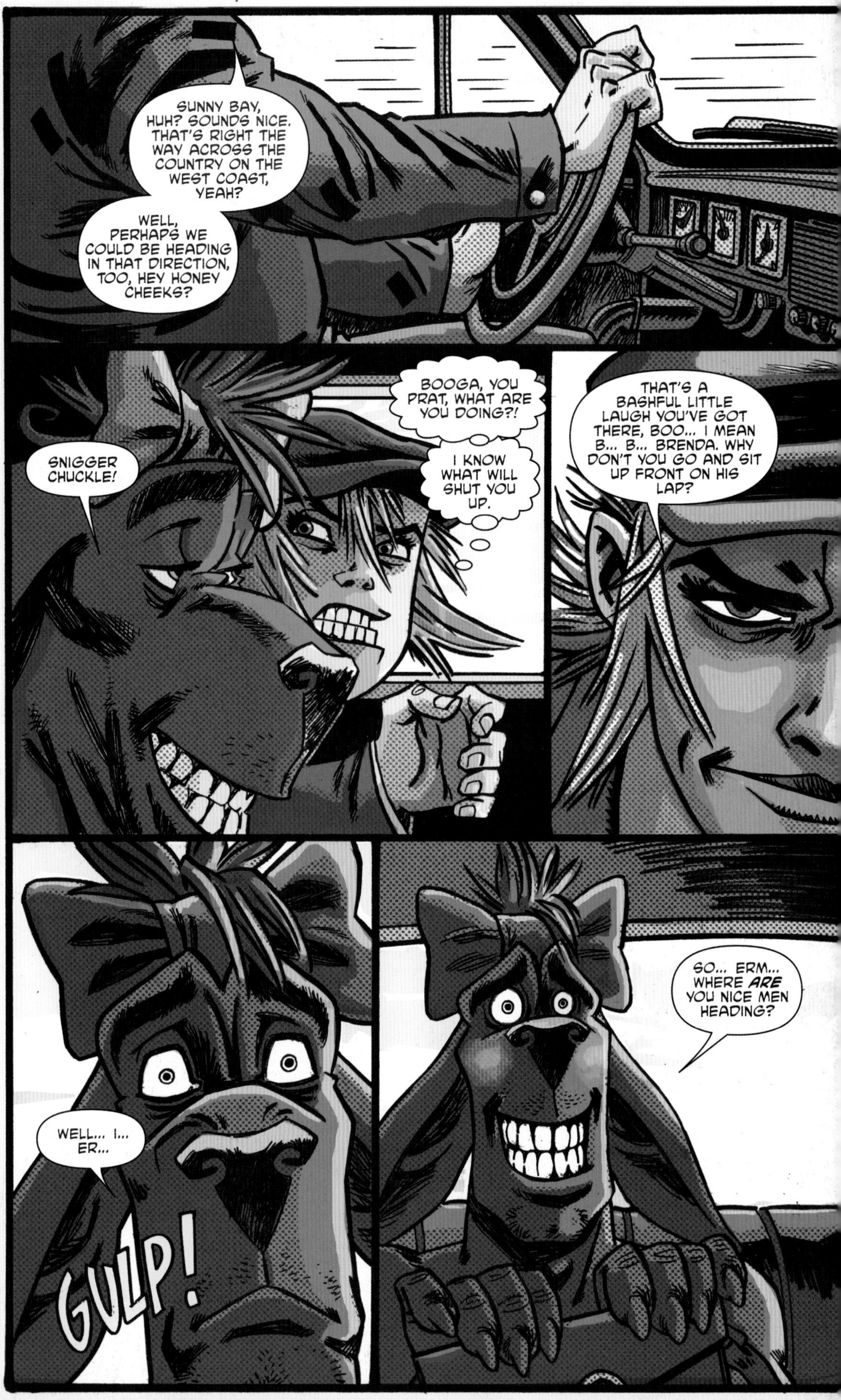
SUNNY BAY, HUH? SOUNDS NICE. THAT'S RIGHT THE WAY ACROSS THE COUNTRY ON THE WEST COAST, YEAH?
WELL, PERHAPS WE COULD BE HEADING IN THAT DIRECTION, TOO, HEY HONEY CHEEKS?
SNIGGER CHUCKLE!
BOOGA, YOU PRAT, WHAT ARE YOU DOING?!
I KNOW WHAT WILL SHUT YOU UP.
THAT'S A BASHFUL LITTLE LAUGH YOU'VE GOT THERE, BOO... I MEAN B... B... BRENDA. WHY DON'T YOU GO AND SIT UP FRONT ON HIS LAP?
WELL... I... ER...
GULP!
SO... ERM... WHERE *ARE* YOU NICE MEN HEADING?

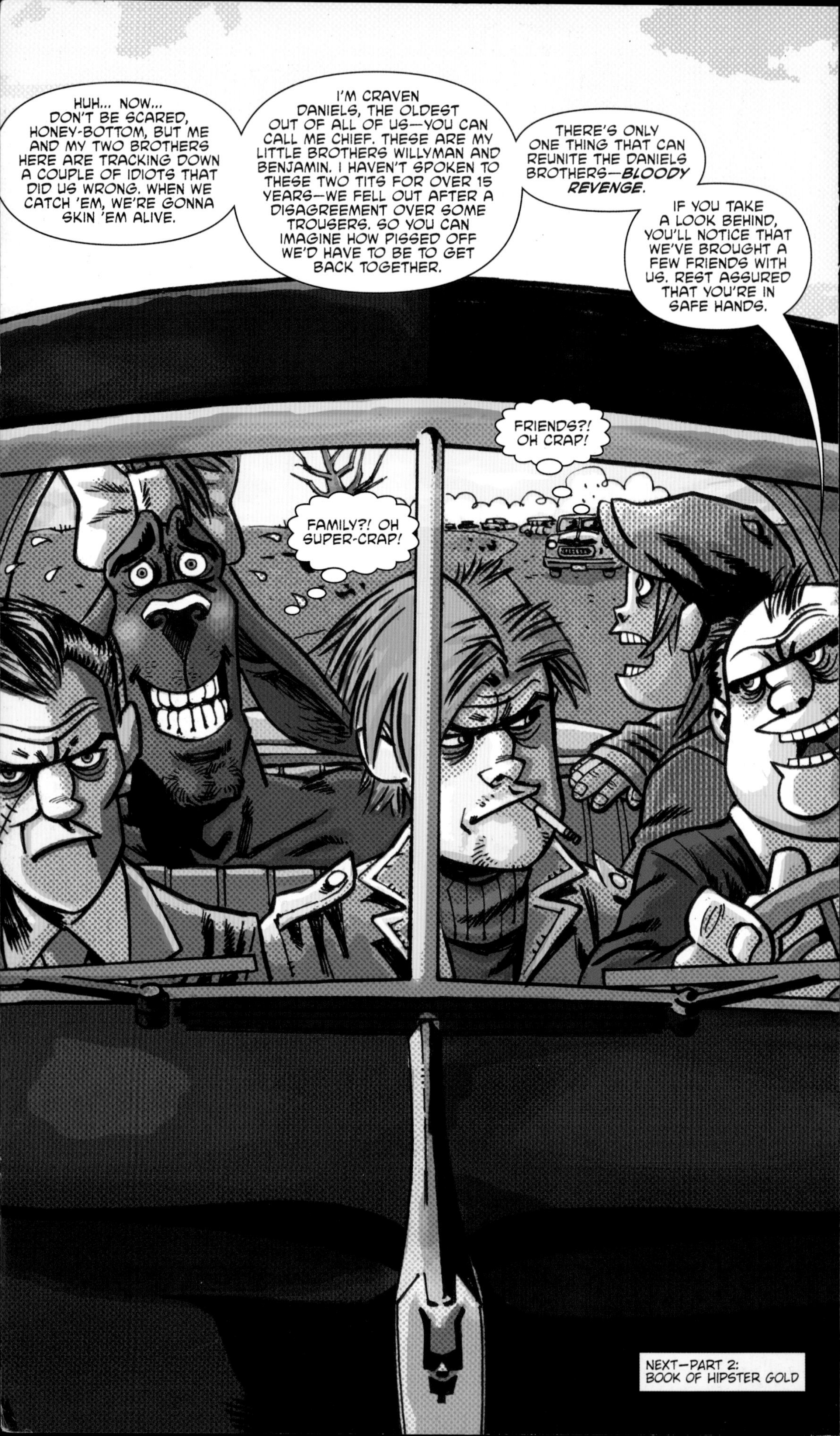
HUH... NOW... DON'T BE SCARED, HONEY-BOTTOM, BUT ME AND MY TWO BROTHERS HERE ARE TRACKING DOWN A COUPLE OF IDIOTS THAT DID US WRONG. WHEN WE CATCH 'EM, WE'RE GONNA SKIN 'EM ALIVE.
I'M CRAVEN DANIELS, THE OLDEST OUT OF ALL OF US—YOU CAN CALL ME CHIEF. THESE ARE MY LITTLE BROTHERS WILLYMAN AND BENJAMIN. I HAVEN'T SPOKEN TO THESE TWO TITS FOR OVER 15 YEARS—WE FELL OUT AFTER A DISAGREEMENT OVER SOME TROUSERS. SO YOU CAN IMAGINE HOW PISSED OFF WE'D HAVE TO BE TO GET BACK TOGETHER.
THERE'S ONLY ONE THING THAT CAN REUNITE THE DANIELS BROTHERS—*BLOODY REVENGE*.
IF YOU TAKE A LOOK BEHIND, YOU'LL NOTICE THAT WE'VE BROUGHT A FEW FRIENDS WITH US. REST ASSURED THAT YOU'RE IN SAFE HANDS.
FRIENDS?! OH CRAP!
FAMILY?! OH SUPER-CRAP!
NEXT—PART 2: BOOK OF HIPSTER GOLD

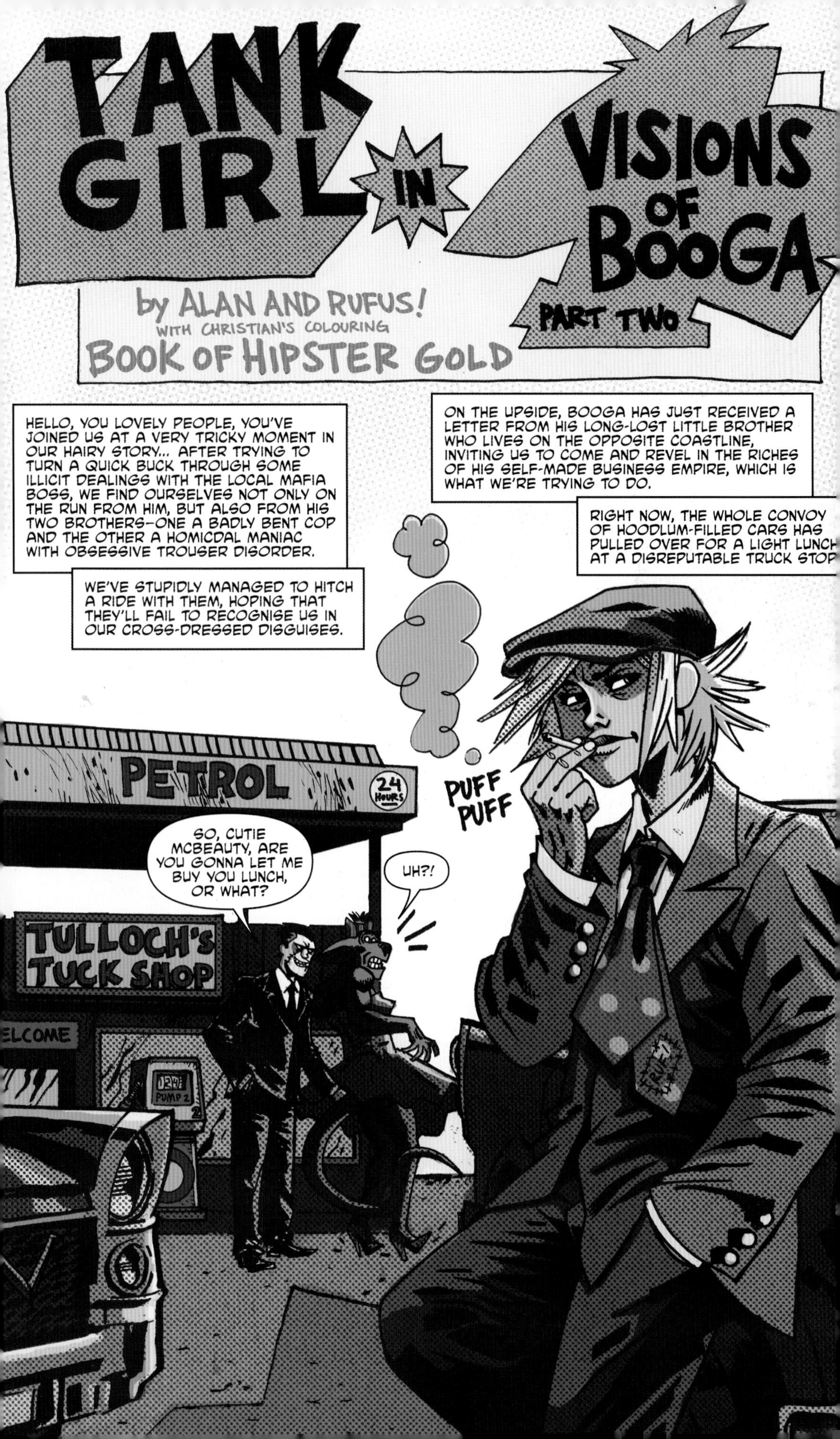
TANK GIRL IN
VISIONS OF BOOGA
PART TWO
by ALAN AND RUFUS!
WITH CHRISTIAN'S COLOURING
BOOK OF HIPSTER GOLD
HELLO, YOU LOVELY PEOPLE, YOU'VE JOINED US AT A VERY TRICKY MOMENT IN OUR HAIRY STORY... AFTER TRYING TO TURN A QUICK BUCK THROUGH SOME ILLICIT DEALINGS WITH THE LOCAL MAFIA BOSS, WE FIND OURSELVES NOT ONLY ON THE RUN FROM HIM, BUT ALSO FROM HIS TWO BROTHERS–ONE A BADLY BENT COP AND THE OTHER A HOMICDAL MANIAC WITH OBSESSIVE TROUSER DISORDER.
WE'VE STUPIDLY MANAGED TO HITCH A RIDE WITH THEM, HOPING THAT THEY'LL FAIL TO RECOGNISE US IN OUR CROSS-DRESSED DISGUISES.
ON THE UPSIDE, BOOGA HAS JUST RECEIVED A LETTER FROM HIS LONG-LOST LITTLE BROTHER WHO LIVES ON THE OPPOSITE COASTLINE, INVITING US TO COME AND REVEL IN THE RICHES OF HIS SELF-MADE BUSINESS EMPIRE, WHICH IS WHAT WE'RE TRYING TO DO.
RIGHT NOW, THE WHOLE CONVOY OF HOODLUM-FILLED CARS HAS PULLED OVER FOR A LIGHT LUNCH AT A DISREPUTABLE TRUCK STOP
PETROL
24 HOURS
PUFF PUFF
SO, CUTIE MCBEAUTY, ARE YOU GONNA LET ME BUY YOU LUNCH, OR WHAT?
UH?!
TULLOCH'S TUCK SHOP

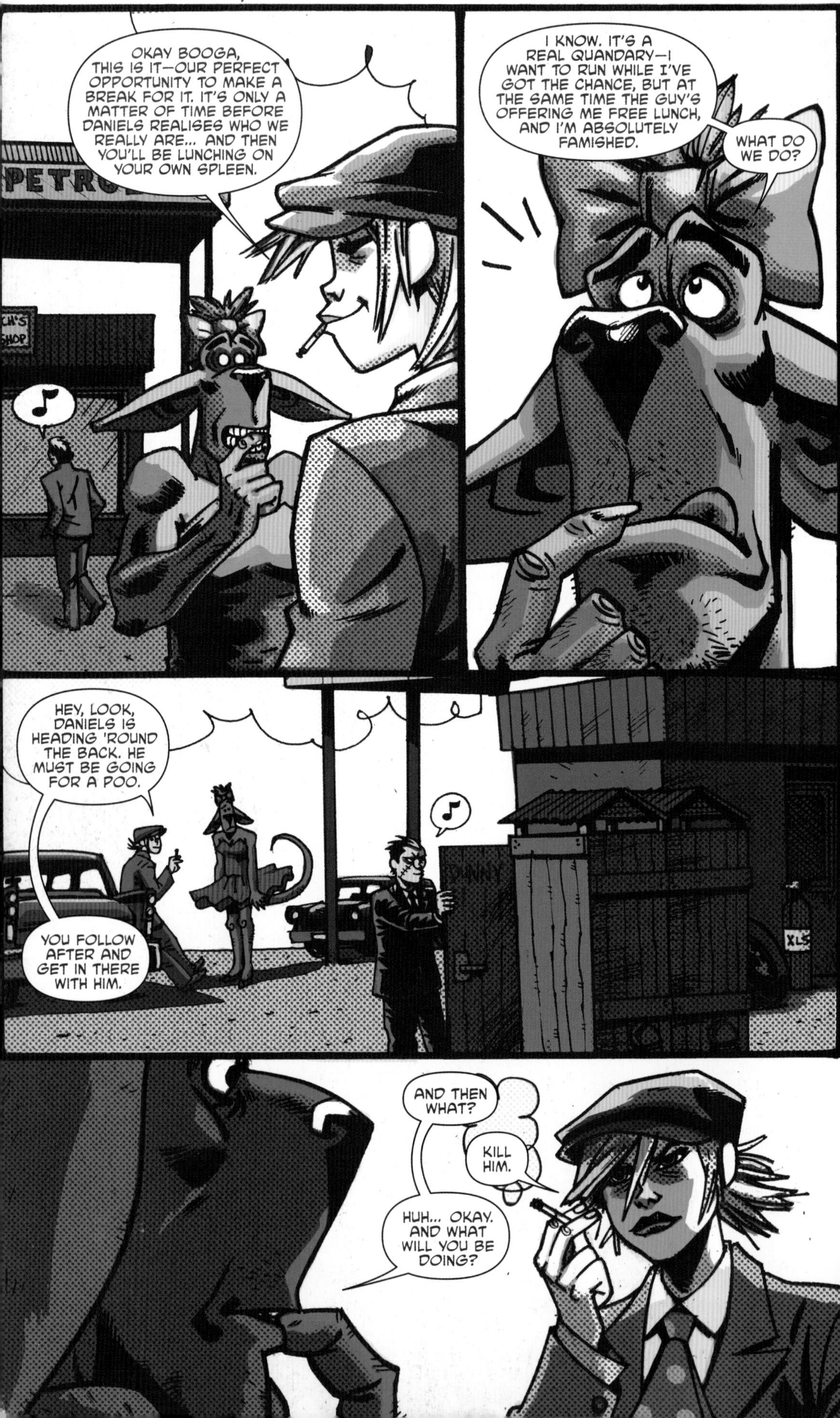
OKAY BOOGA, THIS IS IT—OUR PERFECT OPPORTUNITY TO MAKE A BREAK FOR IT. IT'S ONLY A MATTER OF TIME BEFORE DANIELS REALISES WHO WE REALLY ARE... AND THEN YOU'LL BE LUNCHING ON YOUR OWN SPLEEN.
PETRO
I KNOW. IT'S A REAL QUANDARY—I WANT TO RUN WHILE I'VE GOT THE CHANCE, BUT AT THE SAME TIME THE GUY'S OFFERING ME FREE LUNCH, AND I'M ABSOLUTELY FAMISHED.
WHAT DO WE DO?
HEY, LOOK, DANIELS IS HEADING 'ROUND THE BACK. HE MUST BE GOING FOR A POO.
YOU FOLLOW AFTER AND GET IN THERE WITH HIM.
AND THEN WHAT?
KILL HIM.
HUH... OKAY. AND WHAT WILL YOU BE DOING?

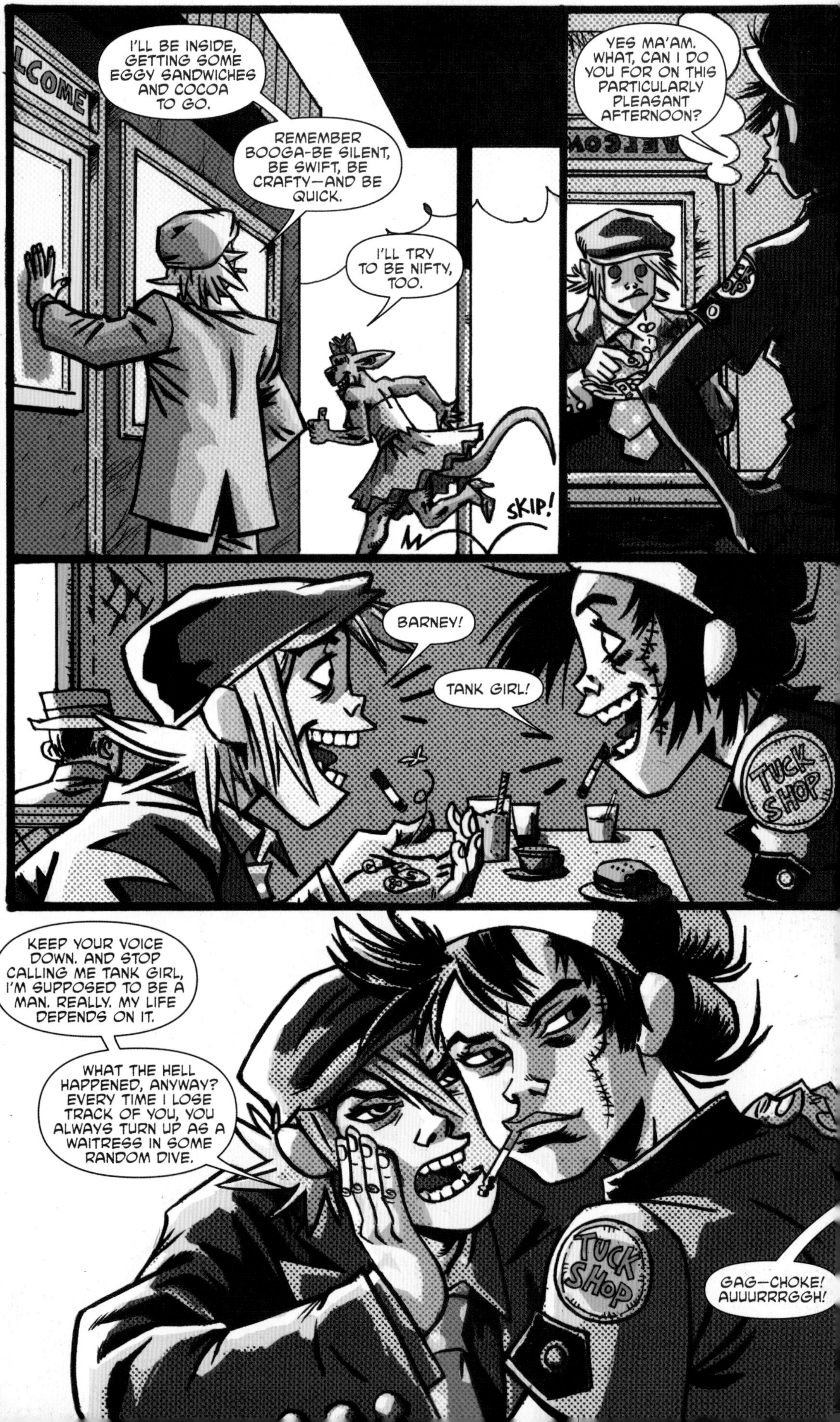
I'LL BE INSIDE, GETTING SOME EGGY SANDWICHES AND COCOA TO GO.
REMEMBER BOOGA–BE SILENT, BE SWIFT, BE CRAFTY—AND BE QUICK.
I'LL TRY TO BE NIFTY, TOO.
SKIP!
YES MA'AM. WHAT, CAN I DO YOU FOR ON THIS PARTICULARLY PLEASANT AFTERNOON?
BARNEY!
TANK GIRL!
TUCK SHOP
KEEP YOUR VOICE DOWN. AND STOP CALLING ME TANK GIRL, I'M SUPPOSED TO BE A MAN. REALLY. MY LIFE DEPENDS ON IT.
WHAT THE HELL HAPPENED, ANYWAY? EVERY TIME I LOSE TRACK OF YOU, YOU ALWAYS TURN UP AS A WAITRESS IN SOME RANDOM DIVE.
TUCK SHOP
GAG—CHOKE! AUUURRRGGH!

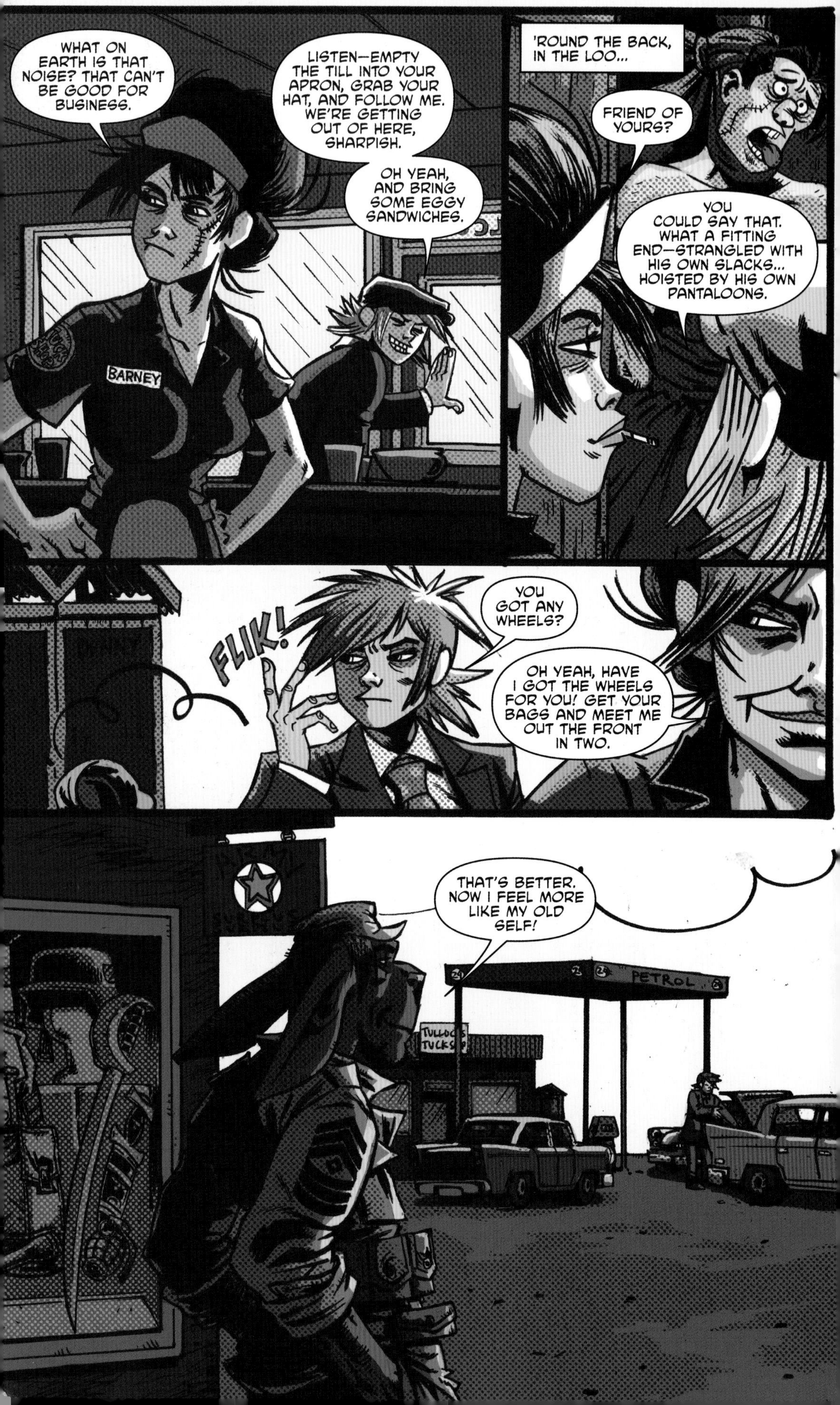
WHAT ON EARTH IS THAT NOISE? THAT CAN'T BE GOOD FOR BUSINESS.
LISTEN—EMPTY THE TILL INTO YOUR APRON, GRAB YOUR HAT, AND FOLLOW ME. WE'RE GETTING OUT OF HERE, SHARPISH.
OH YEAH, AND BRING SOME EGGY SANDWICHES.
BARNEY
'ROUND THE BACK, IN THE LOO...
FRIEND OF YOURS?
YOU COULD SAY THAT. WHAT A FITTING END—STRANGLED WITH HIS OWN SLACKS... HOISTED BY HIS OWN PANTALOONS.
FLIK!
YOU GOT ANY WHEELS?
OH YEAH, HAVE I GOT THE WHEELS FOR YOU! GET YOUR BAGS AND MEET ME OUT THE FRONT IN TWO.
THAT'S BETTER. NOW I FEEL MORE LIKE MY OLD SELF!
PETROL

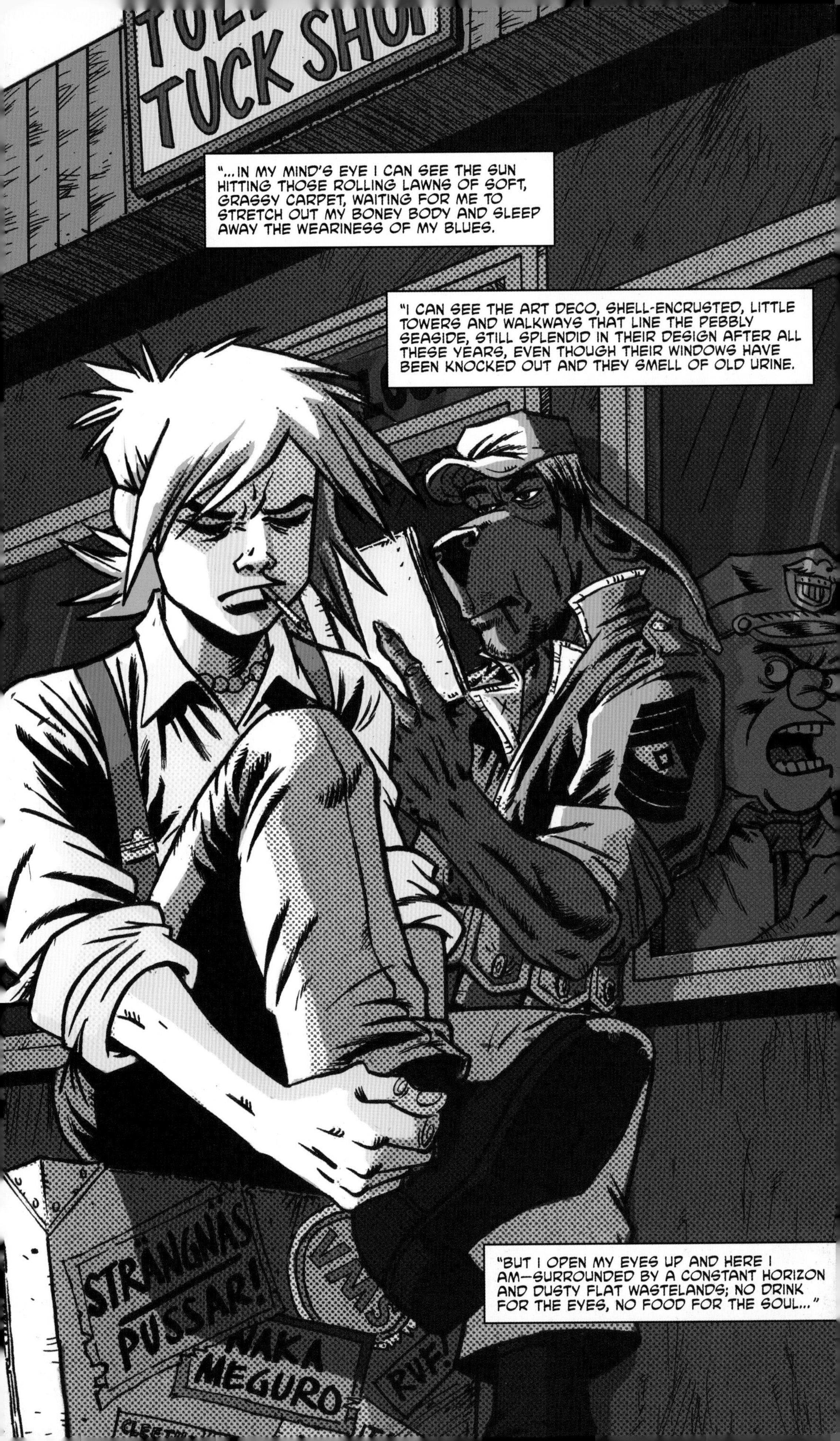

"...IN MY MIND'S EYE I CAN SEE THE SUN HITTING THOSE ROLLING LAWNS OF SOFT, GRASSY CARPET, WAITING FOR ME TO STRETCH OUT MY BONEY BODY AND SLEEP AWAY THE WEARINESS OF MY BLUES.
"I CAN SEE THE ART DECO, SHELL-ENCRUSTED, LITTLE TOWERS AND WALKWAYS THAT LINE THE PEBBLY SEASIDE, STILL SPLENDID IN THEIR DESIGN AFTER ALL THESE YEARS, EVEN THOUGH THEIR WINDOWS HAVE BEEN KNOCKED OUT AND THEY SMELL OF OLD URINE.
"BUT I OPEN MY EYES UP AND HERE I AM—SURROUNDED BY A CONSTANT HORIZON AND DUSTY FLAT WASTELANDS; NO DRINK FOR THE EYES, NO FOOD FOR THE SOUL..."
STRÄNGNÄS PUSSAR!
NAKA MEGURO

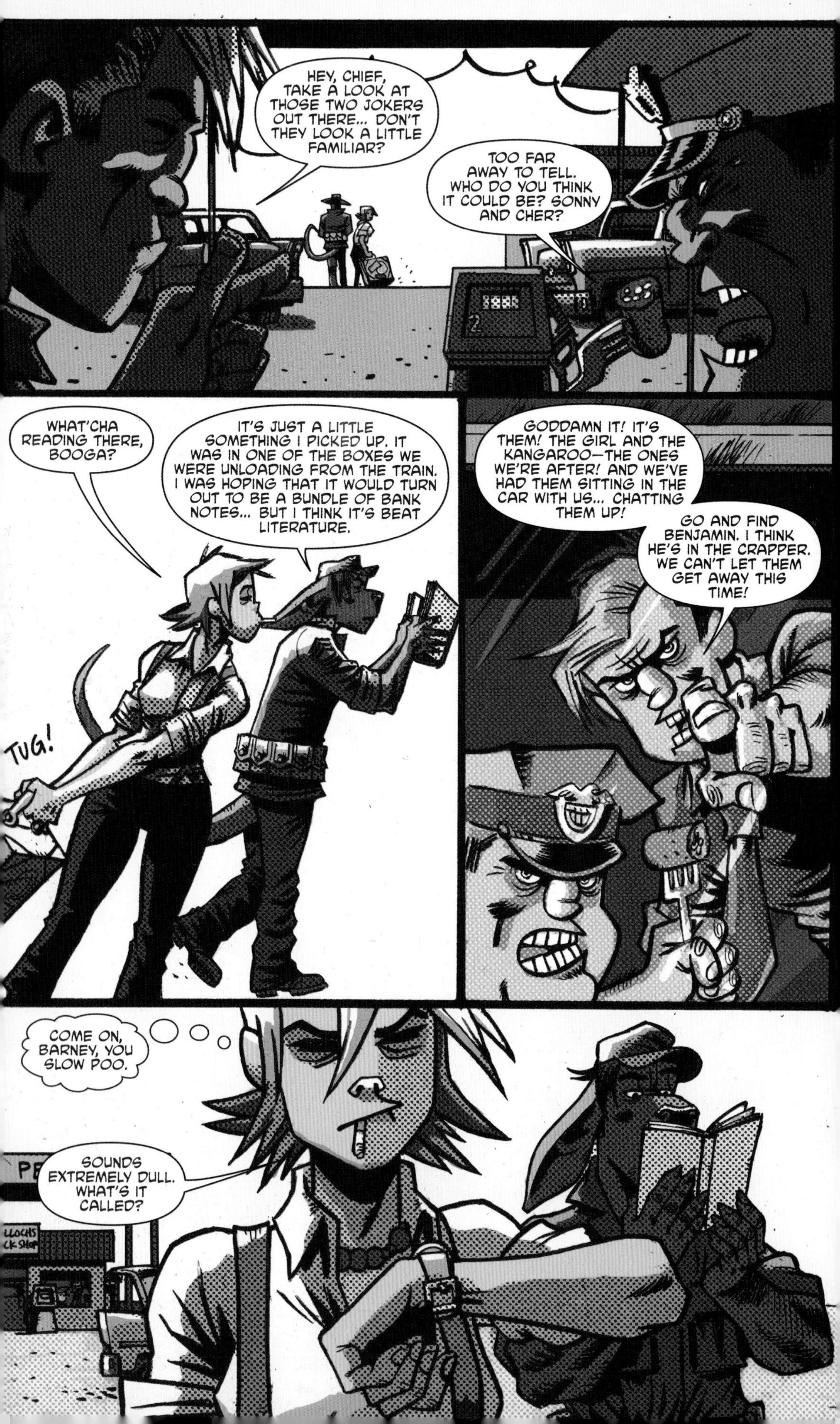
HEY, CHIEF, TAKE A LOOK AT THOSE TWO JOKERS OUT THERE... DON'T THEY LOOK A LITTLE FAMILIAR?
TOO FAR AWAY TO TELL. WHO DO YOU THINK IT COULD BE? SONNY AND CHER?
WHAT'CHA READING THERE, BOOGA?
IT'S JUST A LITTLE SOMETHING I PICKED UP. IT WAS IN ONE OF THE BOXES WE WERE UNLOADING FROM THE TRAIN. I WAS HOPING THAT IT WOULD TURN OUT TO BE A BUNDLE OF BANK NOTES... BUT I THINK IT'S BEAT LITERATURE.
TUG!
GODDAMN IT! IT'S THEM! THE GIRL AND THE KANGAROO—THE ONES WE'RE AFTER! AND WE'VE HAD THEM SITTING IN THE CAR WITH US... CHATTING THEM UP!
GO AND FIND BENJAMIN. I THINK HE'S IN THE CRAPPER. WE CAN'T LET THEM GET AWAY THIS TIME!
COME ON, BARNEY, YOU SLOW POO.
SOUNDS EXTREMELY DULL. WHAT'S IT CALLED?

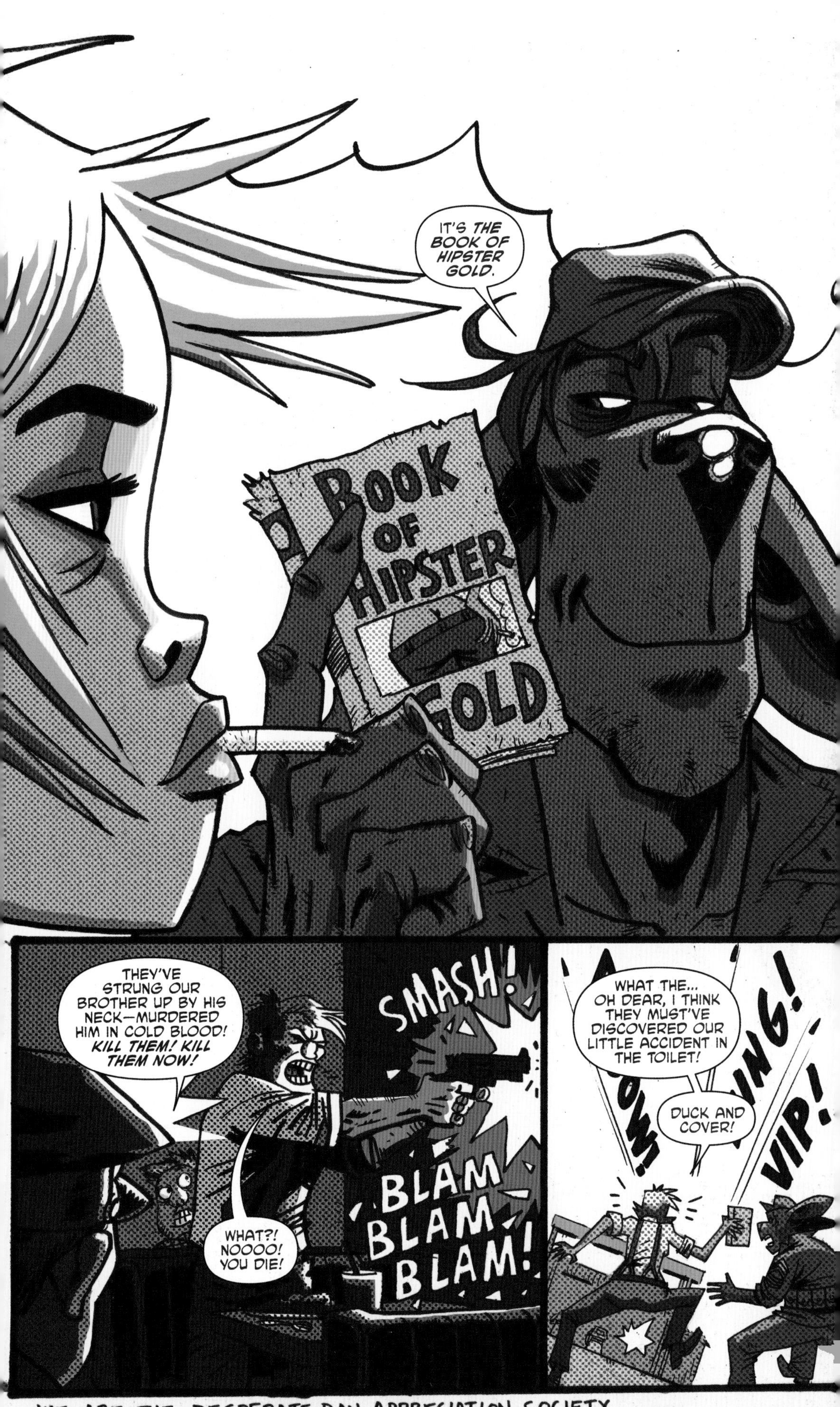
IT'S *THE BOOK OF HIPSTER GOLD.*
BOOK OF HIPSTER GOLD
THEY'VE STRUNG OUR BROTHER UP BY HIS NECK—MURDERED HIM IN COLD BLOOD! ***KILL THEM! KILL THEM NOW!***
WHAT?! NOOOO! YOU DIE!
SMASH!
BLAM BLAM BLAM!
WHAT THE... OH DEAR, I THINK THEY MUST'VE DISCOVERED OUR LITTLE ACCIDENT IN THE TOILET!
DUCK AND COVER!

WE ARE THE DESPERATE DAN APPRECIATION SOCIETY...
GOD SAVE STRAWBERRY JAM, AND ALL THE DIFFERENT VARIETIES

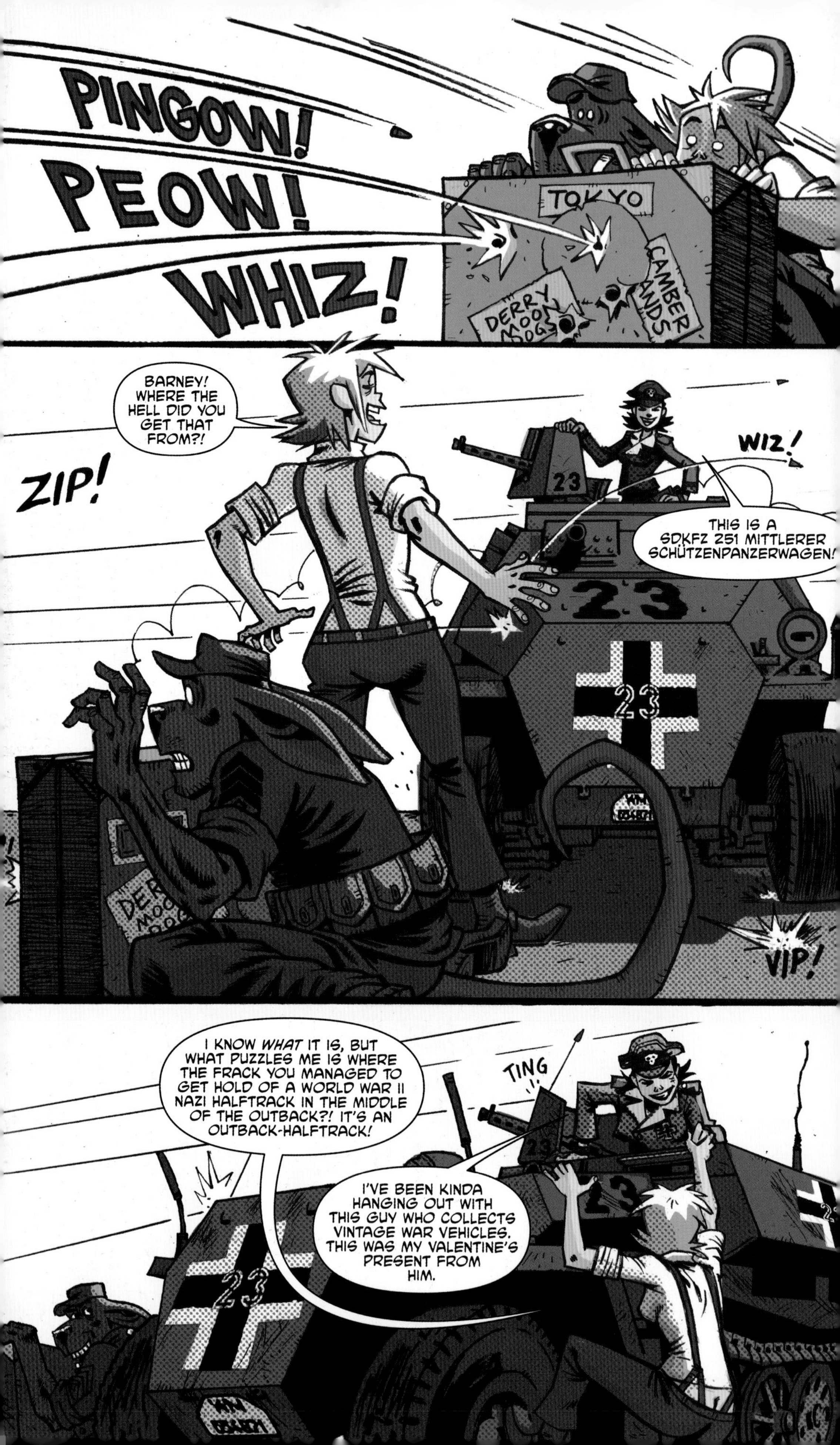
PINGOW!
PEOW!
WHIZ!
TOKYO
CAMBER SANDS
DERRY MOON DOGS
BARNEY! WHERE THE HELL DID YOU GET THAT FROM?!
ZIP!
WIZ!
THIS IS A SDKFZ 251 MITTLERER SCHÜTZENPANZERWAGEN!
23
VIP!
I KNOW *WHAT* IT IS, BUT WHAT PUZZLES ME IS WHERE THE FRACK YOU MANAGED TO GET HOLD OF A WORLD WAR II NAZI HALFTRACK IN THE MIDDLE OF THE OUTBACK?! IT'S AN OUTBACK-HALFTRACK!
TING
I'VE BEEN KINDA HANGING OUT WITH THIS GUY WHO COLLECTS VINTAGE WAR VEHICLES. THIS WAS MY VALENTINE'S PRESENT FROM HIM.

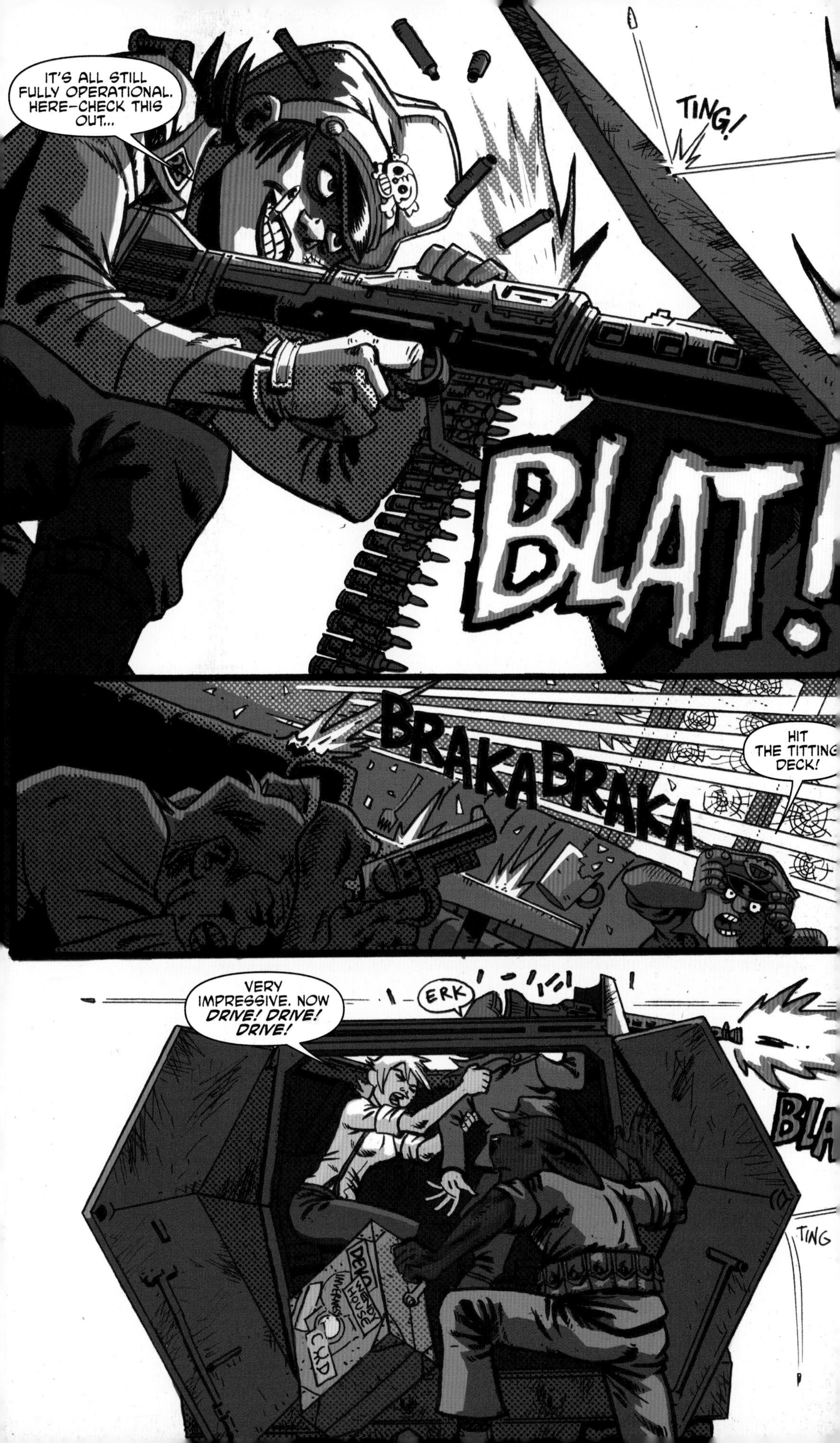
IT'S ALL STILL FULLY OPERATIONAL. HERE—CHECK THIS OUT...
TING!
BLAT!
BRAKABRAKA
HIT THE TITTING DECK!
VERY IMPRESSIVE. NOW DRIVE! DRIVE! DRIVE!
ERK
TING

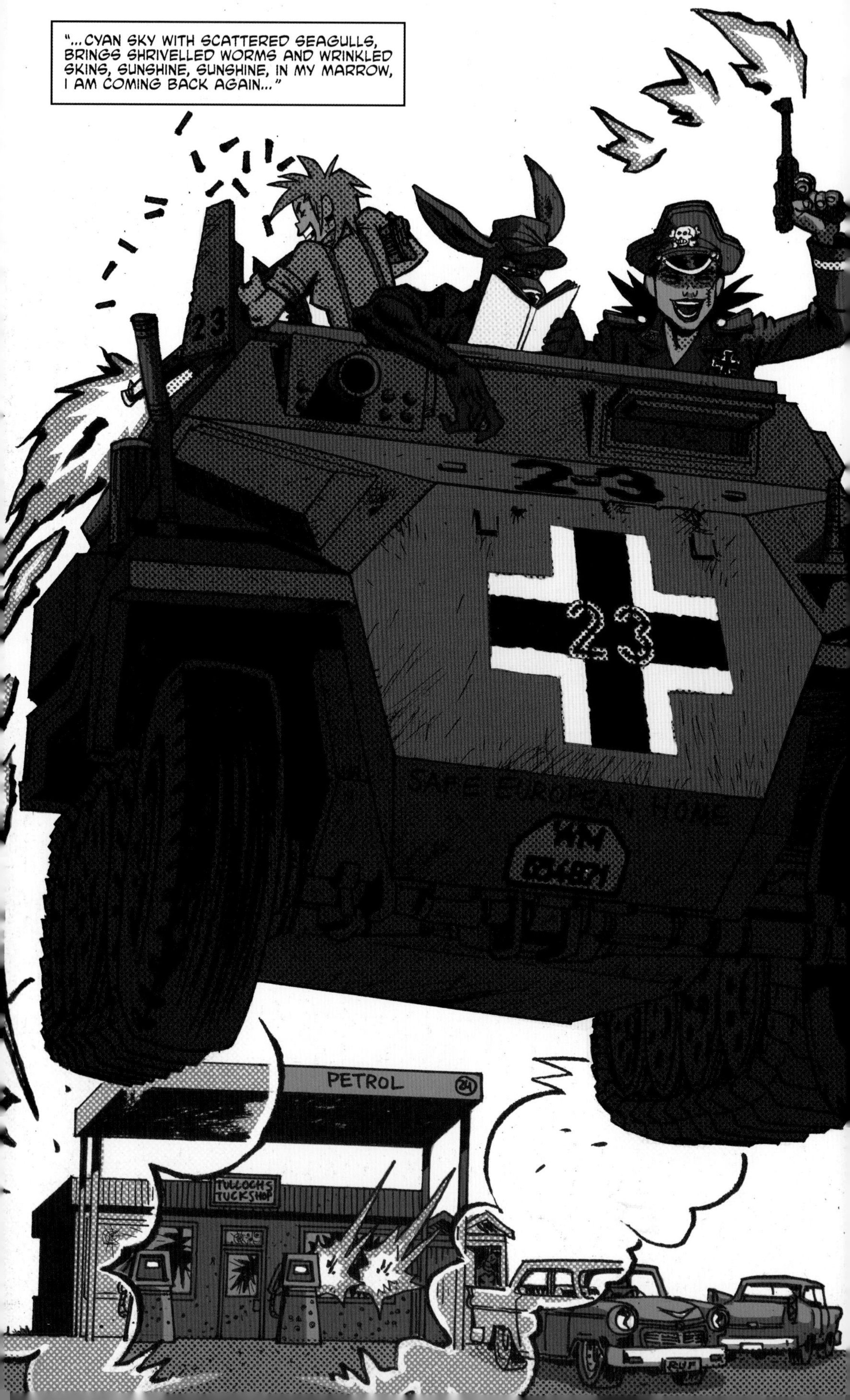
"...CYAN SKY WITH SCATTERED SEAGULLS, BRINGS SHRIVELLED WORMS AND WRINKLED SKINS, SUNSHINE, SUNSHINE, IN MY MARROW, I AM COMING BACK AGAIN..."
23
23
23
PETROL
TULLOCHS TUCKSHOP

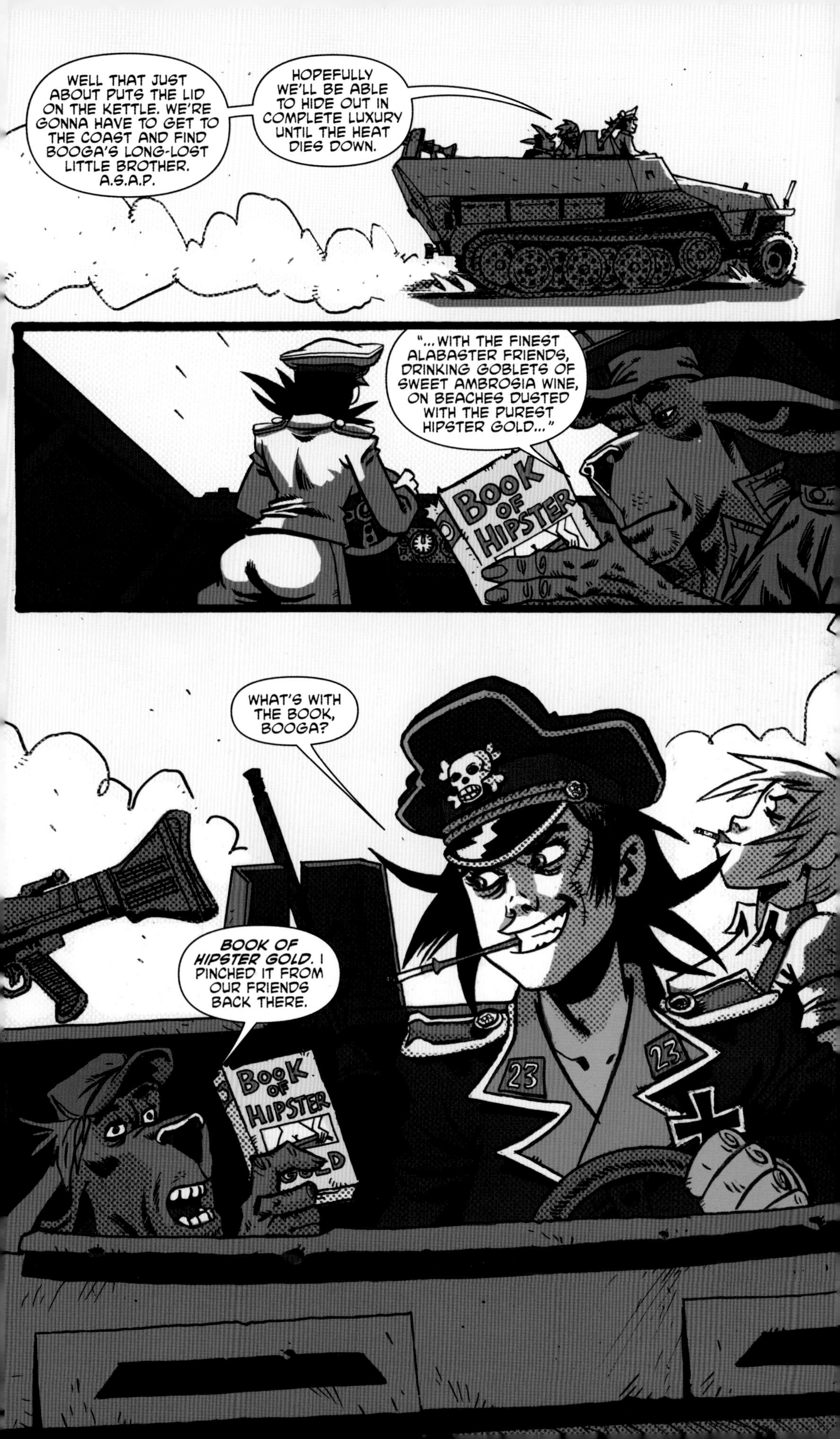
WELL THAT JUST ABOUT PUTS THE LID ON THE KETTLE. WE'RE GONNA HAVE TO GET TO THE COAST AND FIND BOOGA'S LONG-LOST LITTLE BROTHER. A.S.A.P.
HOPEFULLY WE'LL BE ABLE TO HIDE OUT IN COMPLETE LUXURY UNTIL THE HEAT DIES DOWN.
"...WITH THE FINEST ALABASTER FRIENDS, DRINKING GOBLETS OF SWEET AMBROSIA WINE, ON BEACHES DUSTED WITH THE PUREST HIPSTER GOLD..."
BOOK OF HIPSTER
WHAT'S WITH THE BOOK, BOOGA?
BOOK OF HIPSTER GOLD. I PINCHED IT FROM OUR FRIENDS BACK THERE.
23
23
BOOK OF HIPSTER GOLD

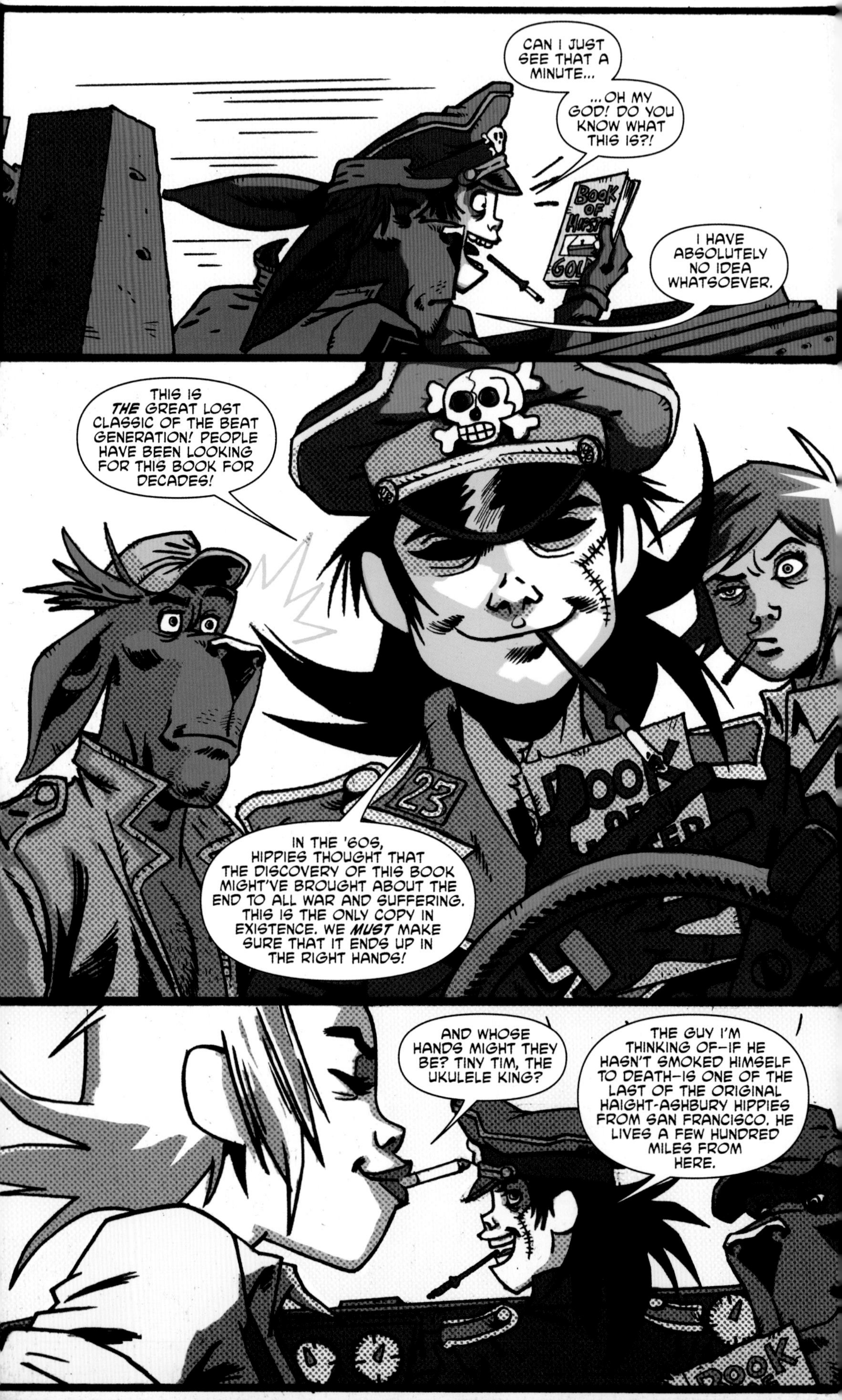
CAN I JUST SEE THAT A MINUTE...
...OH MY GOD! DO YOU KNOW WHAT THIS IS?!
I HAVE ABSOLUTELY NO IDEA WHATSOEVER.
THIS IS *THE* GREAT LOST CLASSIC OF THE BEAT GENERATION! PEOPLE HAVE BEEN LOOKING FOR THIS BOOK FOR DECADES!
IN THE '60S, HIPPIES THOUGHT THAT THE DISCOVERY OF THIS BOOK MIGHT'VE BROUGHT ABOUT THE END TO ALL WAR AND SUFFERING. THIS IS THE ONLY COPY IN EXISTENCE. WE *MUST* MAKE SURE THAT IT ENDS UP IN THE RIGHT HANDS!
AND WHOSE HANDS MIGHT THEY BE? TINY TIM, THE UKULELE KING?
THE GUY I'M THINKING OF—IF HE HASN'T SMOKED HIMSELF TO DEATH—IS ONE OF THE LAST OF THE ORIGINAL HAIGHT-ASHBURY HIPPIES FROM SAN FRANCISCO. HE LIVES A FEW HUNDRED MILES FROM HERE.

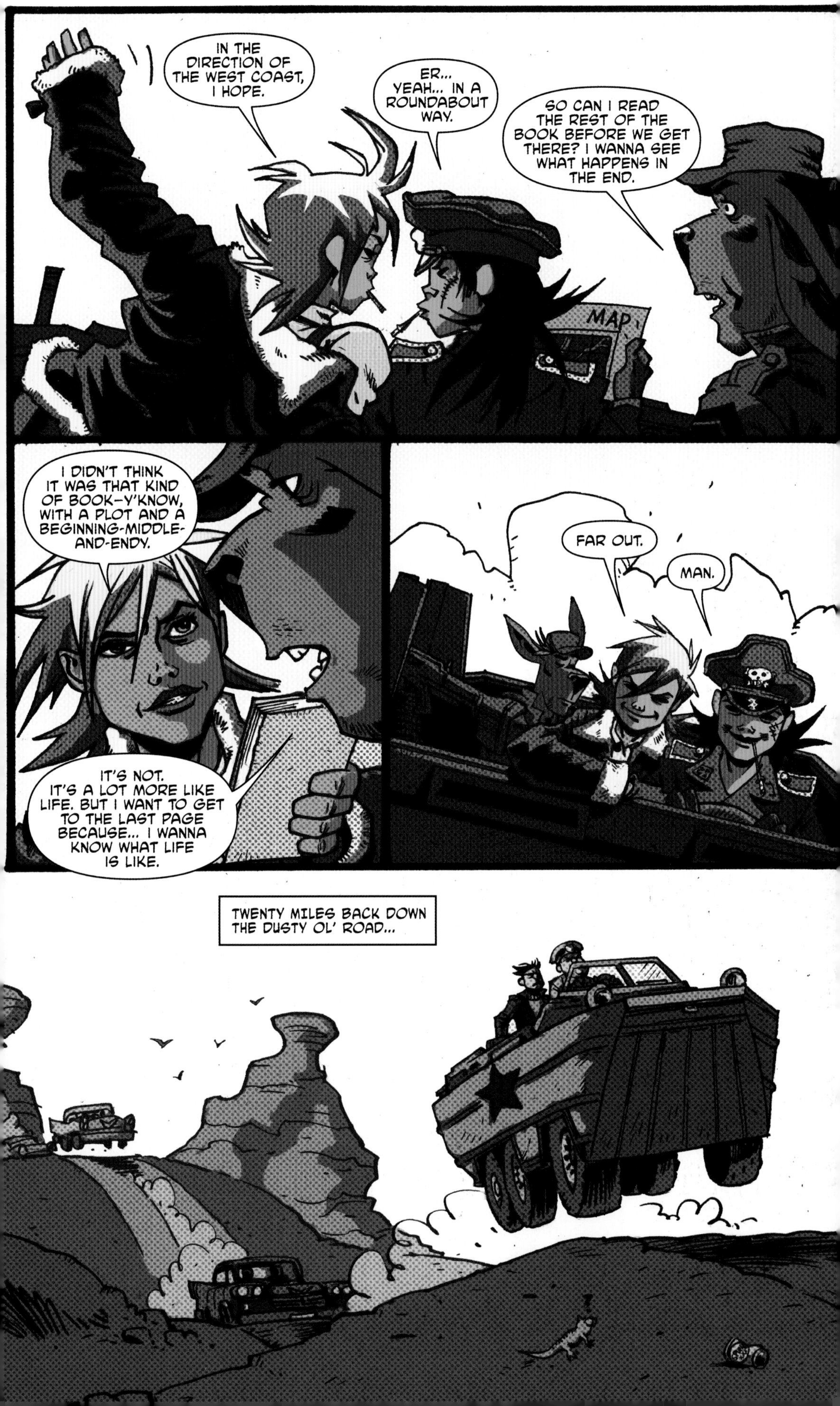
IN THE DIRECTION OF THE WEST COAST, I HOPE.
ER... YEAH... IN A ROUNDABOUT WAY.
SO CAN I READ THE REST OF THE BOOK BEFORE WE GET THERE? I WANNA SEE WHAT HAPPENS IN THE END.
MAP
I DIDN'T THINK IT WAS THAT KIND OF BOOK—Y'KNOW, WITH A PLOT AND A BEGINNING-MIDDLE-AND-ENDY.
IT'S NOT. IT'S A LOT MORE LIKE LIFE. BUT I WANT TO GET TO THE LAST PAGE BECAUSE... I WANNA KNOW WHAT LIFE IS LIKE.
FAR OUT.
MAN.
TWENTY MILES BACK DOWN THE DUSTY OL' ROAD...

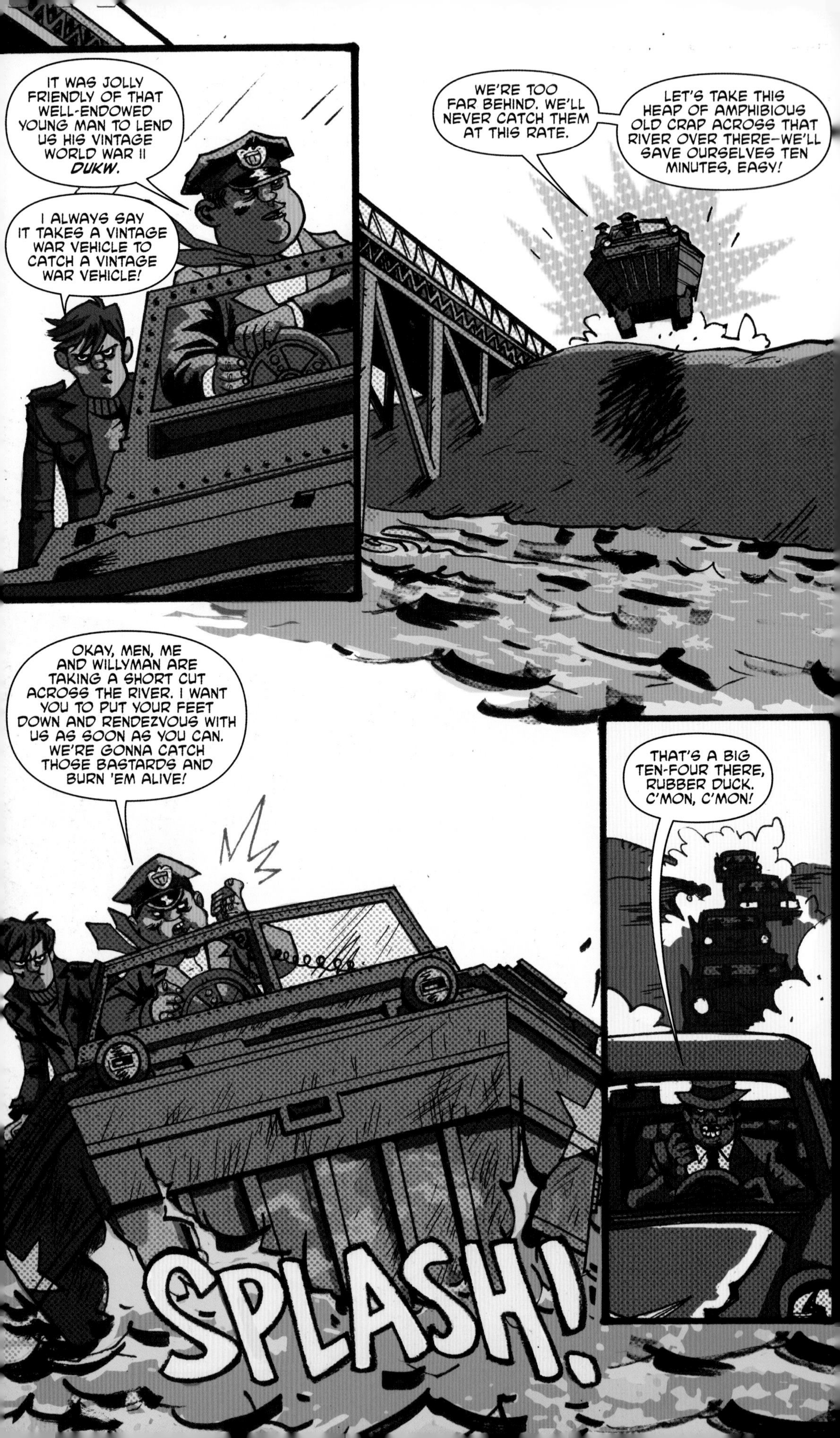
IT WAS JOLLY FRIENDLY OF THAT WELL-ENDOWED YOUNG MAN TO LEND US HIS VINTAGE WORLD WAR II *DUKW*.
I ALWAYS SAY IT TAKES A VINTAGE WAR VEHICLE TO CATCH A VINTAGE WAR VEHICLE!
WE'RE TOO FAR BEHIND. WE'LL NEVER CATCH THEM AT THIS RATE.
LET'S TAKE THIS HEAP OF AMPHIBIOUS OLD CRAP ACROSS THAT RIVER OVER THERE—WE'LL SAVE OURSELVES TEN MINUTES, EASY!
OKAY, MEN, ME AND WILLYMAN ARE TAKING A SHORT CUT ACROSS THE RIVER. I WANT YOU TO PUT YOUR FEET DOWN AND RENDEZVOUS WITH US AS SOON AS YOU CAN. WE'RE GONNA CATCH THOSE BASTARDS AND BURN 'EM ALIVE!
THAT'S A BIG TEN-FOUR THERE, RUBBER DUCK. C'MON, C'MON!
SPLASH!

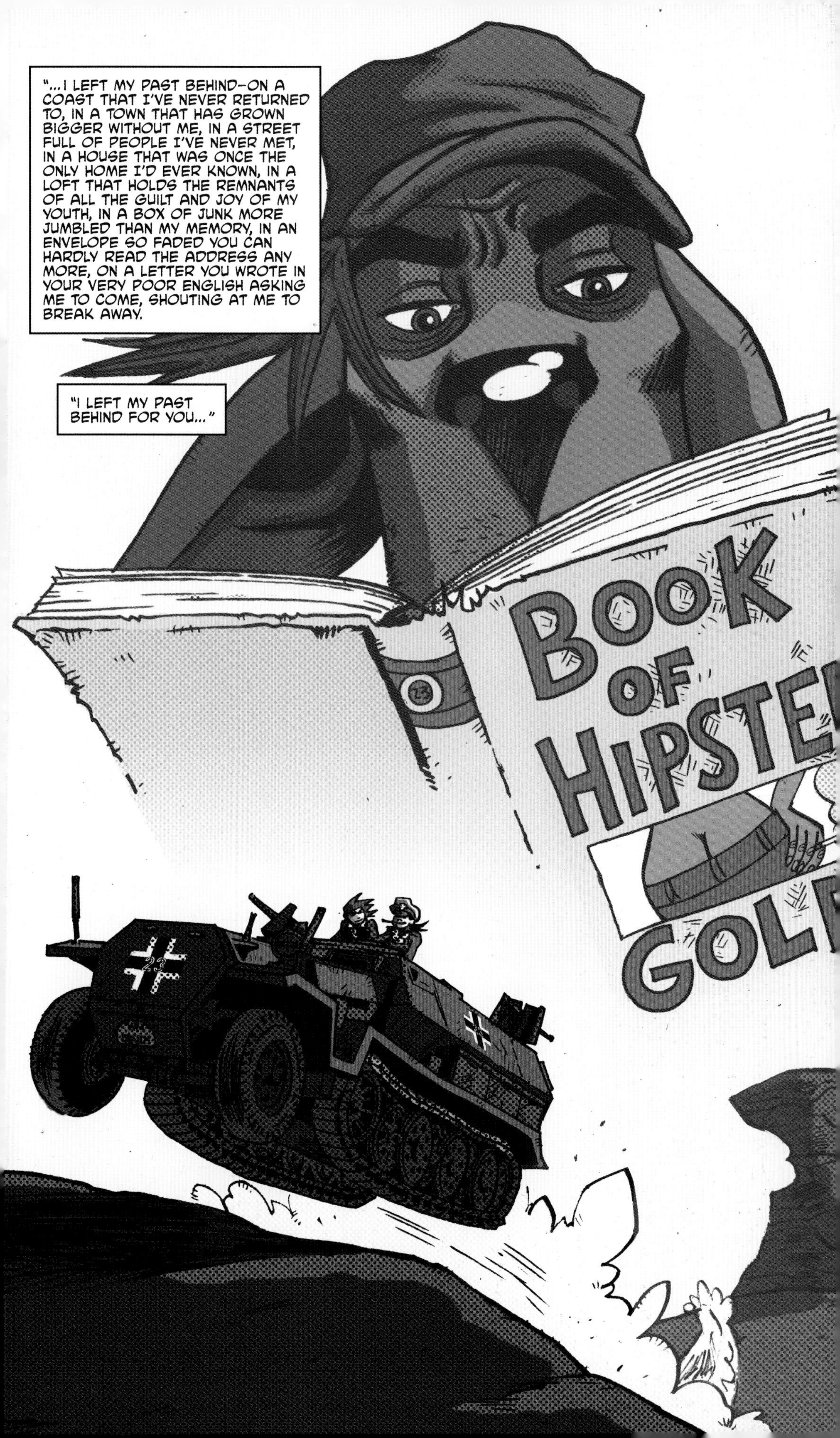
"...I LEFT MY PAST BEHIND–ON A COAST THAT I'VE NEVER RETURNED TO, IN A TOWN THAT HAS GROWN BIGGER WITHOUT ME, IN A STREET FULL OF PEOPLE I'VE NEVER MET, IN A HOUSE THAT WAS ONCE THE ONLY HOME I'D EVER KNOWN, IN A LOFT THAT HOLDS THE REMNANTS OF ALL THE GUILT AND JOY OF MY YOUTH, IN A BOX OF JUNK MORE JUMBLED THAN MY MEMORY, IN AN ENVELOPE SO FADED YOU CAN HARDLY READ THE ADDRESS ANY MORE, ON A LETTER YOU WROTE IN YOUR VERY POOR ENGLISH ASKING ME TO COME, SHOUTING AT ME TO BREAK AWAY.
"I LEFT MY PAST BEHIND FOR YOU..."
BOOK OF HIPSTE
GOL
23

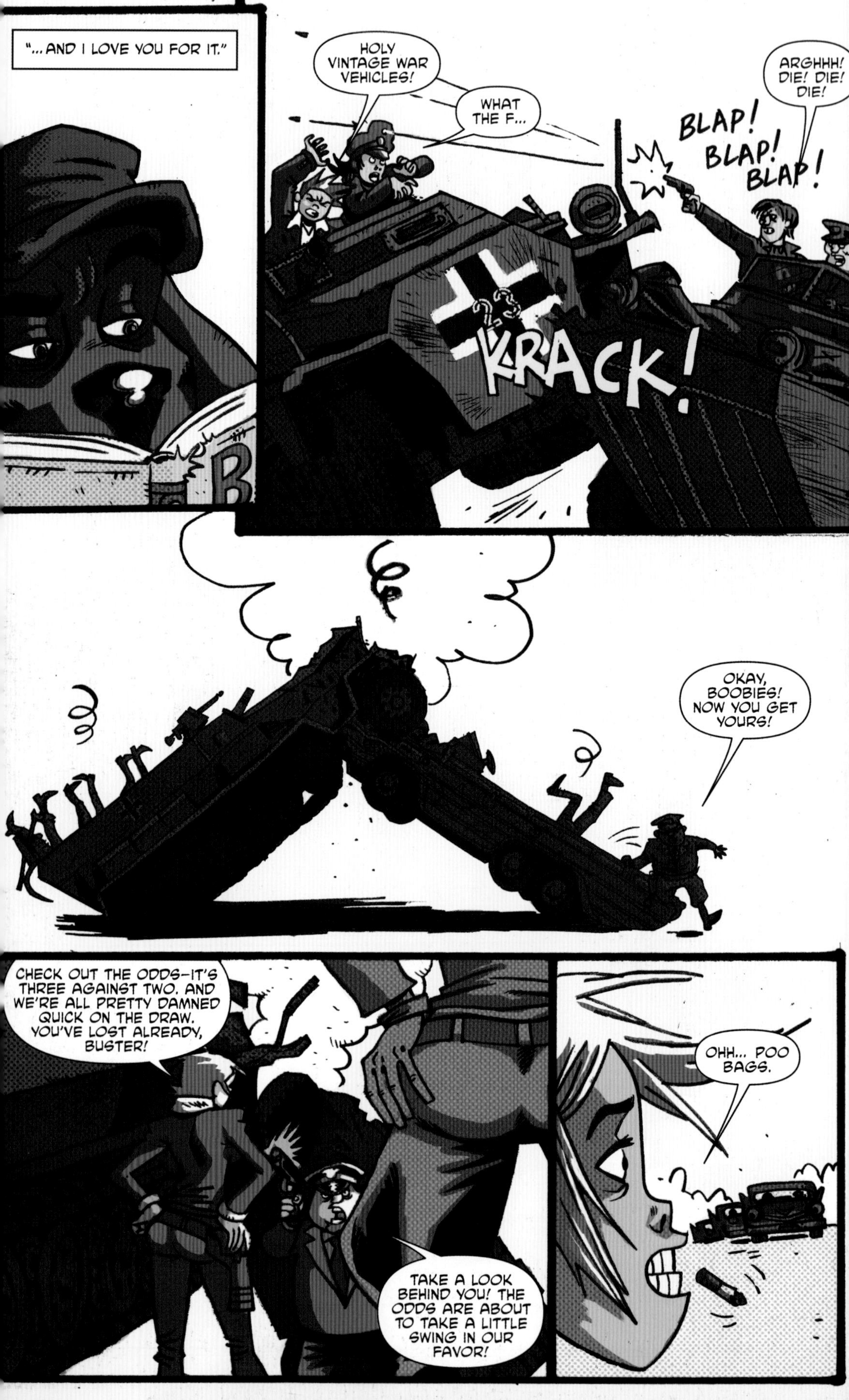
"... AND I LOVE YOU FOR IT."
HOLY VINTAGE WAR VEHICLES!
WHAT THE F...
ARGHHH! DIE! DIE! DIE!
BLAP! BLAP! BLAP!
KRACK!
OKAY, BOOBIES! NOW YOU GET YOURS!
CHECK OUT THE ODDS—IT'S THREE AGAINST TWO. AND WE'RE ALL PRETTY DAMNED QUICK ON THE DRAW. YOU'VE LOST ALREADY, BUSTER!
TAKE A LOOK BEHIND YOU! THE ODDS ARE ABOUT TO TAKE A LITTLE SWING IN OUR FAVOR!
OHH... POO BAGS.

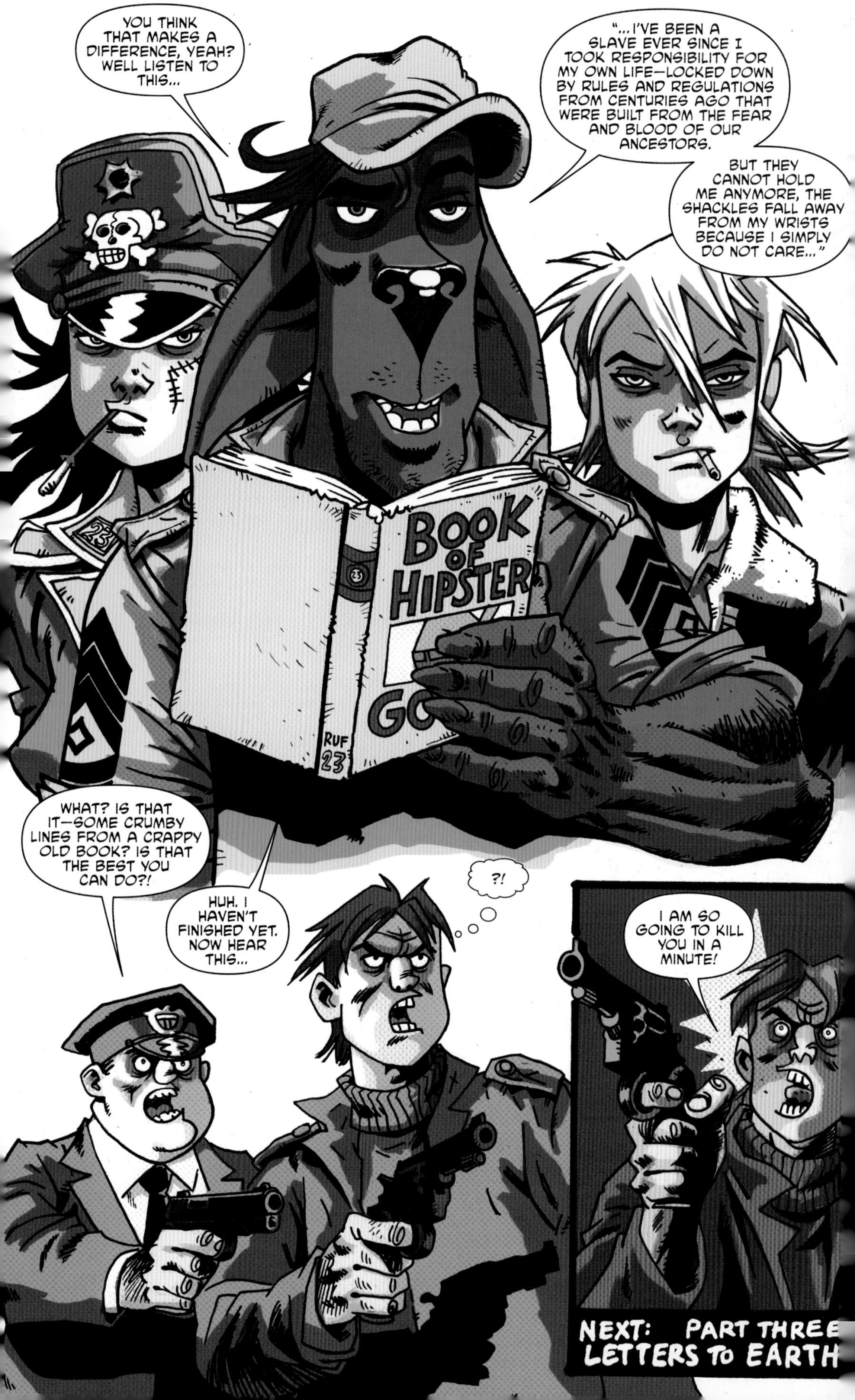
YOU THINK THAT MAKES A DIFFERENCE, YEAH? WELL LISTEN TO THIS...
"...I'VE BEEN A SLAVE EVER SINCE I TOOK RESPONSIBILITY FOR MY OWN LIFE—LOCKED DOWN BY RULES AND REGULATIONS FROM CENTURIES AGO THAT WERE BUILT FROM THE FEAR AND BLOOD OF OUR ANCESTORS.
BUT THEY CANNOT HOLD ME ANYMORE, THE SHACKLES FALL AWAY FROM MY WRISTS BECAUSE I SIMPLY DO NOT CARE..."
BOOK OF HIPSTER
RUF 23
WHAT? IS THAT IT—SOME CRUMBY LINES FROM A CRAPPY OLD BOOK? IS THAT THE BEST YOU CAN DO?!
HUH. I HAVEN'T FINISHED YET. NOW HEAR THIS...
?!
I AM SO GOING TO KILL YOU IN A MINUTE!
NEXT: PART THREE
LETTERS TO EARTH

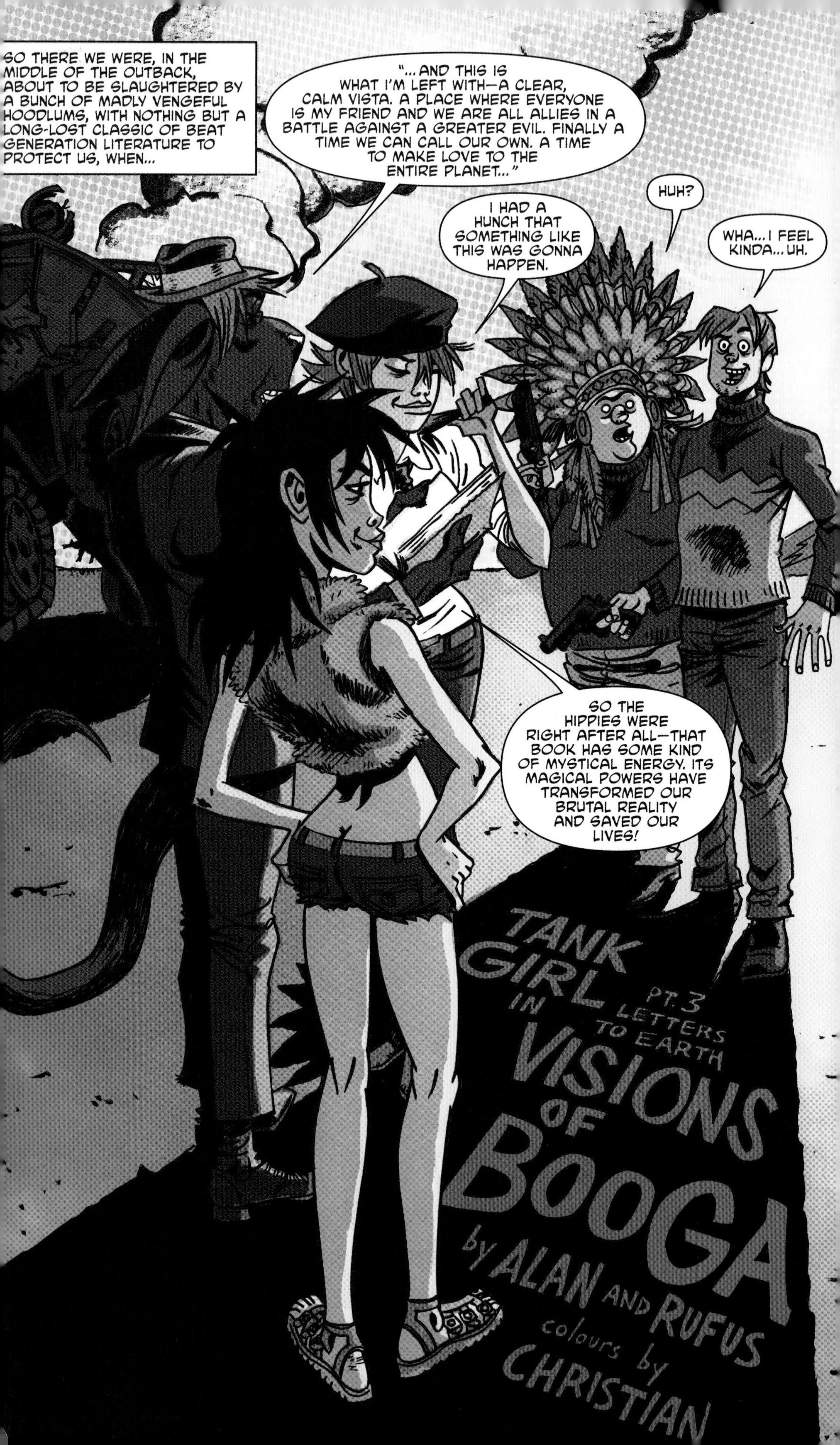
SO THERE WE WERE, IN THE MIDDLE OF THE OUTBACK, ABOUT TO BE SLAUGHTERED BY A BUNCH OF MADLY VENGEFUL HOODLUMS, WITH NOTHING BUT A LONG-LOST CLASSIC OF BEAT GENERATION LITERATURE TO PROTECT US, WHEN...
"...AND THIS IS WHAT I'M LEFT WITH—A CLEAR, CALM VISTA. A PLACE WHERE EVERYONE IS MY FRIEND AND WE ARE ALL ALLIES IN A BATTLE AGAINST A GREATER EVIL. FINALLY A TIME WE CAN CALL OUR OWN. A TIME TO MAKE LOVE TO THE ENTIRE PLANET..."
I HAD A HUNCH THAT SOMETHING LIKE THIS WAS GONNA HAPPEN.
HUH?
WHA... I FEEL KINDA... UH.
SO THE HIPPIES WERE RIGHT AFTER ALL—THAT BOOK HAS SOME KIND OF MYSTICAL ENERGY. ITS MAGICAL POWERS HAVE TRANSFORMED OUR BRUTAL REALITY AND SAVED OUR LIVES!
TANK GIRL IN
PT. 3 LETTERS TO EARTH
VISIONS OF BOOGA
by ALAN AND RUFUS
colours by CHRISTIAN

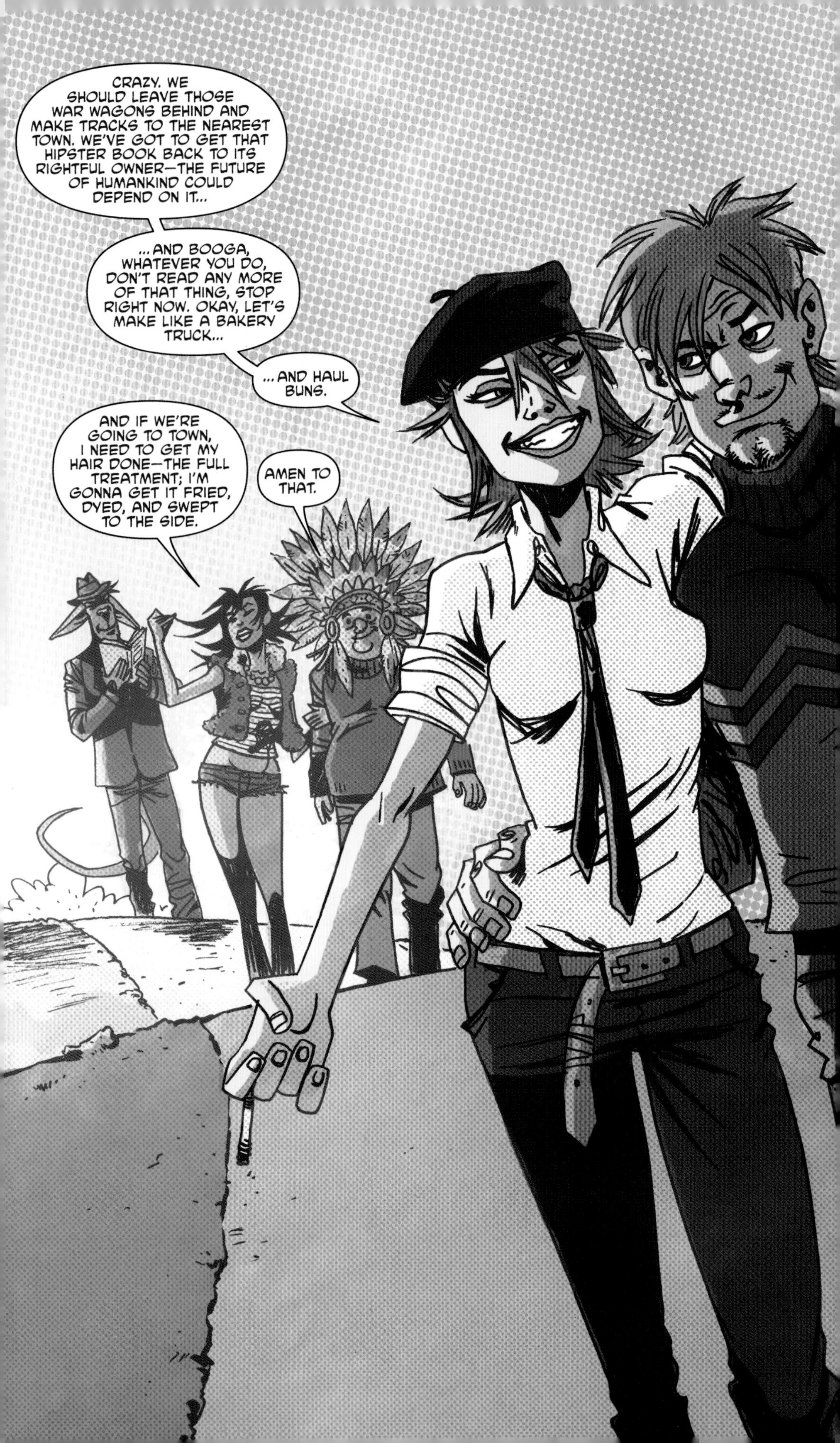
CRAZY. WE SHOULD LEAVE THOSE WAR WAGONS BEHIND AND MAKE TRACKS TO THE NEAREST TOWN. WE'VE GOT TO GET THAT HIPSTER BOOK BACK TO ITS RIGHTFUL OWNER—THE FUTURE OF HUMANKIND COULD DEPEND ON IT...
...AND BOOGA, WHATEVER YOU DO, DON'T READ ANY MORE OF THAT THING, STOP RIGHT NOW. OKAY, LET'S MAKE LIKE A BAKERY TRUCK...
...AND HAUL BUNS.
AND IF WE'RE GOING TO TOWN, I NEED TO GET MY HAIR DONE—THE FULL TREATMENT; I'M GONNA GET IT FRIED, DYED, AND SWEPT TO THE SIDE.
AMEN TO THAT.

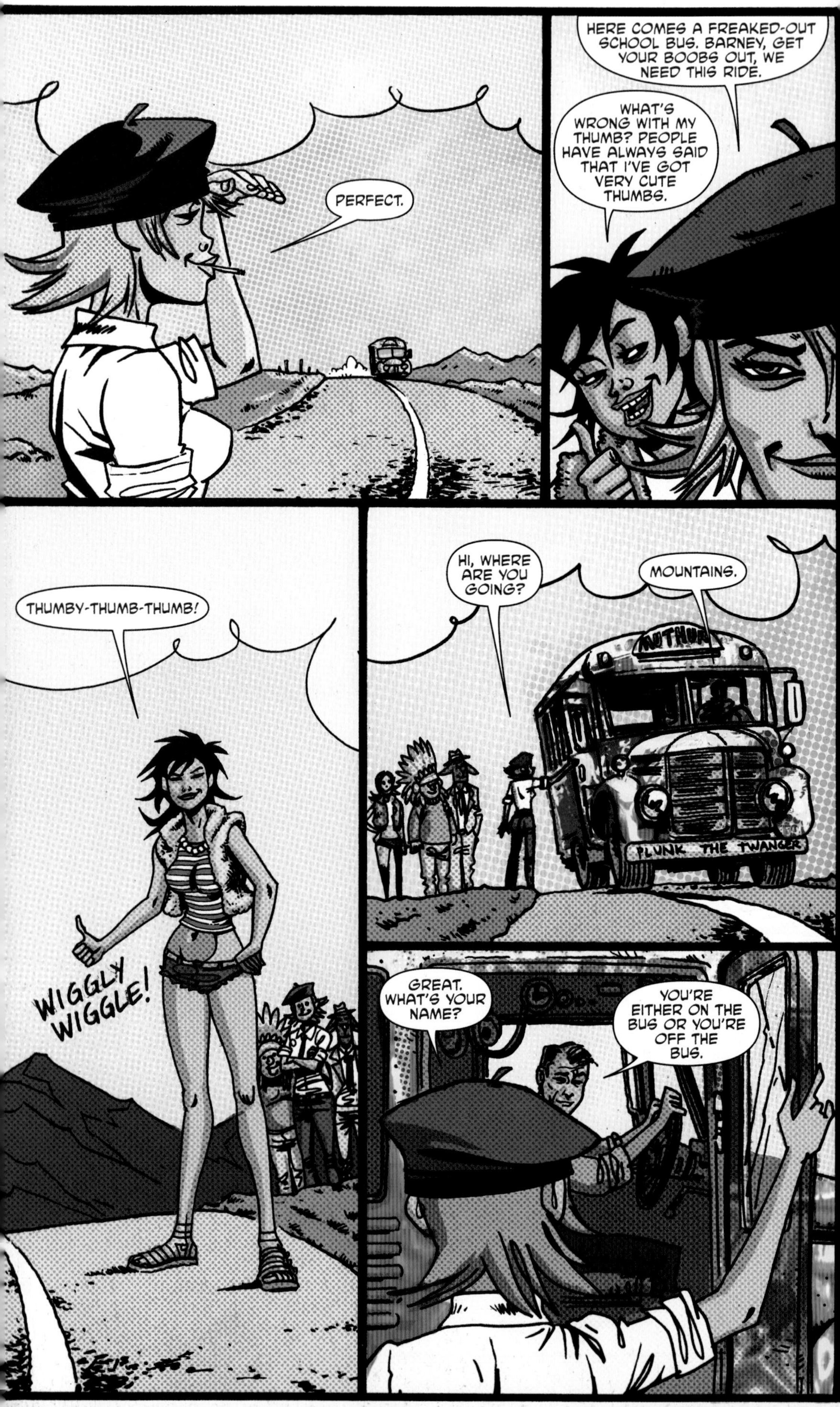
PERFECT.
HERE COMES A FREAKED-OUT SCHOOL BUS. BARNEY, GET YOUR BOOBS OUT, WE NEED THIS RIDE.
WHAT'S WRONG WITH MY THUMB? PEOPLE HAVE ALWAYS SAID THAT I'VE GOT VERY CUTE THUMBS.
THUMBY-THUMB-THUMB!
WIGGLY WIGGLE!
HI, WHERE ARE YOU GOING?
MOUNTAINS.
PLUNK THE TWANGER
GREAT. WHAT'S YOUR NAME?
YOU'RE EITHER ON THE BUS OR YOU'RE OFF THE BUS.

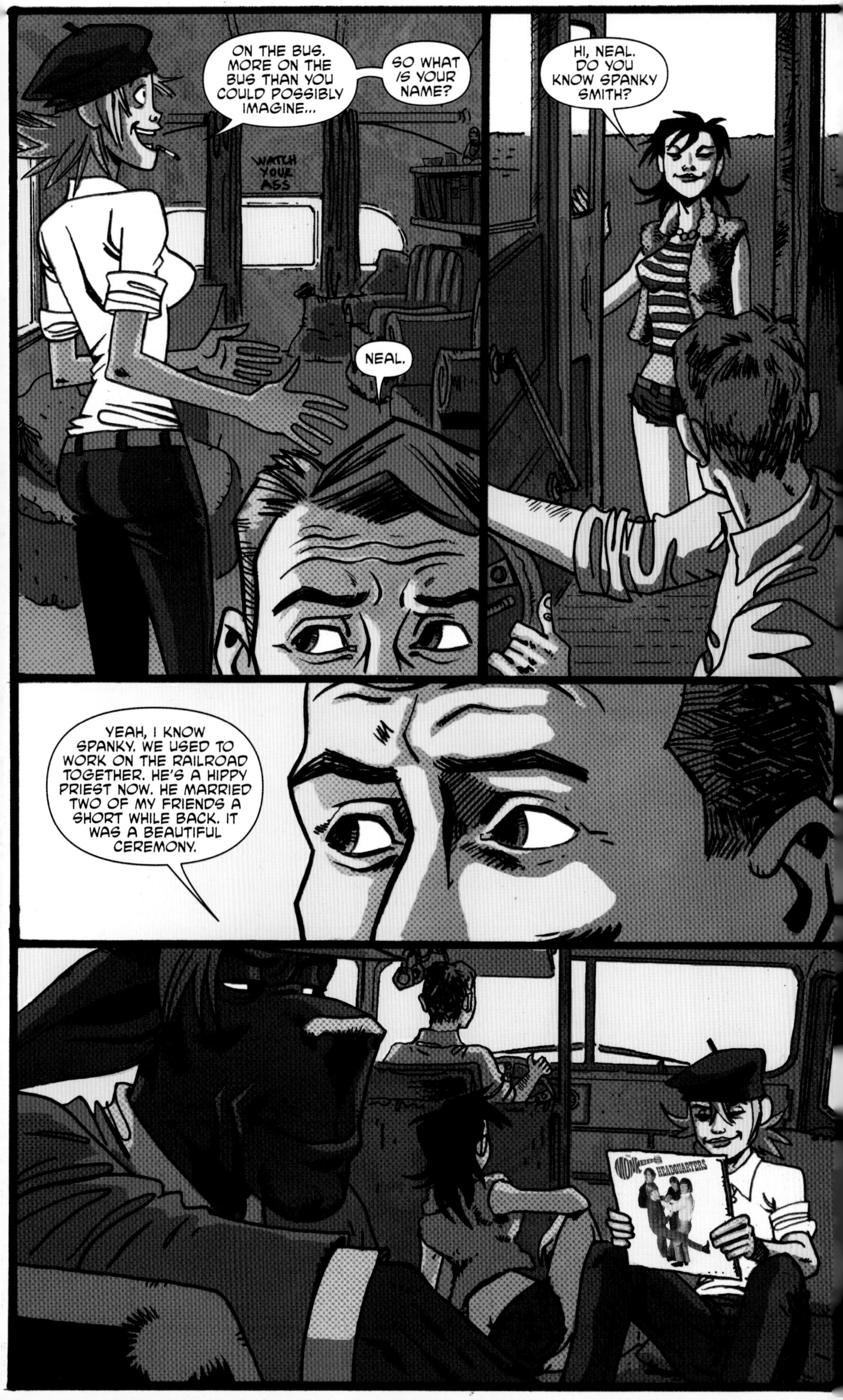
ON THE BUS. MORE ON THE BUS THAN YOU COULD POSSIBLY IMAGINE...
SO WHAT IS YOUR NAME?
WATCH YOUR ASS
NEAL.
HI, NEAL. DO YOU KNOW SPANKY SMITH?
YEAH, I KNOW SPANKY. WE USED TO WORK ON THE RAILROAD TOGETHER. HE'S A HIPPY PRIEST NOW. HE MARRIED TWO OF MY FRIENDS A SHORT WHILE BACK. IT WAS A BEAUTIFUL CEREMONY.
HEADQUARTERS

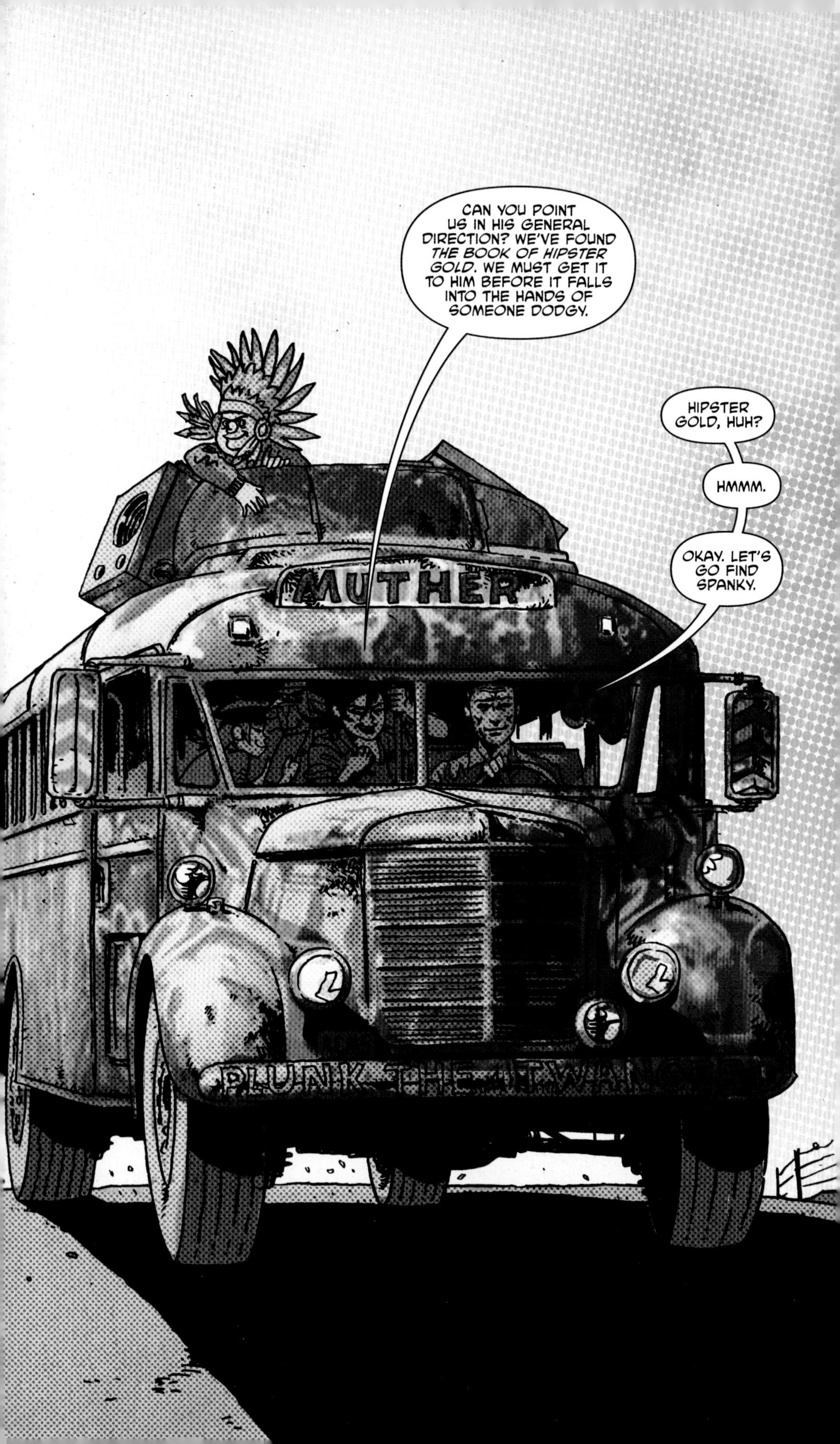
CAN YOU POINT US IN HIS GENERAL DIRECTION? WE'VE FOUND *THE BOOK OF HIPSTER GOLD*. WE MUST GET IT TO HIM BEFORE IT FALLS INTO THE HANDS OF SOMEONE DODGY.
HIPSTER GOLD, HUH?
HMMM.
OKAY. LET'S GO FIND SPANKY.
MUTHER

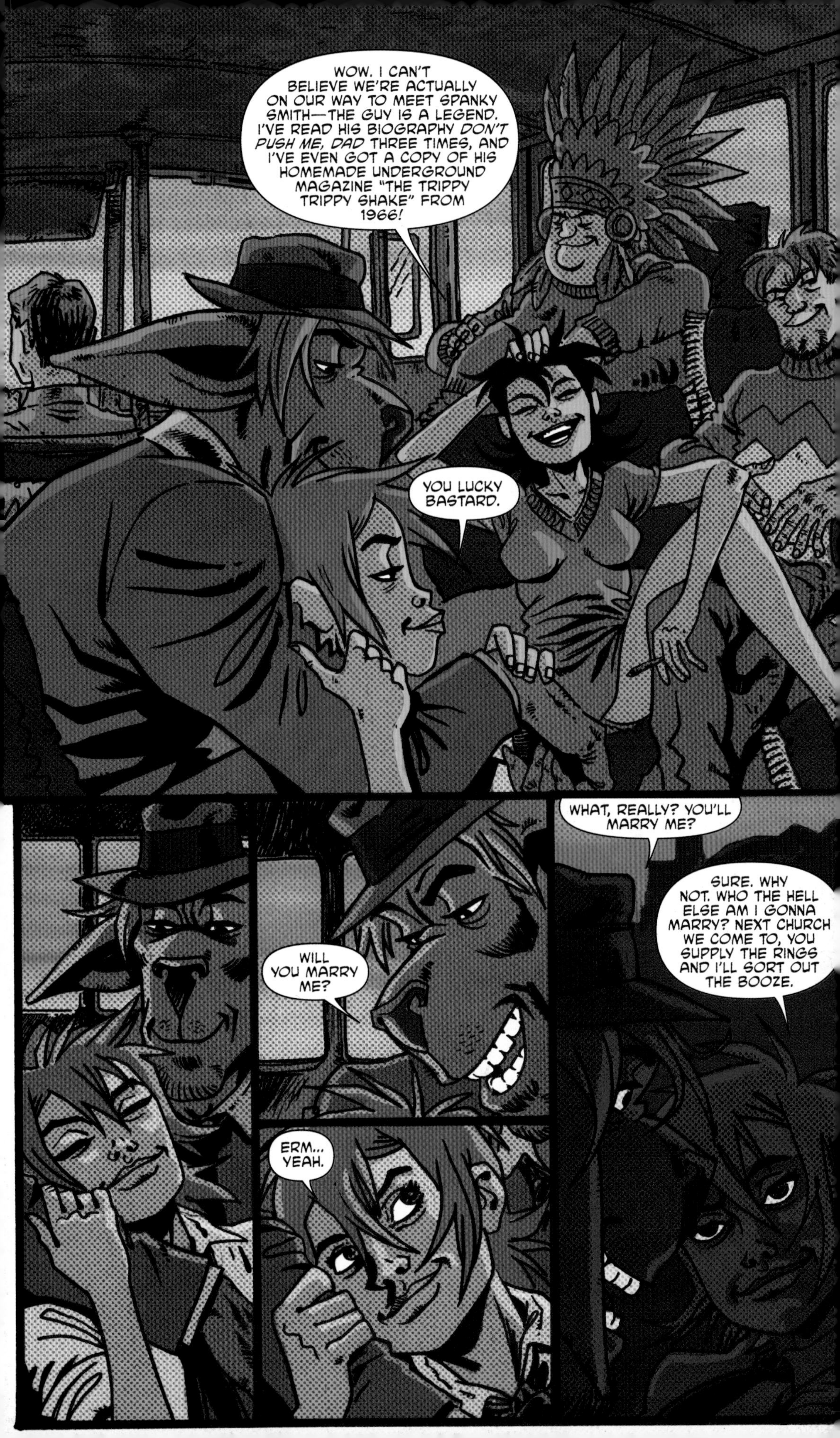
WOW. I CAN'T BELIEVE WE'RE ACTUALLY ON OUR WAY TO MEET SPANKY SMITH—THE GUY IS A LEGEND. I'VE READ HIS BIOGRAPHY *DON'T PUSH ME, DAD* THREE TIMES, AND I'VE EVEN GOT A COPY OF HIS HOMEMADE UNDERGROUND MAGAZINE "THE TRIPPY TRIPPY SHAKE" FROM 1966!
YOU LUCKY BASTARD.
WILL YOU MARRY ME?
ERM... YEAH.
WHAT, REALLY? YOU'LL MARRY ME?
SURE. WHY NOT. WHO THE HELL ELSE AM I GONNA MARRY? NEXT CHURCH WE COME TO, YOU SUPPLY THE RINGS AND I'LL SORT OUT THE BOOZE.

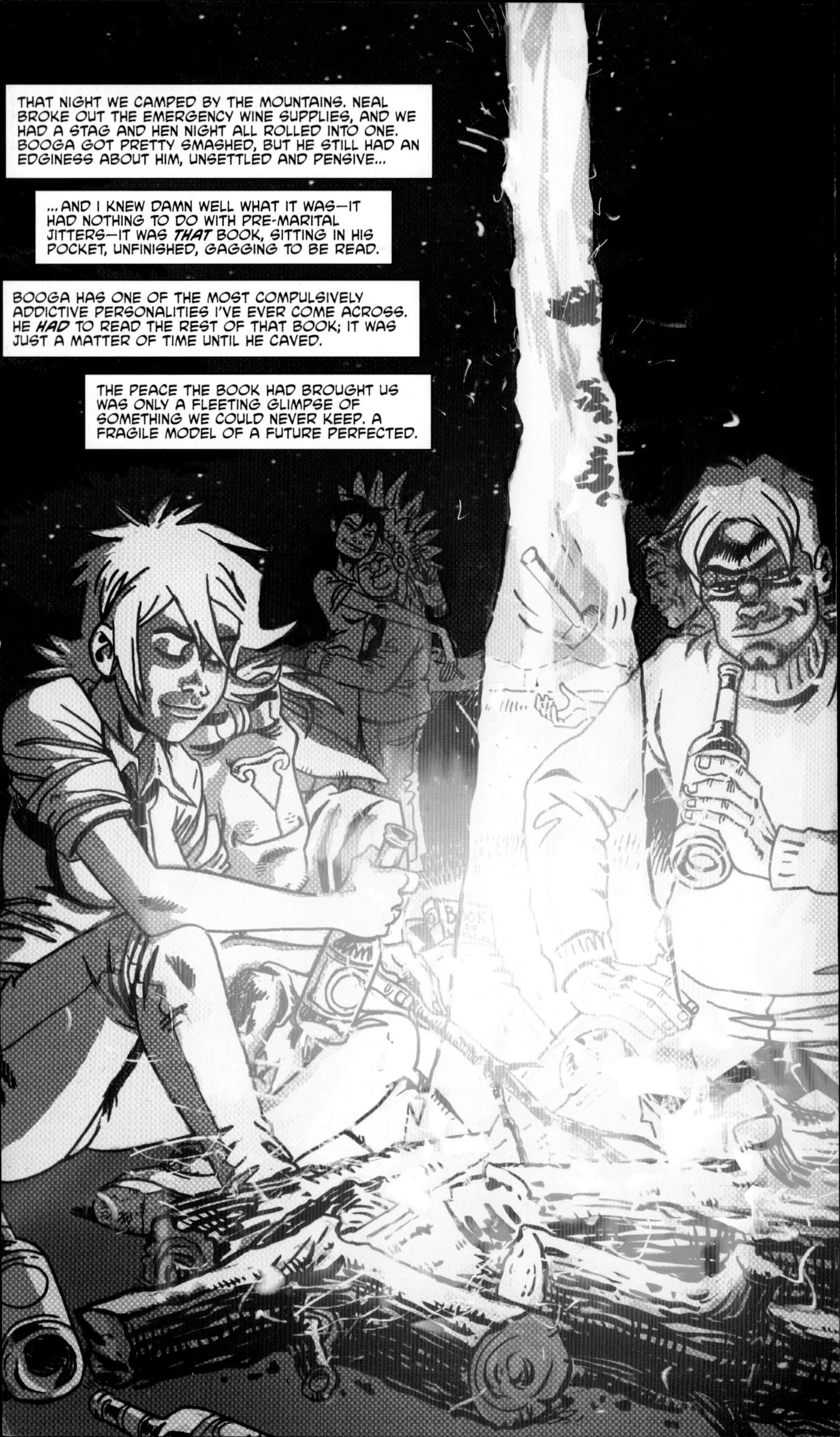
THAT NIGHT WE CAMPED BY THE MOUNTAINS. NEAL BROKE OUT THE EMERGENCY WINE SUPPLIES, AND WE HAD A STAG AND HEN NIGHT ALL ROLLED INTO ONE. BOOGA GOT PRETTY SMASHED, BUT HE STILL HAD AN EDGINESS ABOUT HIM, UNSETTLED AND PENSIVE...
...AND I KNEW DAMN WELL WHAT IT WAS—IT HAD NOTHING TO DO WITH PRE-MARITAL JITTERS—IT WAS *THAT* BOOK, SITTING IN HIS POCKET, UNFINISHED, GAGGING TO BE READ.
BOOGA HAS ONE OF THE MOST COMPULSIVELY ADDICTIVE PERSONALITIES I'VE EVER COME ACROSS. HE *HAD* TO READ THE REST OF THAT BOOK; IT WAS JUST A MATTER OF TIME UNTIL HE CAVED.
THE PEACE THE BOOK HAD BROUGHT US WAS ONLY A FLEETING GLIMPSE OF SOMETHING WE COULD NEVER KEEP. A FRAGILE MODEL OF A FUTURE PERFECTED.

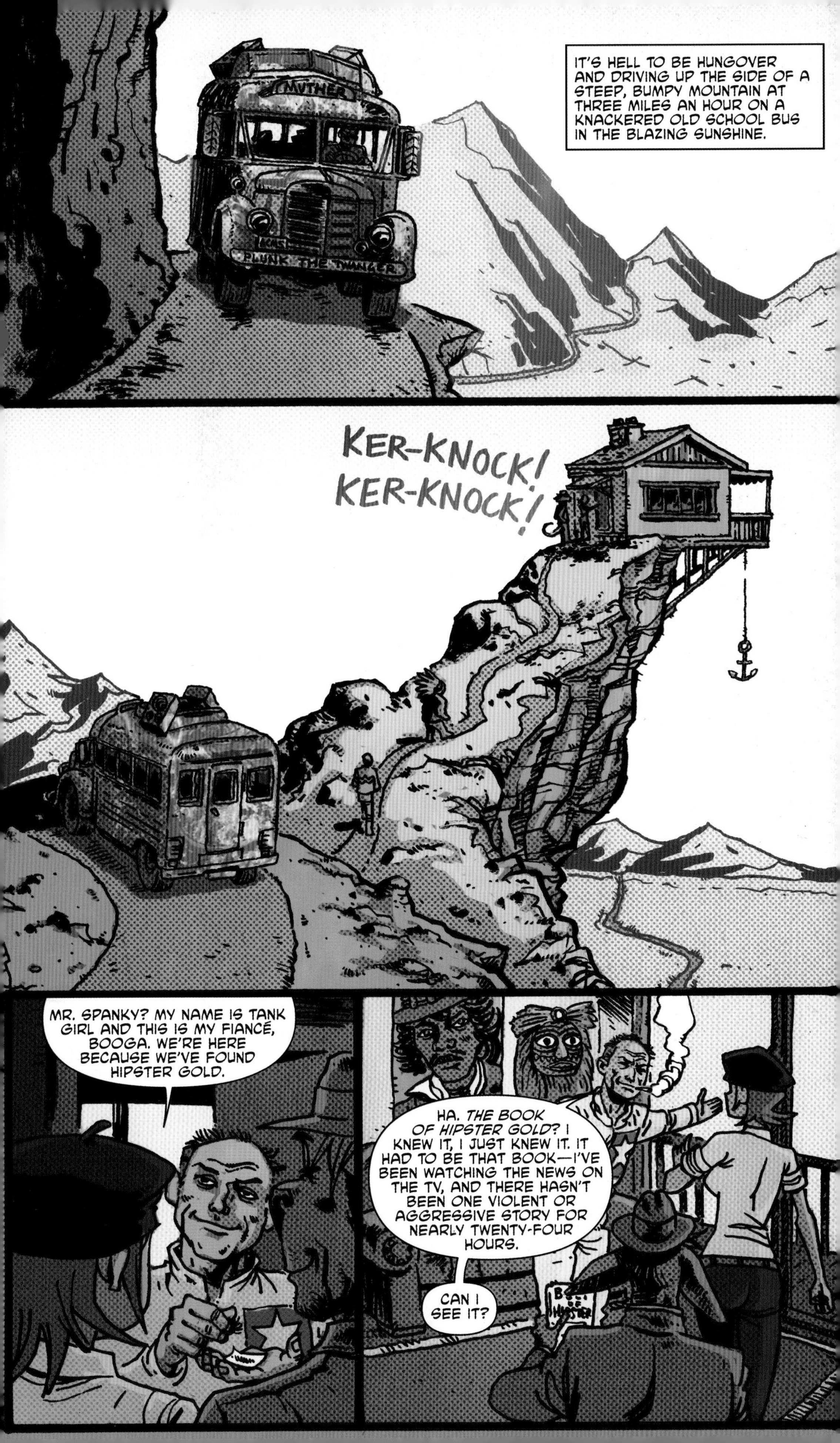

IT'S HELL TO BE HUNGOVER AND DRIVING UP THE SIDE OF A STEEP, BUMPY MOUNTAIN AT THREE MILES AN HOUR ON A KNACKERED OLD SCHOOL BUS IN THE BLAZING SUNSHINE.
MUTHER
PLUNK THE TWANGER
KER-KNOCK! KER-KNOCK!
MR. SPANKY? MY NAME IS TANK GIRL AND THIS IS MY FIANCÉ, BOOGA. WE'RE HERE BECAUSE WE'VE FOUND HIPSTER GOLD.
HA. *THE BOOK OF HIPSTER GOLD*? I KNEW IT, I JUST KNEW IT. IT HAD TO BE THAT BOOK—I'VE BEEN WATCHING THE NEWS ON THE TV, AND THERE HASN'T BEEN ONE VIOLENT OR AGGRESSIVE STORY FOR NEARLY TWENTY-FOUR HOURS.
CAN I SEE IT?

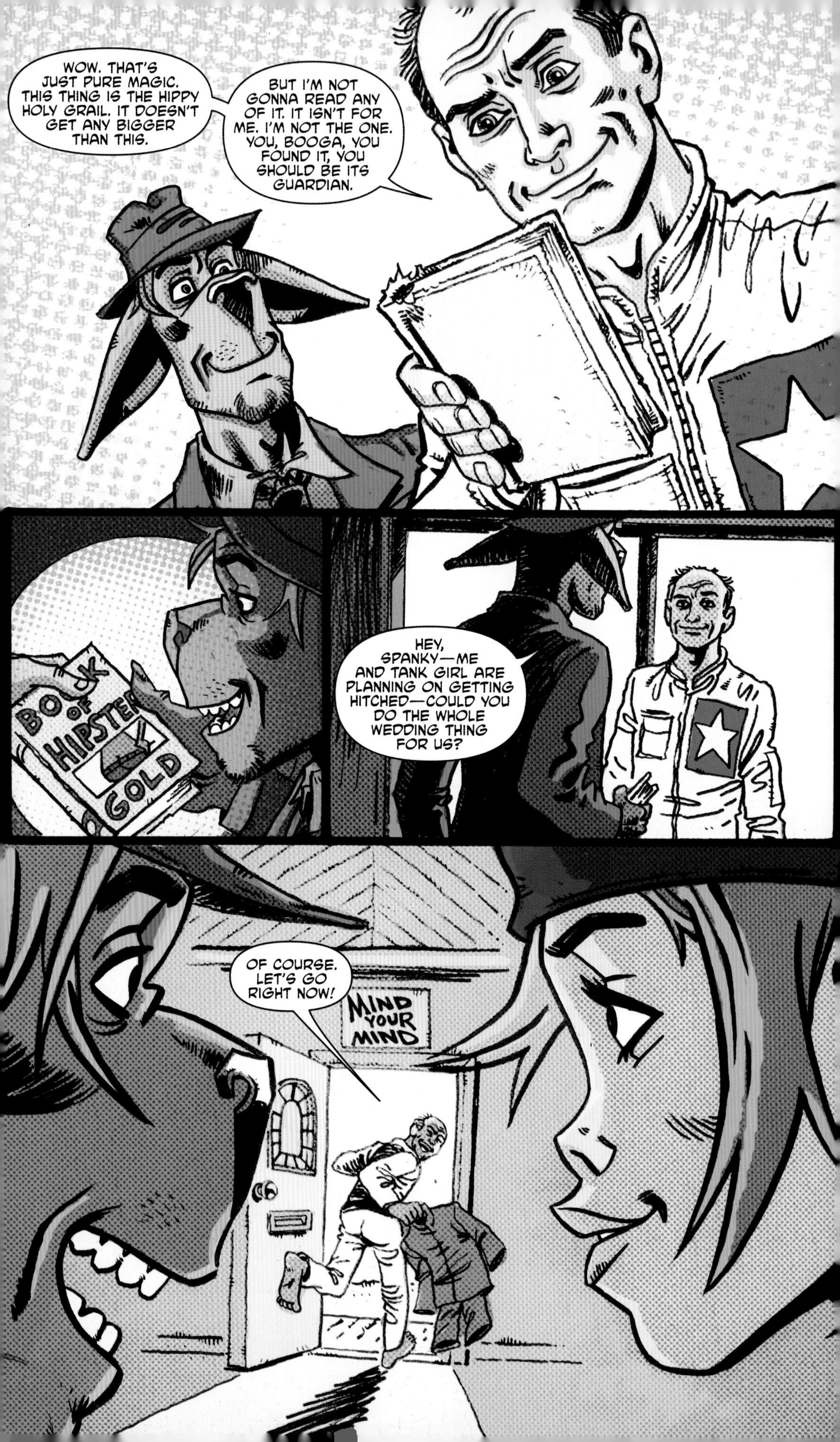
WOW. THAT'S JUST PURE MAGIC. THIS THING IS THE HIPPY HOLY GRAIL. IT DOESN'T GET ANY BIGGER THAN THIS.
BUT I'M NOT GONNA READ ANY OF IT. IT ISN'T FOR ME. I'M NOT THE ONE. YOU, BOOGA, YOU FOUND IT, YOU SHOULD BE ITS GUARDIAN.
BOOK OF HIPSTER GOLD
HEY, SPANKY—ME AND TANK GIRL ARE PLANNING ON GETTING HITCHED—COULD YOU DO THE WHOLE WEDDING THING FOR US?
OF COURSE. LET'S GO RIGHT NOW!
MIND YOUR MIND

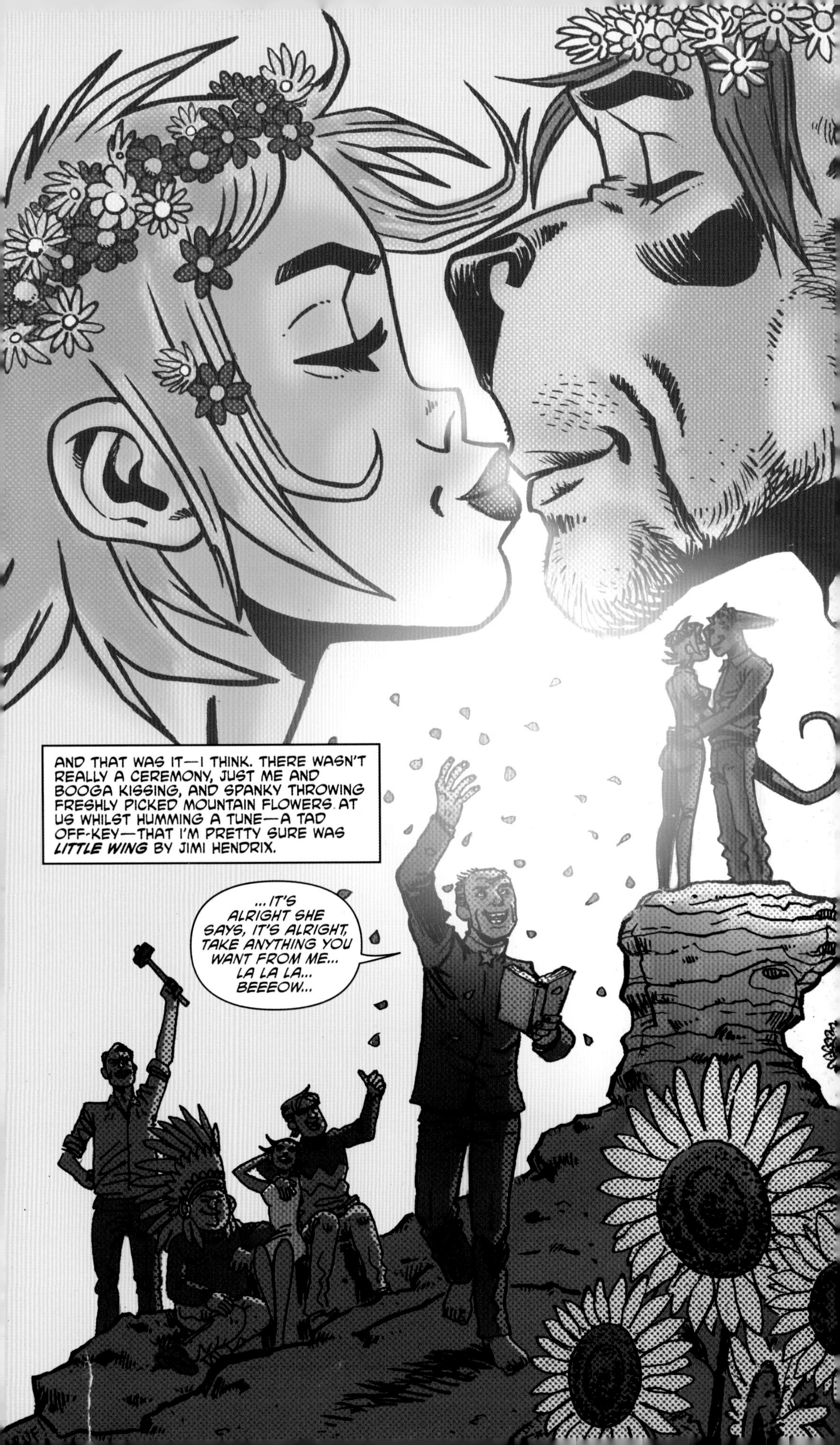
AND THAT WAS IT—I THINK. THERE WASN'T REALLY A CEREMONY, JUST ME AND BOOGA KISSING, AND SPANKY THROWING FRESHLY PICKED MOUNTAIN FLOWERS AT US WHILST HUMMING A TUNE—A TAD OFF-KEY—THAT I'M PRETTY SURE WAS *LITTLE WING* BY JIMI HENDRIX.
...IT'S ALRIGHT SHE SAYS, IT'S ALRIGHT, TAKE ANYTHING YOU WANT FROM ME... LA LA LA... BEEEOW...

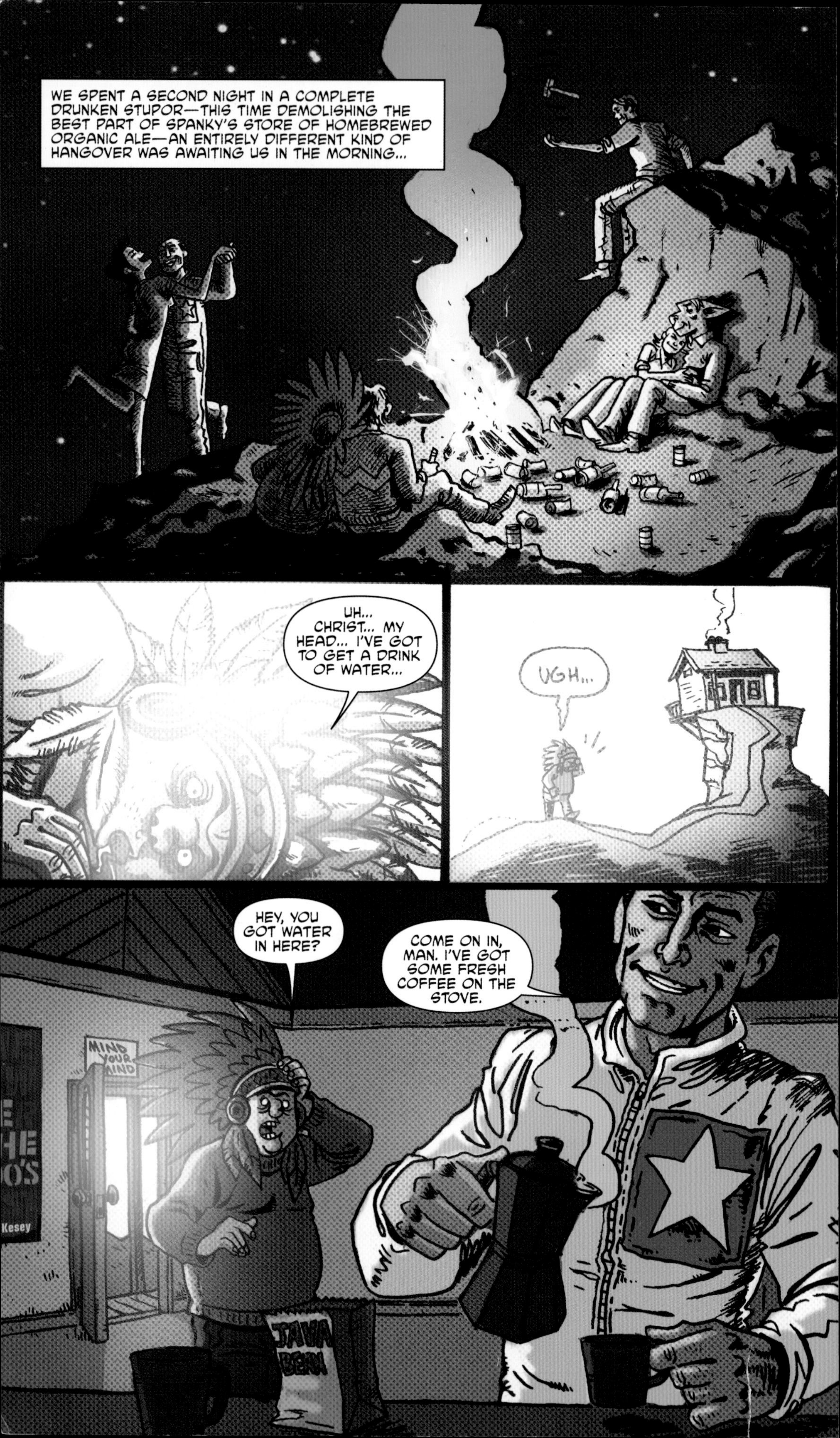
WE SPENT A SECOND NIGHT IN A COMPLETE DRUNKEN STUPOR—THIS TIME DEMOLISHING THE BEST PART OF SPANKY'S STORE OF HOMEBREWED ORGANIC ALE—AN ENTIRELY DIFFERENT KIND OF HANGOVER WAS AWAITING US IN THE MORNING...
UH... CHRIST... MY HEAD... I'VE GOT TO GET A DRINK OF WATER...
UGH...
HEY, YOU GOT WATER IN HERE?
COME ON IN, MAN. I'VE GOT SOME FRESH COFFEE ON THE STOVE.
MIND YOUR MIND
Kesey

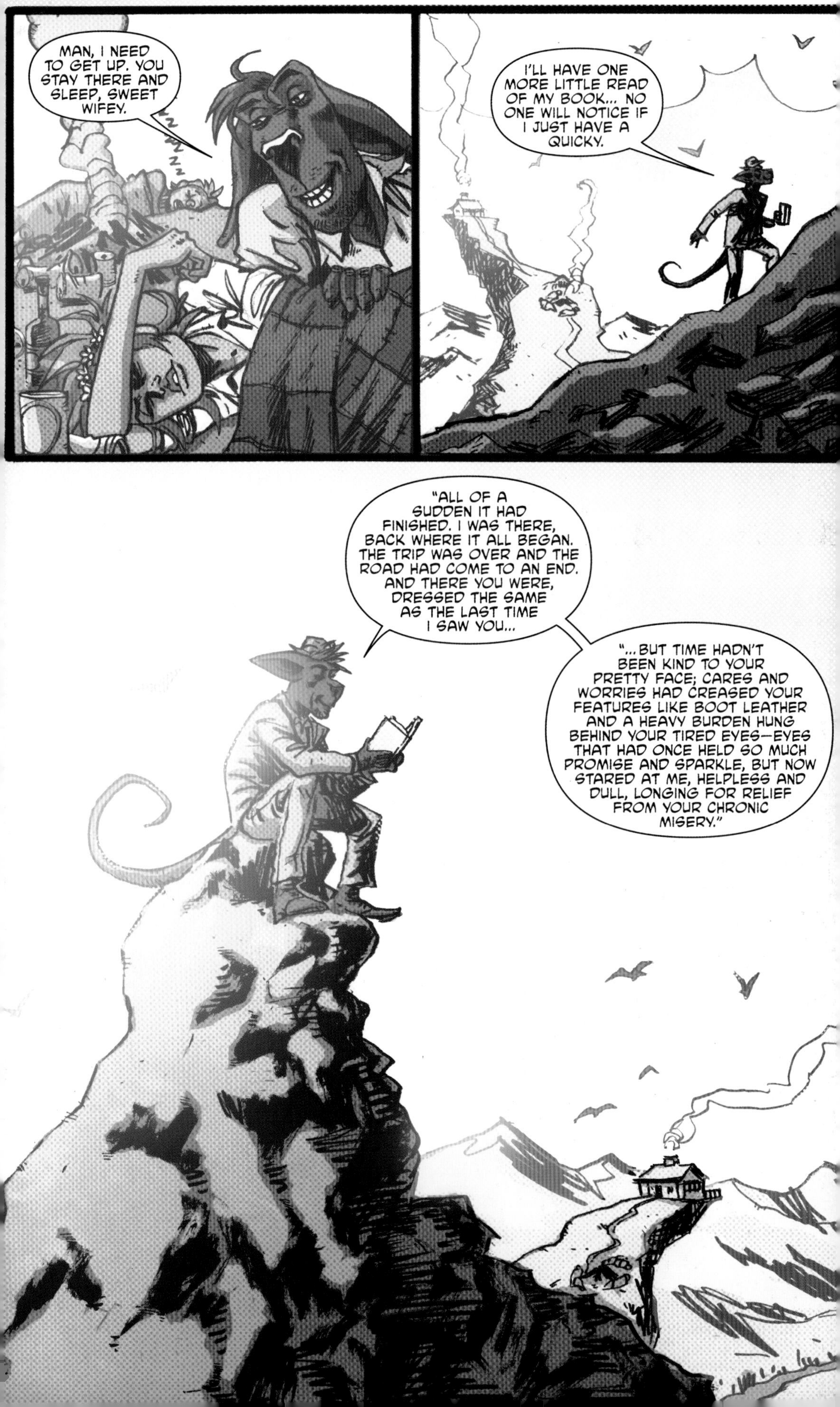
MAN, I NEED TO GET UP. YOU STAY THERE AND SLEEP, SWEET WIFEY.
I'LL HAVE ONE MORE LITTLE READ OF MY BOOK... NO ONE WILL NOTICE IF I JUST HAVE A QUICKY.
"ALL OF A SUDDEN IT HAD FINISHED. I WAS THERE, BACK WHERE IT ALL BEGAN. THE TRIP WAS OVER AND THE ROAD HAD COME TO AN END. AND THERE YOU WERE, DRESSED THE SAME AS THE LAST TIME I SAW YOU...
"...BUT TIME HADN'T BEEN KIND TO YOUR PRETTY FACE; CARES AND WORRIES HAD CREASED YOUR FEATURES LIKE BOOT LEATHER AND A HEAVY BURDEN HUNG BEHIND YOUR TIRED EYES—EYES THAT HAD ONCE HELD SO MUCH PROMISE AND SPARKLE, BUT NOW STARED AT ME, HELPLESS AND DULL, LONGING FOR RELIEF FROM YOUR CHRONIC MISERY."

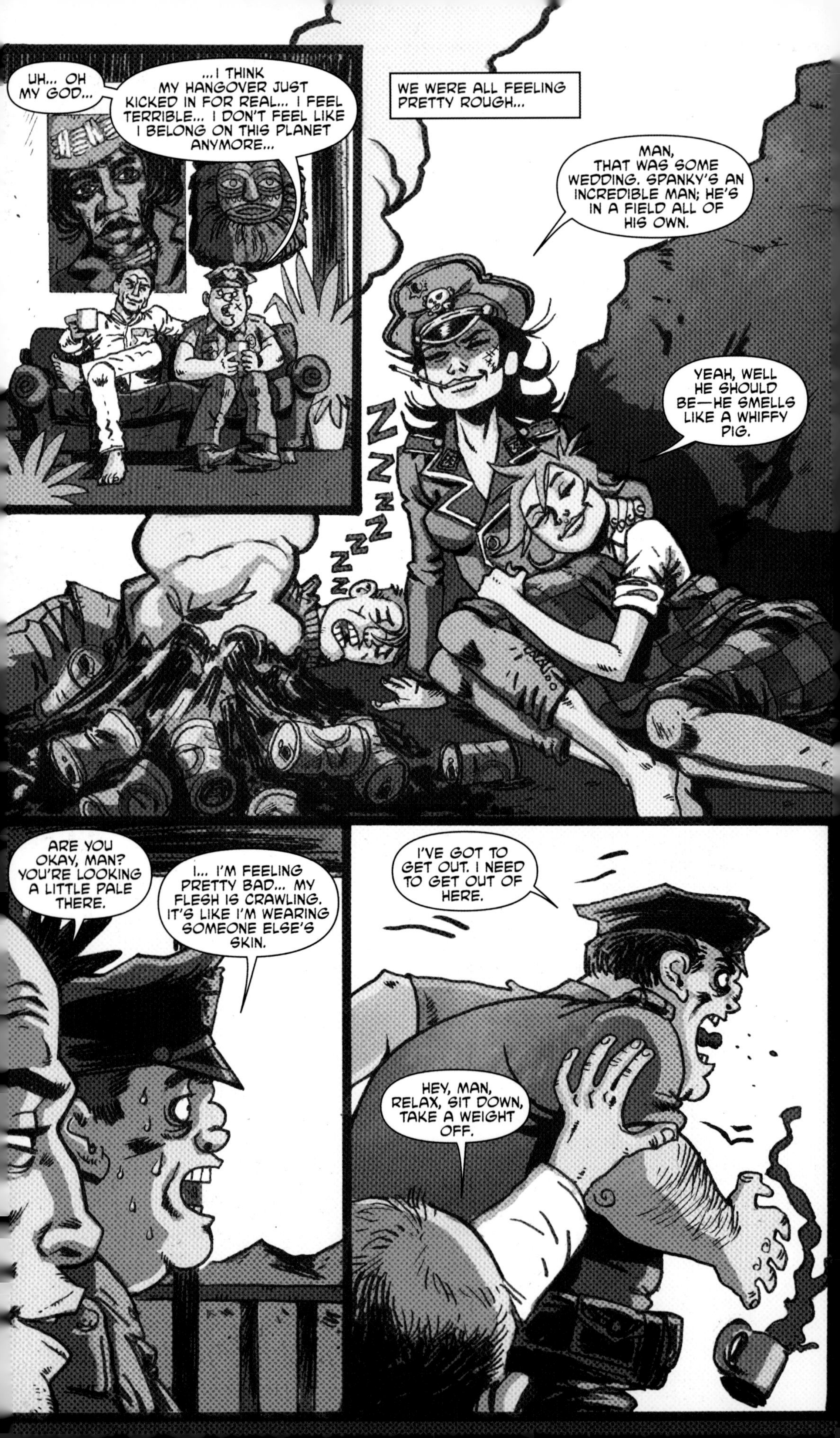
UH... OH MY GOD...
...I THINK MY HANGOVER JUST KICKED IN FOR REAL... I FEEL TERRIBLE... I DON'T FEEL LIKE I BELONG ON THIS PLANET ANYMORE...
WE WERE ALL FEELING PRETTY ROUGH...
MAN, THAT WAS SOME WEDDING. SPANKY'S AN INCREDIBLE MAN; HE'S IN A FIELD ALL OF HIS OWN.
YEAH, WELL HE SHOULD BE—HE SMELLS LIKE A WHIFFY PIG.
ZZZZZZZ
ARE YOU OKAY, MAN? YOU'RE LOOKING A LITTLE PALE THERE.
I... I'M FEELING PRETTY BAD... MY FLESH IS CRAWLING. IT'S LIKE I'M WEARING SOMEONE ELSE'S SKIN.
I'VE GOT TO GET OUT. I NEED TO GET OUT OF HERE.
HEY, MAN, RELAX, SIT DOWN, TAKE A WEIGHT OFF.

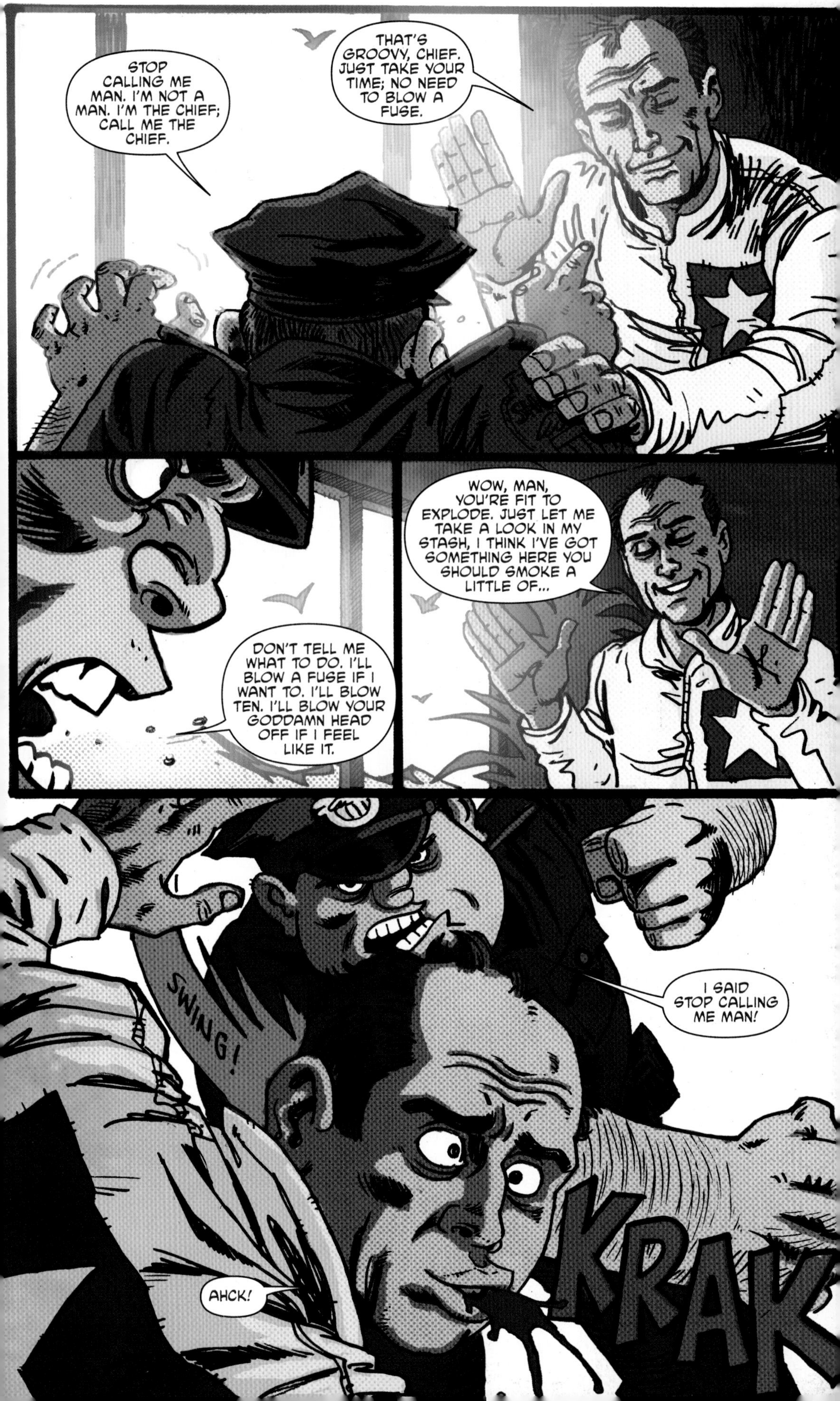
STOP CALLING ME MAN. I'M NOT A MAN. I'M THE CHIEF; CALL ME THE CHIEF.
THAT'S GROOVY, CHIEF. JUST TAKE YOUR TIME; NO NEED TO BLOW A FUSE.
DON'T TELL ME WHAT TO DO. I'LL BLOW A FUSE IF I WANT TO. I'LL BLOW TEN. I'LL BLOW YOUR GODDAMN HEAD OFF IF I FEEL LIKE IT.
WOW, MAN, YOU'RE FIT TO EXPLODE. JUST LET ME TAKE A LOOK IN MY STASH, I THINK I'VE GOT SOMETHING HERE YOU SHOULD SMOKE A LITTLE OF...
SWING!
I SAID STOP CALLING ME MAN!
AHCK!
KRAK

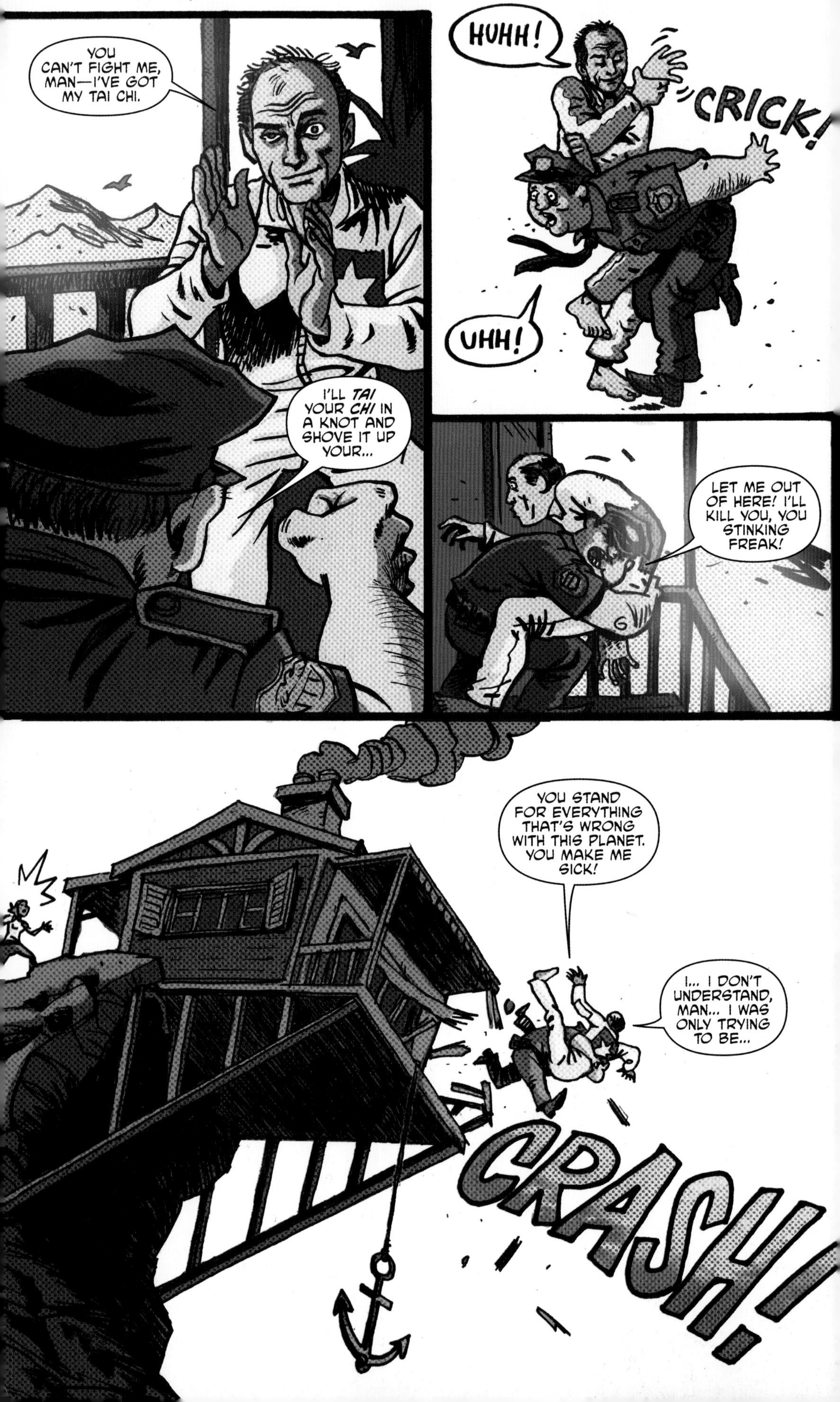
YOU CAN'T FIGHT ME, MAN—I'VE GOT MY TAI CHI.
I'LL TAI YOUR CHI IN A KNOT AND SHOVE IT UP YOUR...
HUHH!
CRICK!
UHH!
LET ME OUT OF HERE! I'LL KILL YOU, YOU STINKING FREAK!
YOU STAND FOR EVERYTHING THAT'S WRONG WITH THIS PLANET. YOU MAKE ME SICK!
I... I DON'T UNDERSTAND, MAN... I WAS ONLY TRYING TO BE...
CRASH!

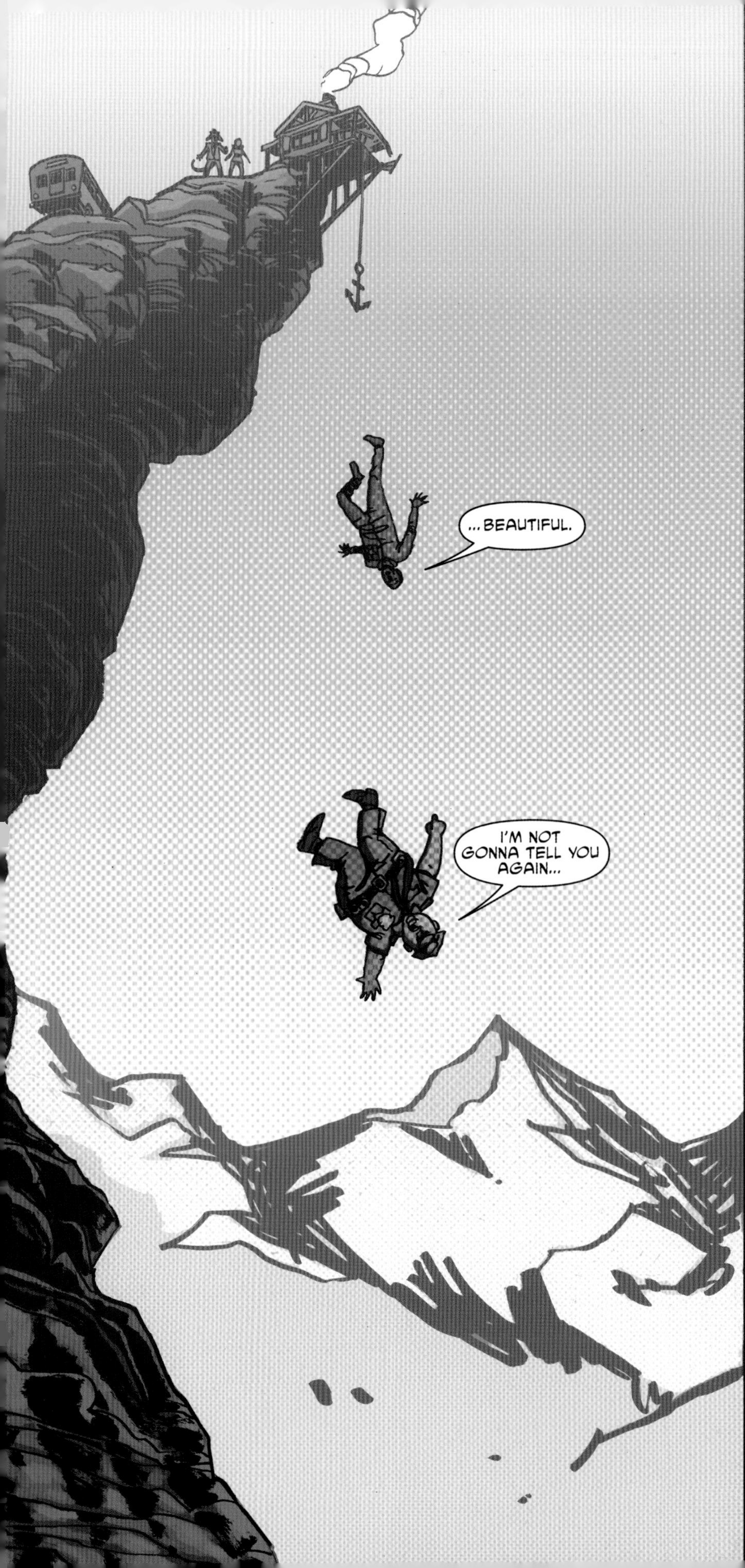
...BEAUTIFUL.
I'M NOT GONNA TELL YOU AGAIN...

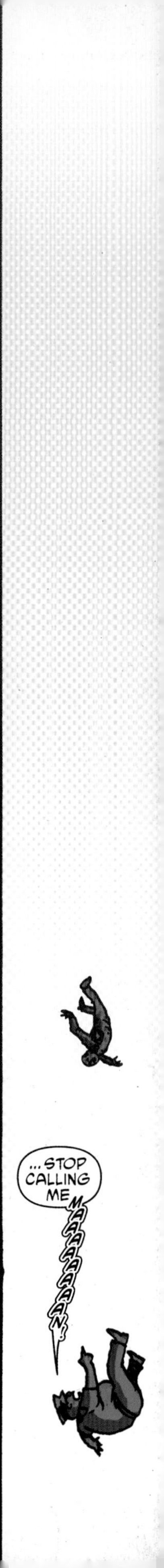
...STOP CALLING ME MAAAAAAAAAN!

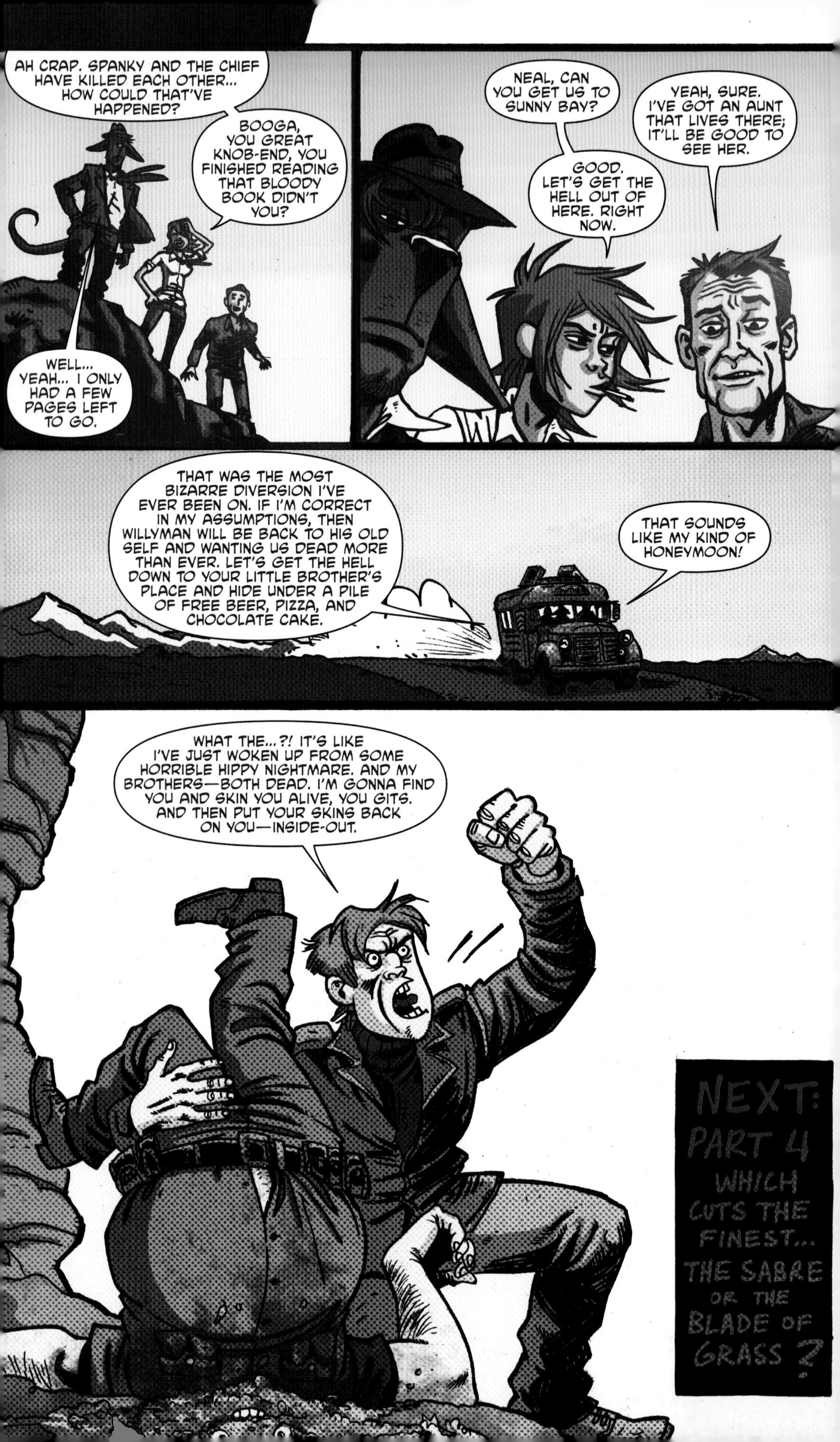
AH CRAP. SPANKY AND THE CHIEF HAVE KILLED EACH OTHER... HOW COULD THAT'VE HAPPENED?
BOOGA, YOU GREAT KNOB-END, YOU FINISHED READING THAT BLOODY BOOK DIDN'T YOU?
WELL... YEAH... I ONLY HAD A FEW PAGES LEFT TO GO.
NEAL, CAN YOU GET US TO SUNNY BAY?
YEAH, SURE. I'VE GOT AN AUNT THAT LIVES THERE; IT'LL BE GOOD TO SEE HER.
GOOD. LET'S GET THE HELL OUT OF HERE. RIGHT NOW.
THAT WAS THE MOST BIZARRE DIVERSION I'VE EVER BEEN ON. IF I'M CORRECT IN MY ASSUMPTIONS, THEN WILLYMAN WILL BE BACK TO HIS OLD SELF AND WANTING US DEAD MORE THAN EVER. LET'S GET THE HELL DOWN TO YOUR LITTLE BROTHER'S PLACE AND HIDE UNDER A PILE OF FREE BEER, PIZZA, AND CHOCOLATE CAKE.
THAT SOUNDS LIKE MY KIND OF HONEYMOON!
WHAT THE...?! IT'S LIKE I'VE JUST WOKEN UP FROM SOME HORRIBLE HIPPY NIGHTMARE. AND MY BROTHERS—BOTH DEAD. I'M GONNA FIND YOU AND SKIN YOU ALIVE, YOU GITS. AND THEN PUT YOUR SKINS BACK ON YOU—INSIDE-OUT.
NEXT: PART 4 WHICH CUTS THE FINEST... THE SABRE OR THE BLADE OF GRASS?

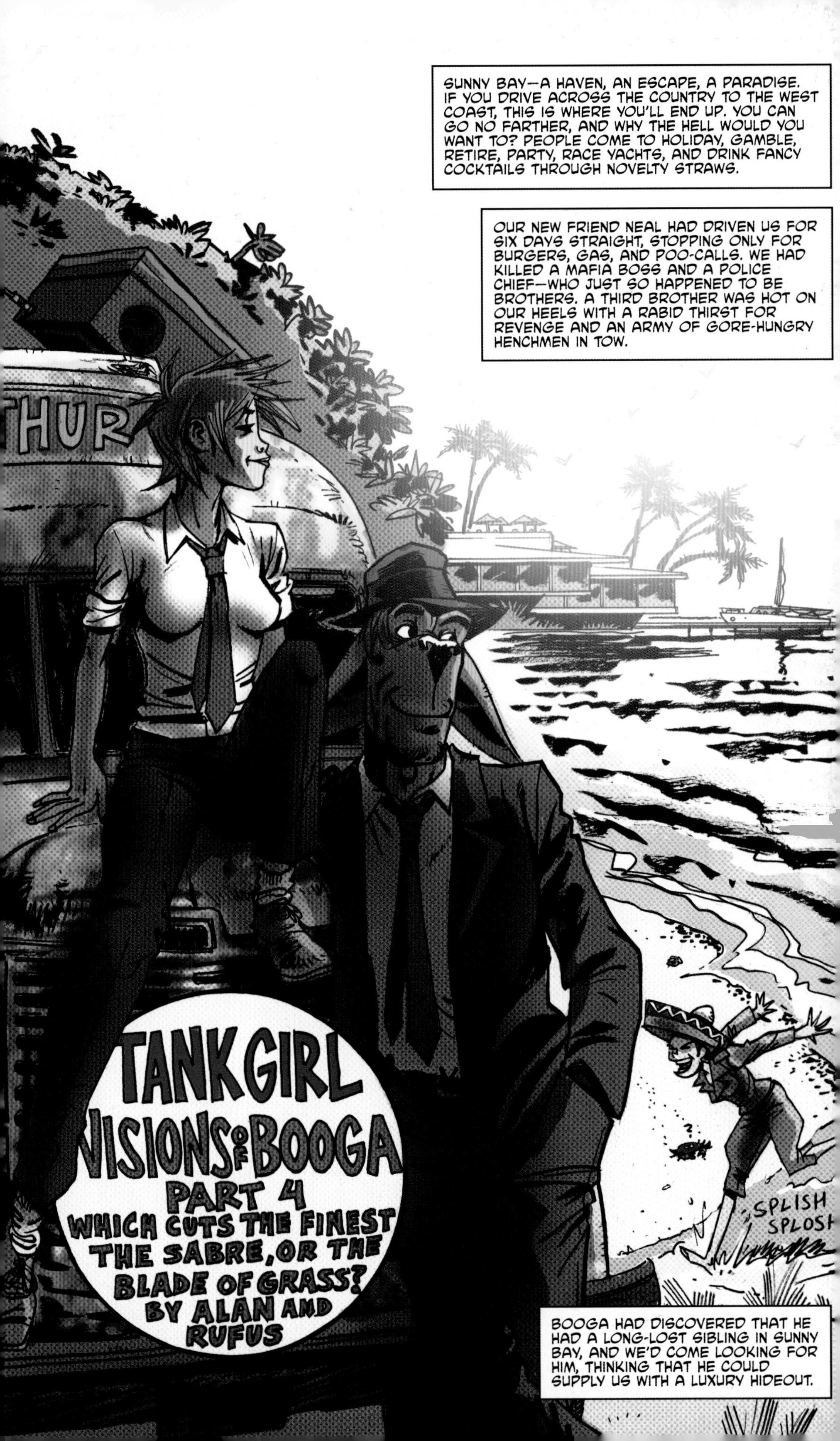

SUNNY BAY—A HAVEN, AN ESCAPE, A PARADISE. IF YOU DRIVE ACROSS THE COUNTRY TO THE WEST COAST, THIS IS WHERE YOU'LL END UP. YOU CAN GO NO FARTHER, AND WHY THE HELL WOULD YOU WANT TO? PEOPLE COME TO HOLIDAY, GAMBLE, RETIRE, PARTY, RACE YACHTS, AND DRINK FANCY COCKTAILS THROUGH NOVELTY STRAWS.
OUR NEW FRIEND NEAL HAD DRIVEN US FOR SIX DAYS STRAIGHT, STOPPING ONLY FOR BURGERS, GAS, AND POO-CALLS. WE HAD KILLED A MAFIA BOSS AND A POLICE CHIEF—WHO JUST SO HAPPENED TO BE BROTHERS. A THIRD BROTHER WAS HOT ON OUR HEELS WITH A RABID THIRST FOR REVENGE AND AN ARMY OF GORE-HUNGRY HENCHMEN IN TOW.
THUR
TANK GIRL
VISIONS OF BOOGA
PART 4
WHICH CUTS THE FINEST THE SABRE, OR THE BLADE OF GRASS?
BY ALAN AND RUFUS
SPLISH
SPLOSH
BOOGA HAD DISCOVERED THAT HE HAD A LONG-LOST SIBLING IN SUNNY BAY, AND WE'D COME LOOKING FOR HIM, THINKING THAT HE COULD SUPPLY US WITH A LUXURY HIDEOUT.

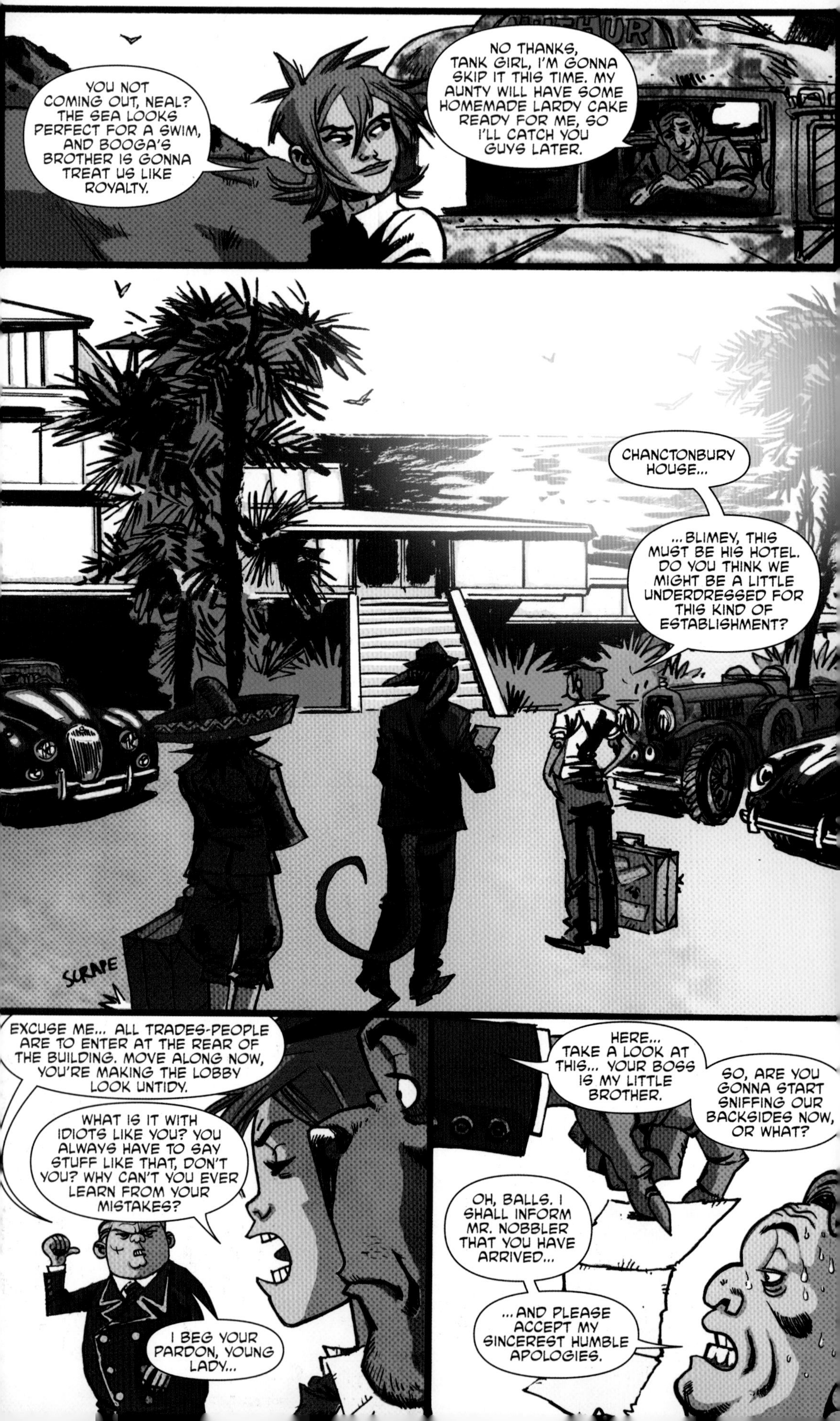

YOU NOT COMING OUT, NEAL? THE SEA LOOKS PERFECT FOR A SWIM, AND BOOGA'S BROTHER IS GONNA TREAT US LIKE ROYALTY.
NO THANKS, TANK GIRL, I'M GONNA SKIP IT THIS TIME. MY AUNTY WILL HAVE SOME HOMEMADE LARDY CAKE READY FOR ME, SO I'LL CATCH YOU GUYS LATER.
CHANCTONBURY HOUSE...
...BLIMEY, THIS MUST BE HIS HOTEL. DO YOU THINK WE MIGHT BE A LITTLE UNDERDRESSED FOR THIS KIND OF ESTABLISHMENT?
SCRAPE
EXCUSE ME... ALL TRADES-PEOPLE ARE TO ENTER AT THE REAR OF THE BUILDING. MOVE ALONG NOW, YOU'RE MAKING THE LOBBY LOOK UNTIDY.
WHAT IS IT WITH IDIOTS LIKE YOU? YOU ALWAYS HAVE TO SAY STUFF LIKE THAT, DON'T YOU? WHY CAN'T YOU EVER LEARN FROM YOUR MISTAKES?
I BEG YOUR PARDON, YOUNG LADY...
HERE... TAKE A LOOK AT THIS... YOUR BOSS IS MY LITTLE BROTHER.
SO, ARE YOU GONNA START SNIFFING OUR BACKSIDES NOW, OR WHAT?
OH, BALLS. I SHALL INFORM MR. NOBBLER THAT YOU HAVE ARRIVED...
...AND PLEASE ACCEPT MY SINCEREST HUMBLE APOLOGIES.

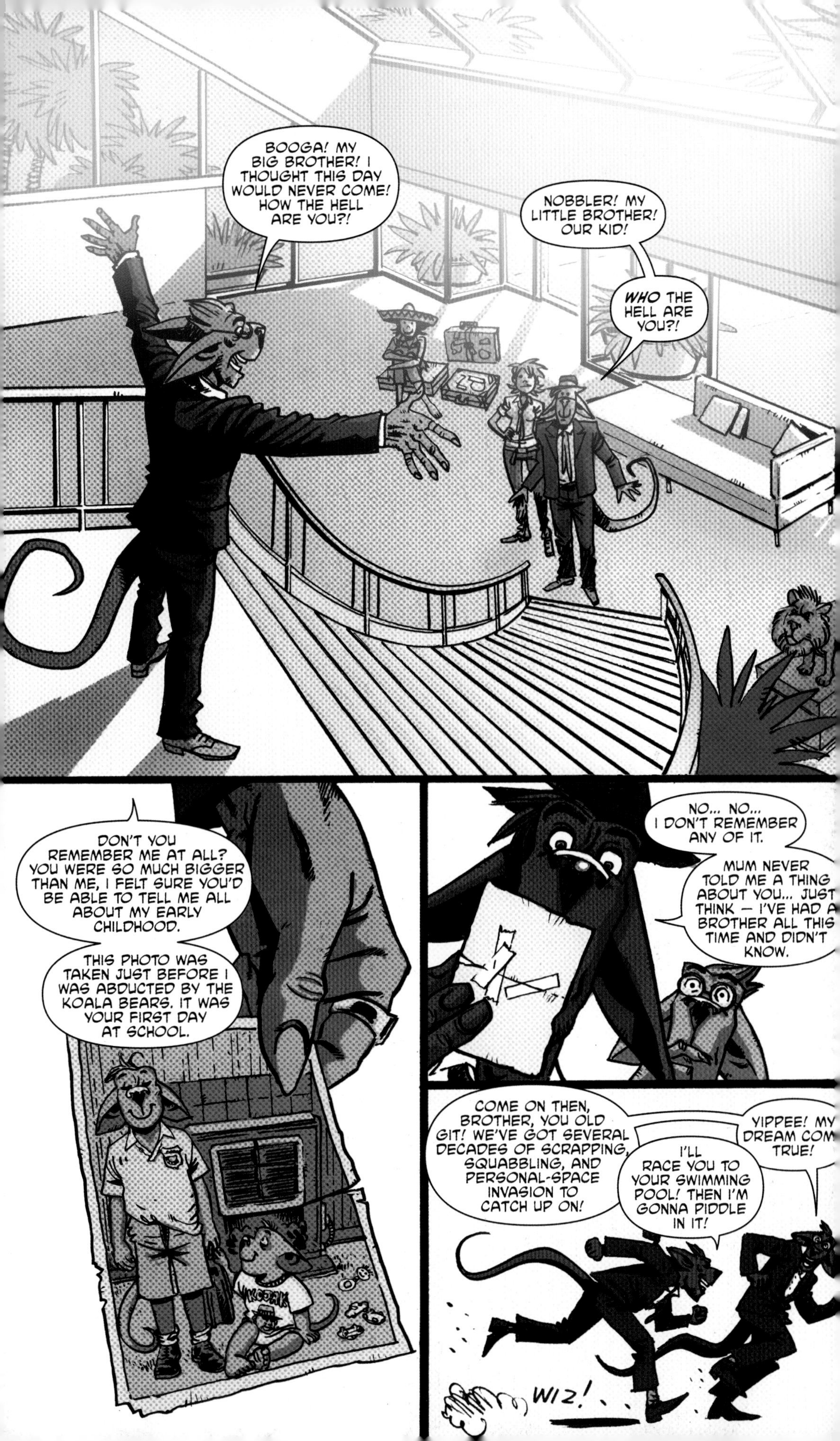
BOOGA! MY BIG BROTHER! I THOUGHT THIS DAY WOULD NEVER COME! HOW THE HELL ARE YOU?!
NOBBLER! MY LITTLE BROTHER! OUR KID!
WHO THE HELL ARE YOU?!
DON'T YOU REMEMBER ME AT ALL? YOU WERE SO MUCH BIGGER THAN ME, I FELT SURE YOU'D BE ABLE TO TELL ME ALL ABOUT MY EARLY CHILDHOOD.
THIS PHOTO WAS TAKEN JUST BEFORE I WAS ABDUCTED BY THE KOALA BEARS. IT WAS YOUR FIRST DAY AT SCHOOL.
NO... NO... I DON'T REMEMBER ANY OF IT.
MUM NEVER TOLD ME A THING ABOUT YOU... JUST THINK — I'VE HAD A BROTHER ALL THIS TIME AND DIDN'T KNOW.
COME ON THEN, BROTHER, YOU OLD GIT! WE'VE GOT SEVERAL DECADES OF SCRAPPING, SQUABBLING, AND PERSONAL-SPACE INVASION TO CATCH UP ON!
YIPPEE! MY DREAM COM TRUE!
I'LL RACE YOU TO YOUR SWIMMING POOL! THEN I'M GONNA PIDDLE IN IT!
WIZ!

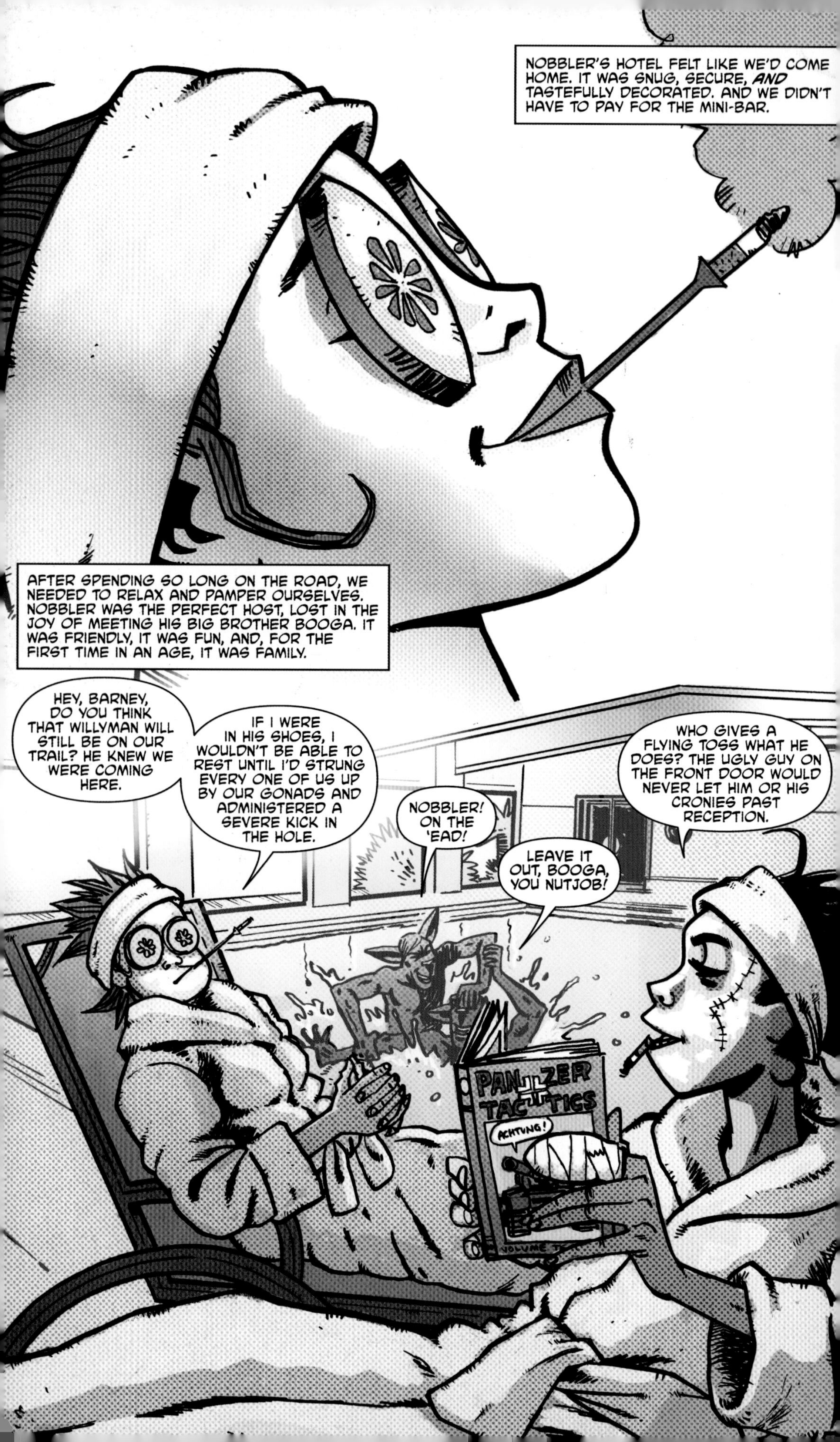

NOBBLER'S HOTEL FELT LIKE WE'D COME HOME. IT WAS SNUG, SECURE, *AND* TASTEFULLY DECORATED. AND WE DIDN'T HAVE TO PAY FOR THE MINI-BAR.
AFTER SPENDING SO LONG ON THE ROAD, WE NEEDED TO RELAX AND PAMPER OURSELVES. NOBBLER WAS THE PERFECT HOST, LOST IN THE JOY OF MEETING HIS BIG BROTHER BOOGA. IT WAS FRIENDLY, IT WAS FUN, AND, FOR THE FIRST TIME IN AN AGE, IT WAS FAMILY.
HEY, BARNEY, DO YOU THINK THAT WILLYMAN WILL STILL BE ON OUR TRAIL? HE KNEW WE WERE COMING HERE.
IF I WERE IN HIS SHOES, I WOULDN'T BE ABLE TO REST UNTIL I'D STRUNG EVERY ONE OF US UP BY OUR GONADS AND ADMINISTERED A SEVERE KICK IN THE HOLE.
NOBBLER! ON THE 'EAD!
LEAVE IT OUT, BOOGA, YOU NUTJOB!
WHO GIVES A FLYING TOSS WHAT HE DOES? THE UGLY GUY ON THE FRONT DOOR WOULD NEVER LET HIM OR HIS CRONIES PAST RECEPTION.
PANZER TACTICS
ACHTUNG!

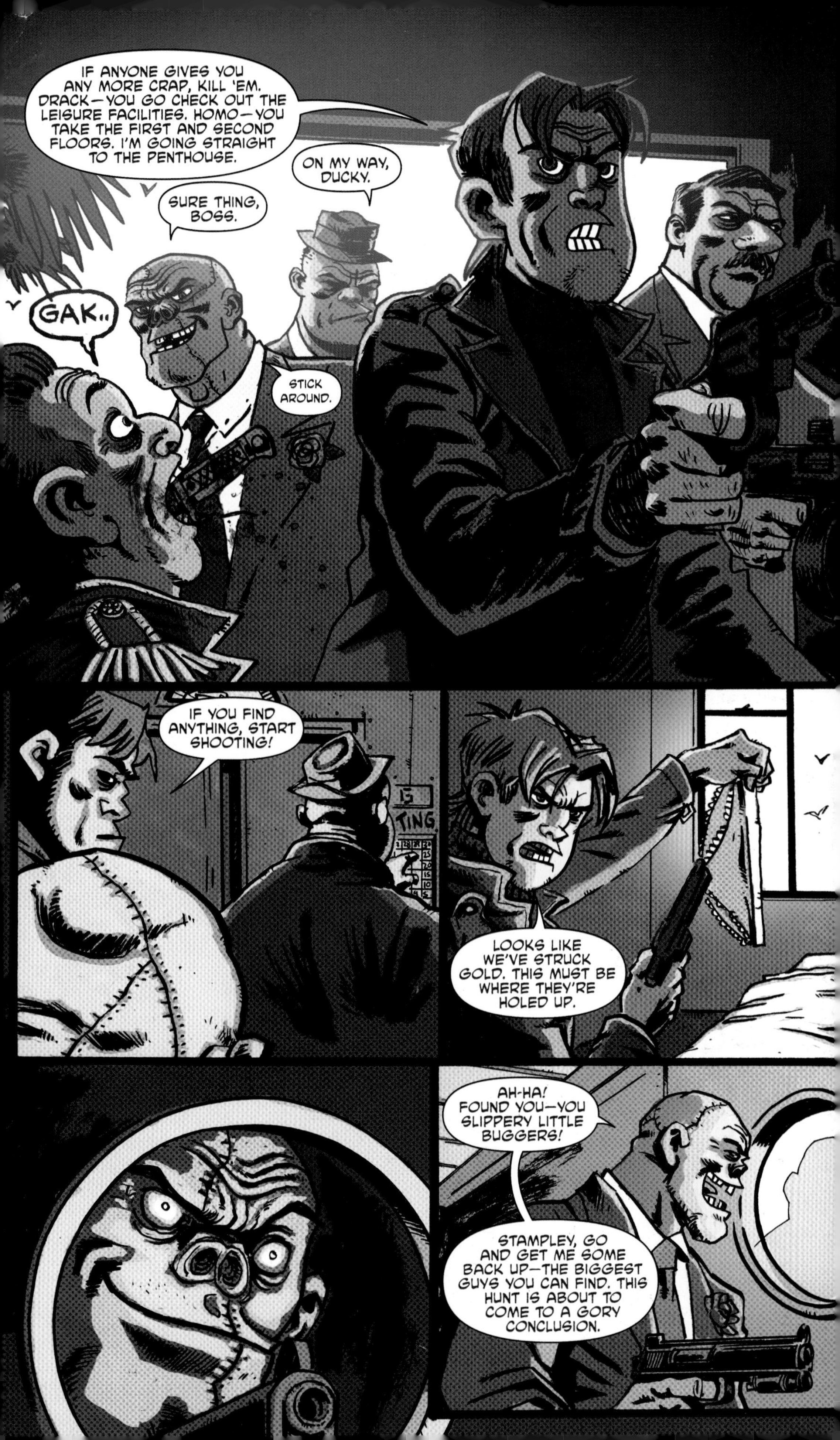
IF ANYONE GIVES YOU ANY MORE CRAP, KILL 'EM. DRACK—YOU GO CHECK OUT THE LEISURE FACILITIES. HOMO—YOU TAKE THE FIRST AND SECOND FLOORS. I'M GOING STRAIGHT TO THE PENTHOUSE.
ON MY WAY, DUCKY.
SURE THING, BOSS.
GAK..
STICK AROUND.
IF YOU FIND ANYTHING, START SHOOTING!
LOOKS LIKE WE'VE STRUCK GOLD. THIS MUST BE WHERE THEY'RE HOLED UP.
AH-HA! FOUND YOU—YOU SLIPPERY LITTLE BUGGERS!
STAMPLEY, GO AND GET ME SOME BACK UP—THE BIGGEST GUYS YOU CAN FIND. THIS HUNT IS ABOUT TO COME TO A GORY CONCLUSION.

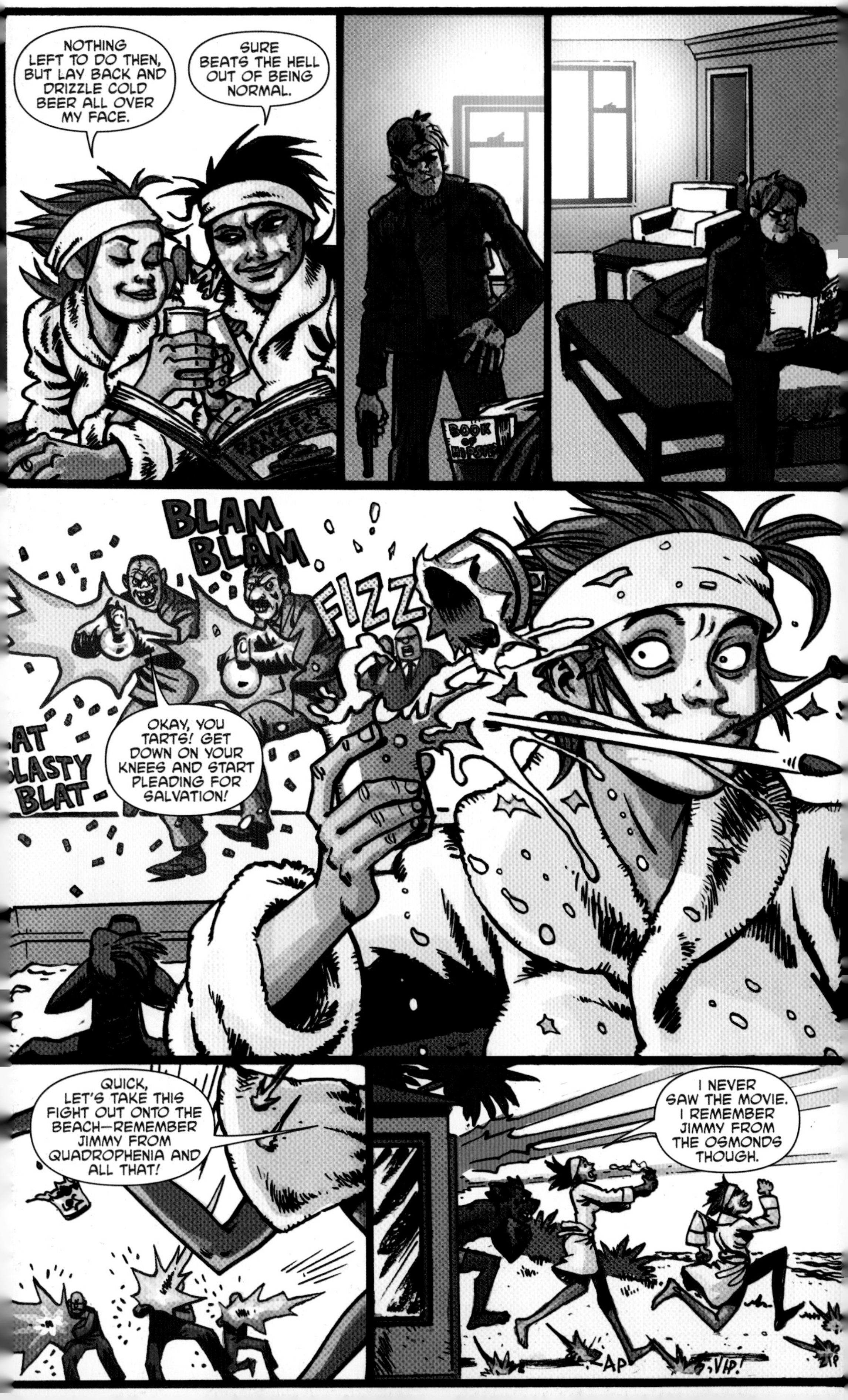
NOTHING LEFT TO DO THEN, BUT LAY BACK AND DRIZZLE COLD BEER ALL OVER MY FACE.
SURE BEATS THE HELL OUT OF BEING NORMAL.
PANZER TACTICS
BOOK OF HIPSTER
BLAM BLAM
FIZZ
OKAY, YOU TARTS! GET DOWN ON YOUR KNEES AND START PLEADING FOR SALVATION!
QUICK, LET'S TAKE THIS FIGHT OUT ONTO THE BEACH—REMEMBER JIMMY FROM QUADROPHENIA AND ALL THAT!
I NEVER SAW THE MOVIE. I REMEMBER JIMMY FROM THE OSMONDS THOUGH.

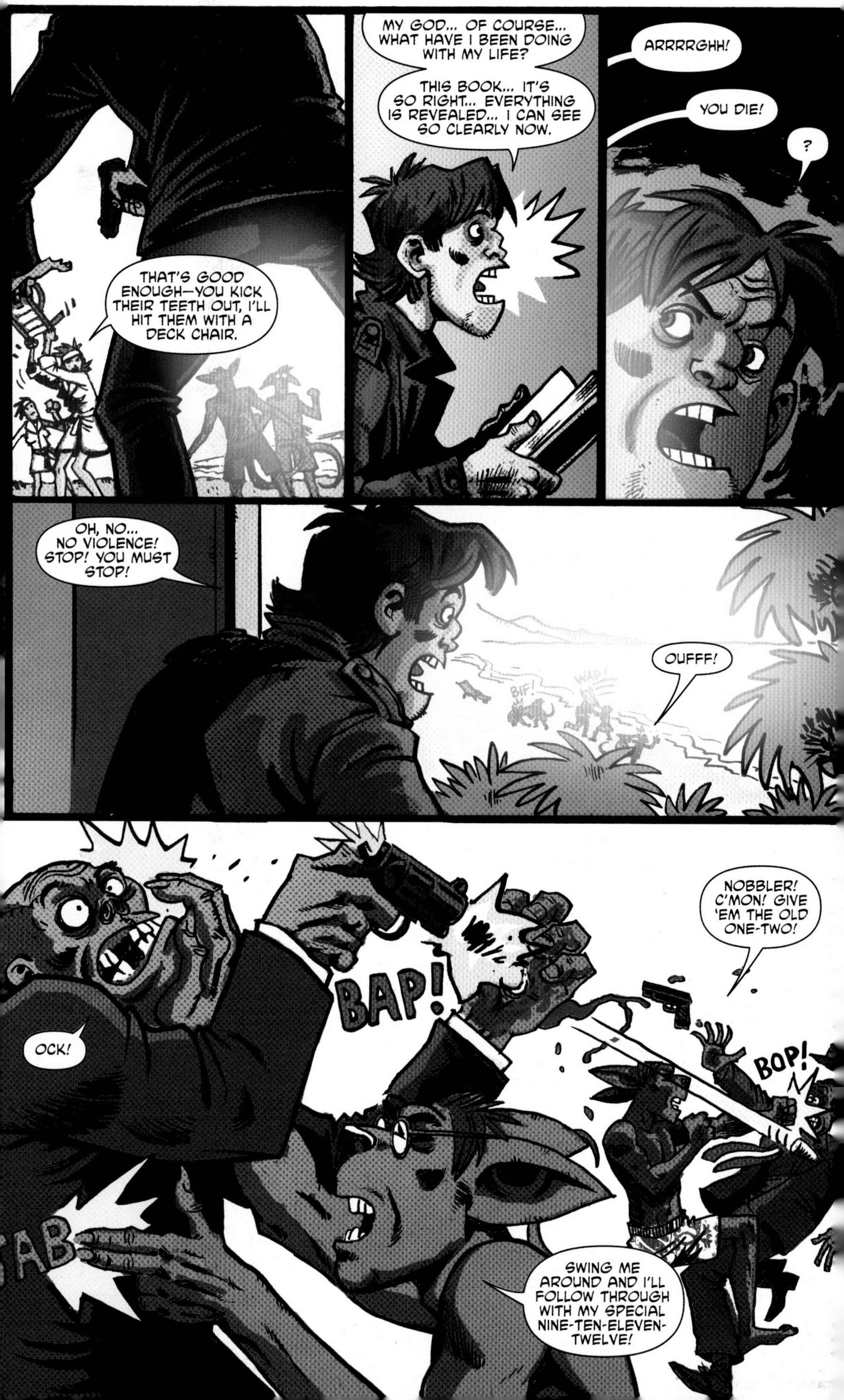
THAT'S GOOD ENOUGH—YOU KICK THEIR TEETH OUT, I'LL HIT THEM WITH A DECK CHAIR.
MY GOD... OF COURSE... WHAT HAVE I BEEN DOING WITH MY LIFE?
THIS BOOK... IT'S SO RIGHT... EVERYTHING IS REVEALED... I CAN SEE SO CLEARLY NOW.
ARRRRGHH!
YOU DIE!
?
OH, NO... NO VIOLENCE! STOP! YOU MUST STOP!
BIF!
WAP!
OUFFF!
BAP!
OCK!
NOBBLER! C'MON! GIVE 'EM THE OLD ONE-TWO!
BOP!
AB
SWING ME AROUND AND I'LL FOLLOW THROUGH WITH MY SPECIAL NINE-TEN-ELEVEN-TWELVE!

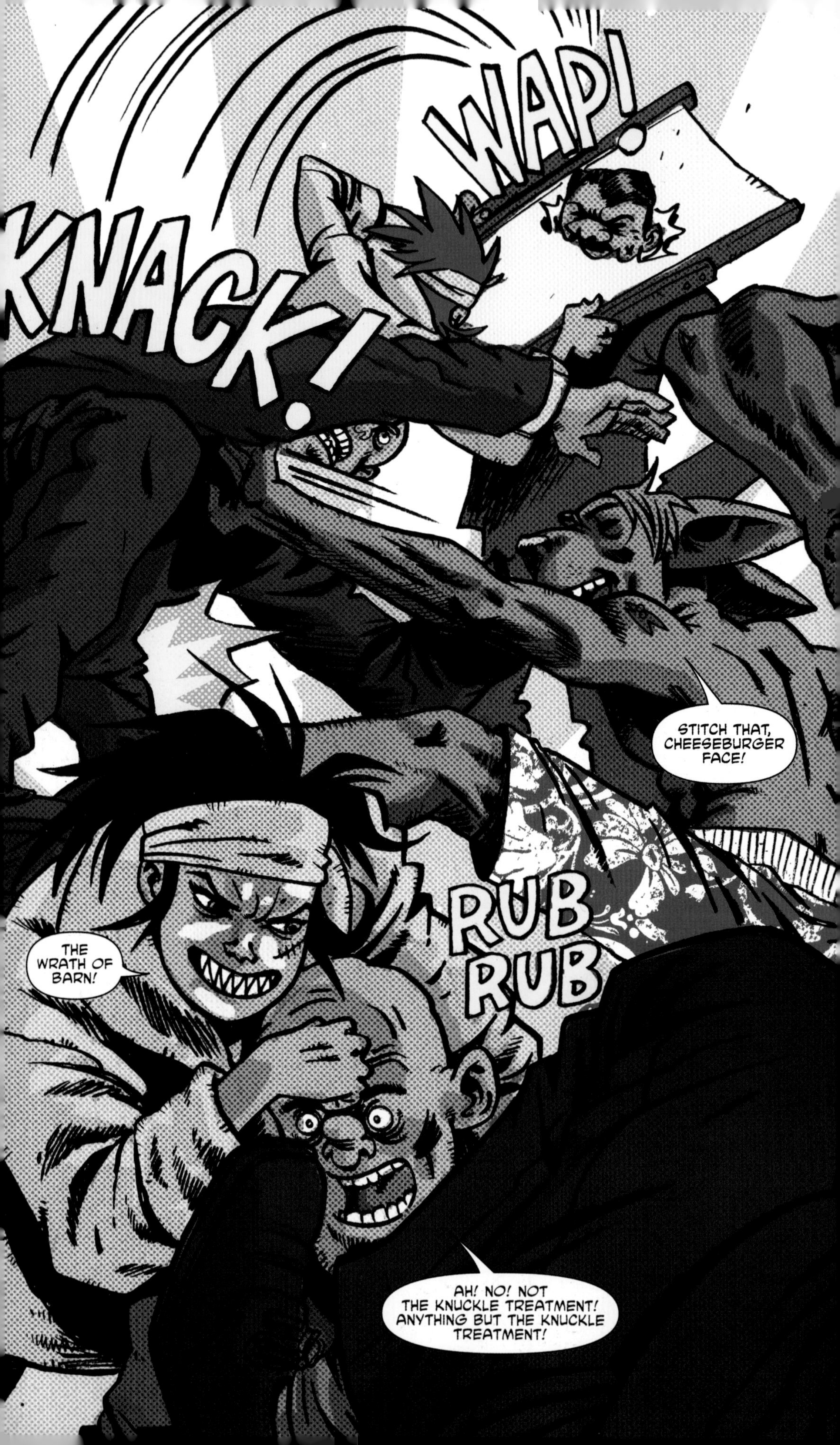
WAP!
KNACK!
STITCH THAT, CHEESEBURGER FACE!
RUB RUB
THE WRATH OF BARN!
AH! NO! NOT THE KNUCKLE TREATMENT! ANYTHING BUT THE KNUCKLE TREATMENT!

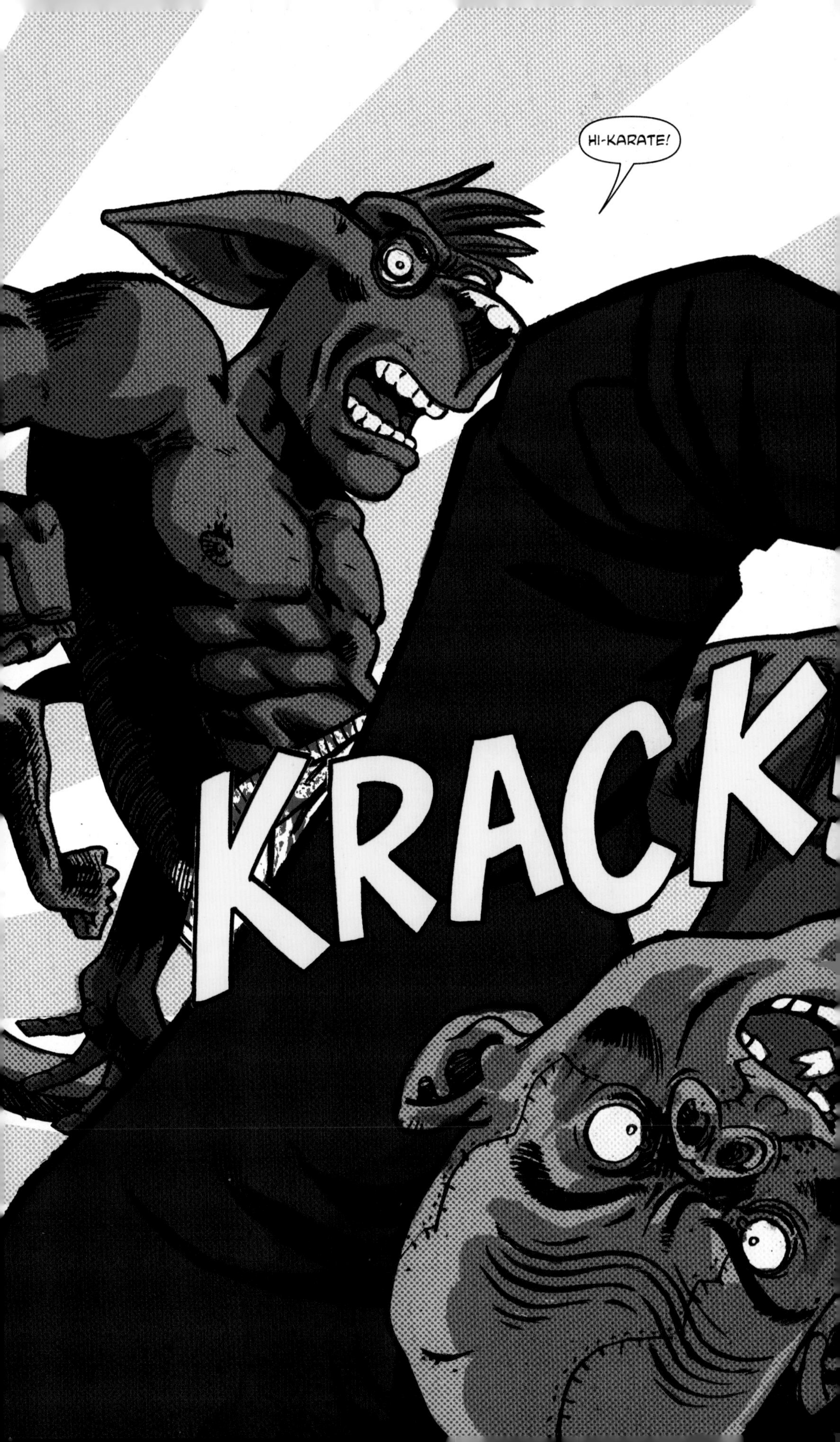
HI-KARATE!
KRACK!

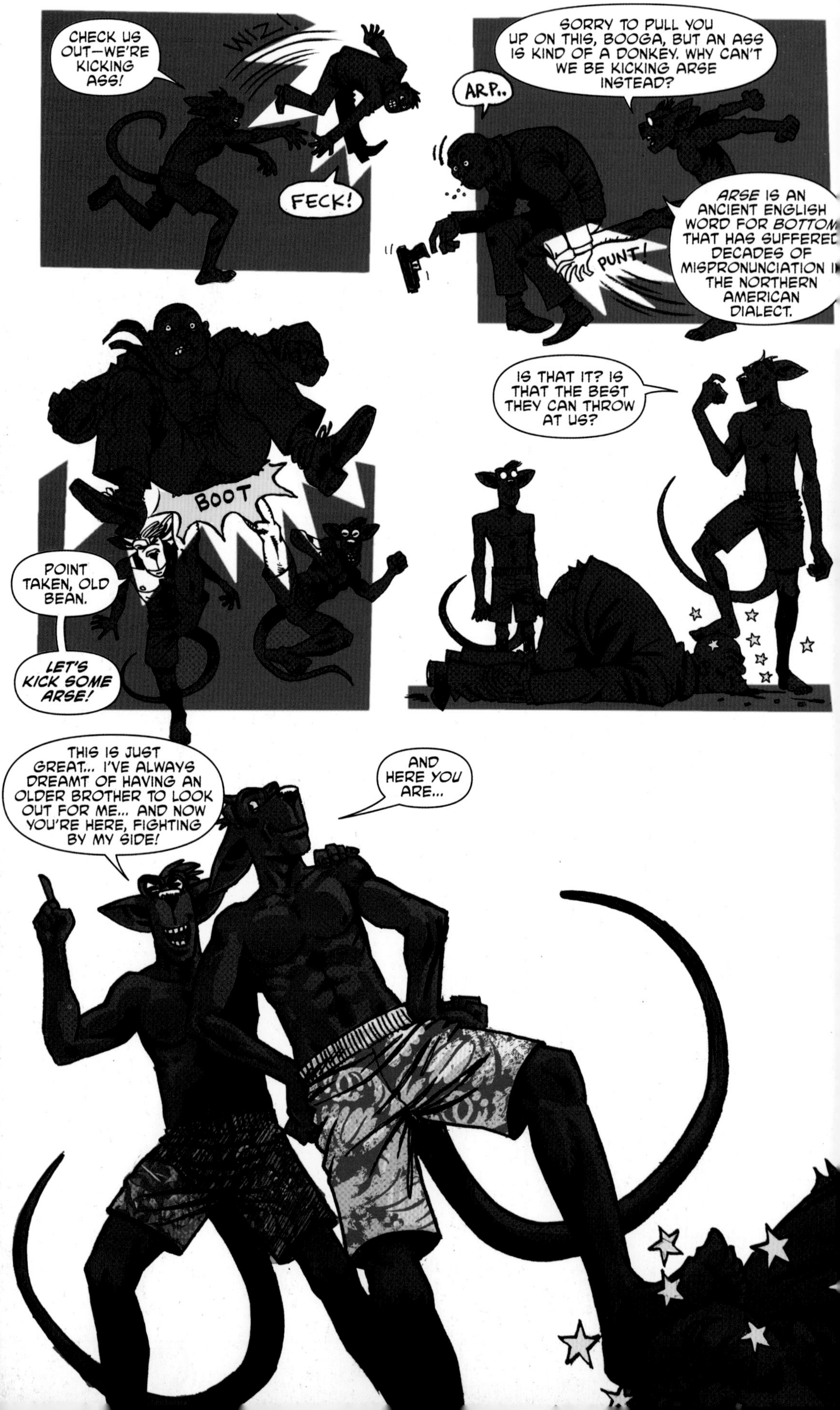
CHECK US OUT—WE'RE KICKING ASS!
WIZ!
FECK!
SORRY TO PULL YOU UP ON THIS, BOOGA, BUT AN ASS IS KIND OF A DONKEY. WHY CAN'T WE BE KICKING ARSE INSTEAD?
ARP..
PUNT!
ARSE IS AN ANCIENT ENGLISH WORD FOR *BOTTOM* THAT HAS SUFFERED DECADES OF MISPRONUNCIATION IN THE NORTHERN AMERICAN DIALECT.
BOOT
POINT TAKEN, OLD BEAN.
LET'S KICK SOME ARSE!
IS THAT IT? IS THAT THE BEST THEY CAN THROW AT US?
THIS IS JUST GREAT... I'VE ALWAYS DREAMT OF HAVING AN OLDER BROTHER TO LOOK OUT FOR ME... AND NOW YOU'RE HERE, FIGHTING BY MY SIDE!
AND HERE *YOU* ARE...

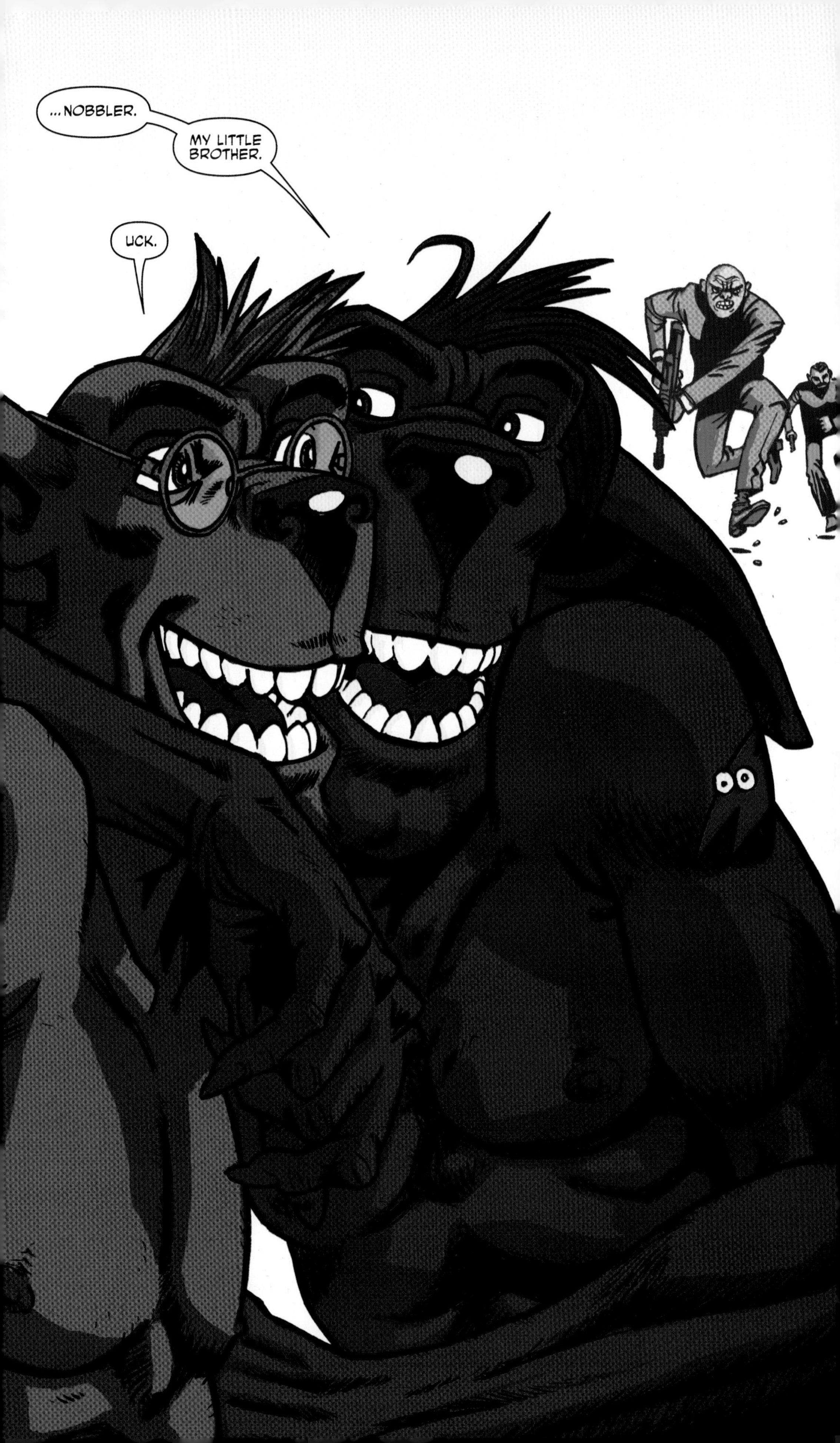
...NOBBLER.
MY LITTLE BROTHER.
UCK.

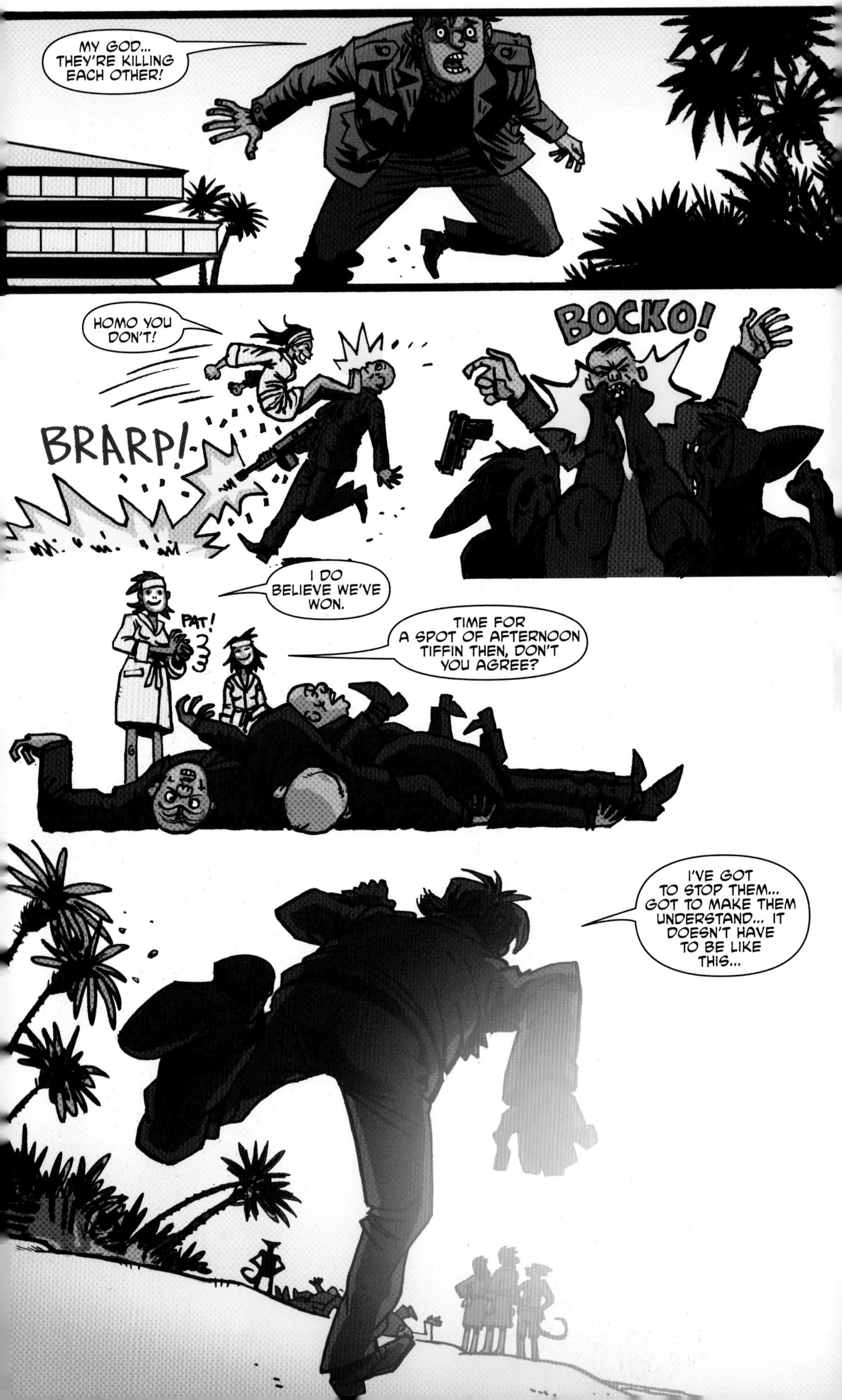
MY GOD... THEY'RE KILLING EACH OTHER!
HOMO YOU DON'T!
BOCKO!
BRARP!
I DO BELIEVE WE'VE WON.
PAT!
TIME FOR A SPOT OF AFTERNOON TIFFIN THEN, DON'T YOU AGREE?
I'VE GOT TO STOP THEM... GOT TO MAKE THEM UNDERSTAND... IT DOESN'T HAVE TO BE LIKE THIS...

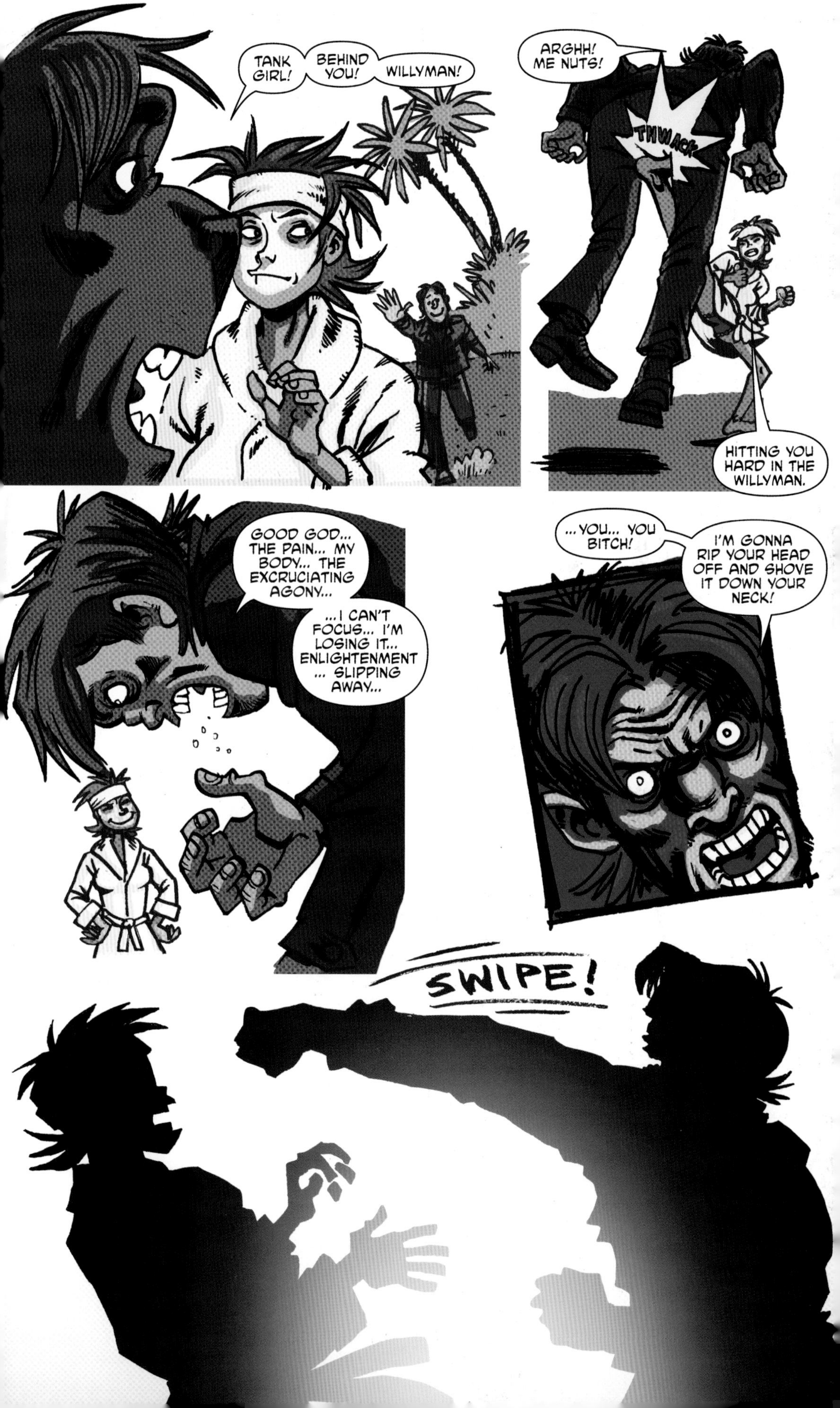
TANK GIRL!
BEHIND YOU!
WILLYMAN!
ARGHH! ME NUTS!
THWACK
HITTING YOU HARD IN THE WILLYMAN.
GOOD GOD... THE PAIN... MY BODY... THE EXCRUCIATING AGONY...
...I CAN'T FOCUS... I'M LOSING IT... ENLIGHTENMENT ... SLIPPING AWAY...
...YOU... YOU BITCH!
I'M GONNA RIP YOUR HEAD OFF AND SHOVE IT DOWN YOUR NECK!
SWIPE!

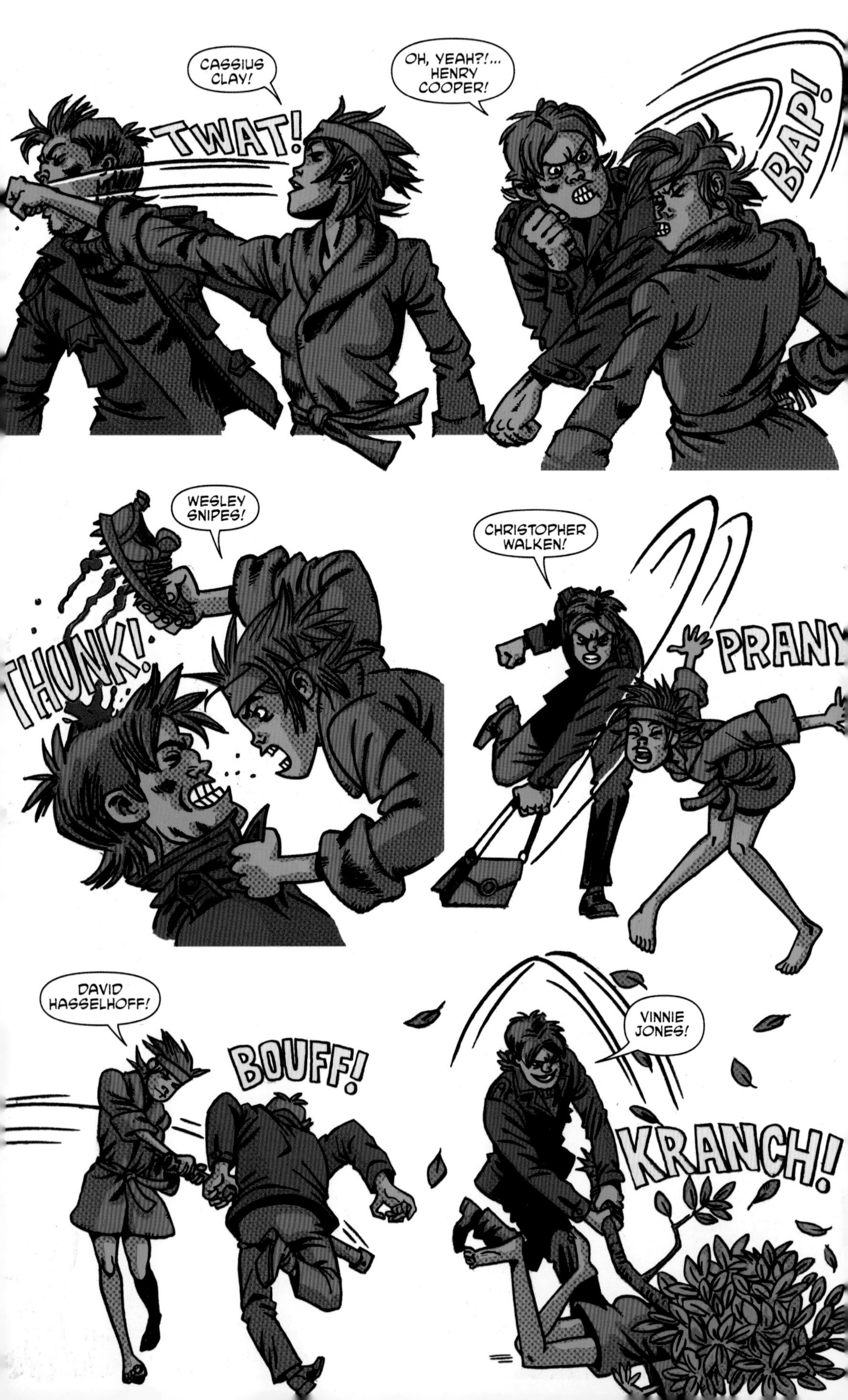
CASSIUS CLAY!
TWAT!
OH, YEAH?!... HENRY COOPER!
BAP!
WESLEY SNIPES!
THUNK!
CHRISTOPHER WALKEN!
PRANY
DAVID HASSELHOFF!
BOUFF!
VINNIE JONES!
KRANCH!

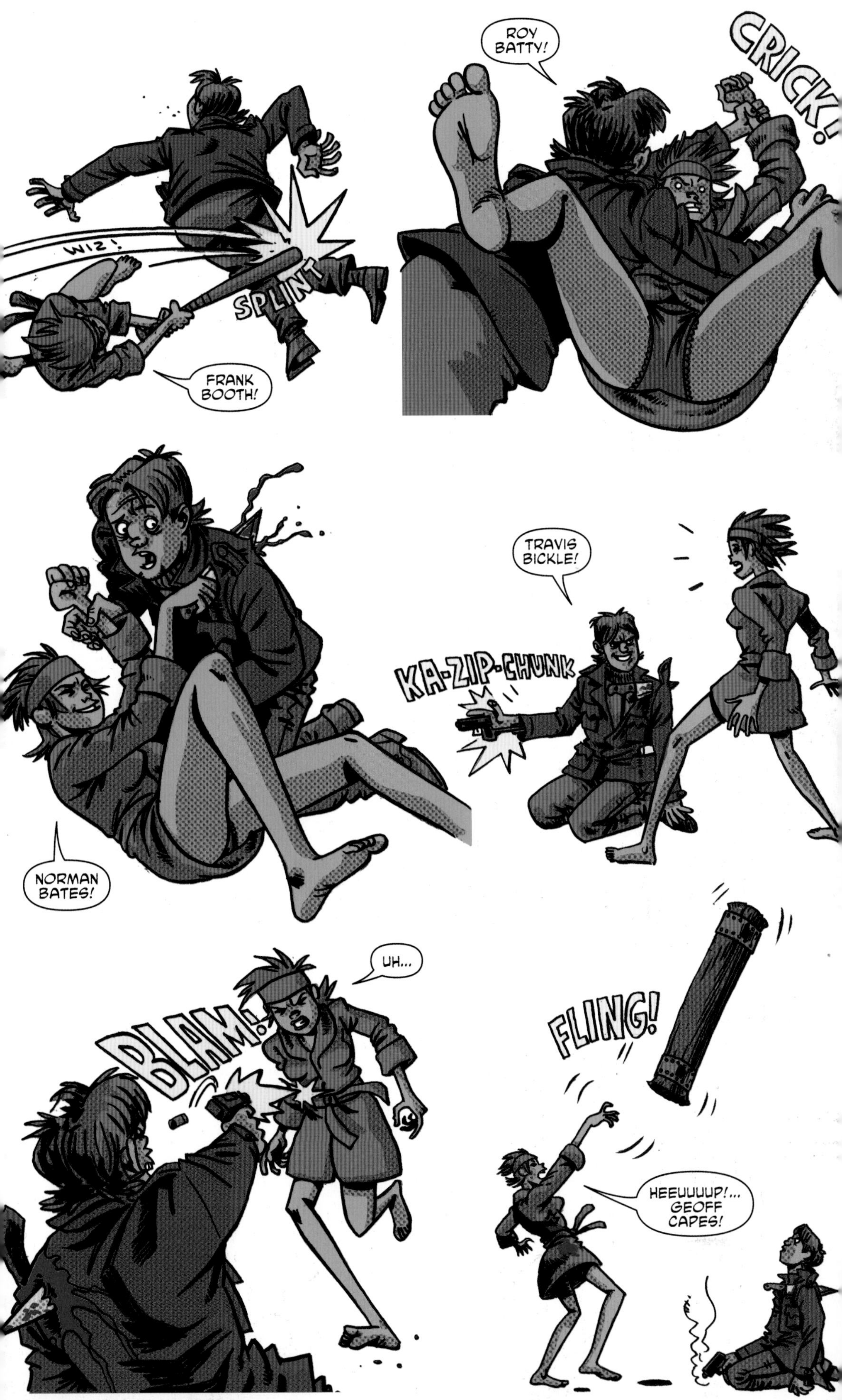
WIZ!
SPLINT
FRANK BOOTH!
ROY BATTY!
CRICK!
NORMAN BATES!
TRAVIS BICKLE!
KA-ZIP-CHUNK
UH...
BLAM!
FLING!
HEEUUUUP!... GEOFF CAPES!

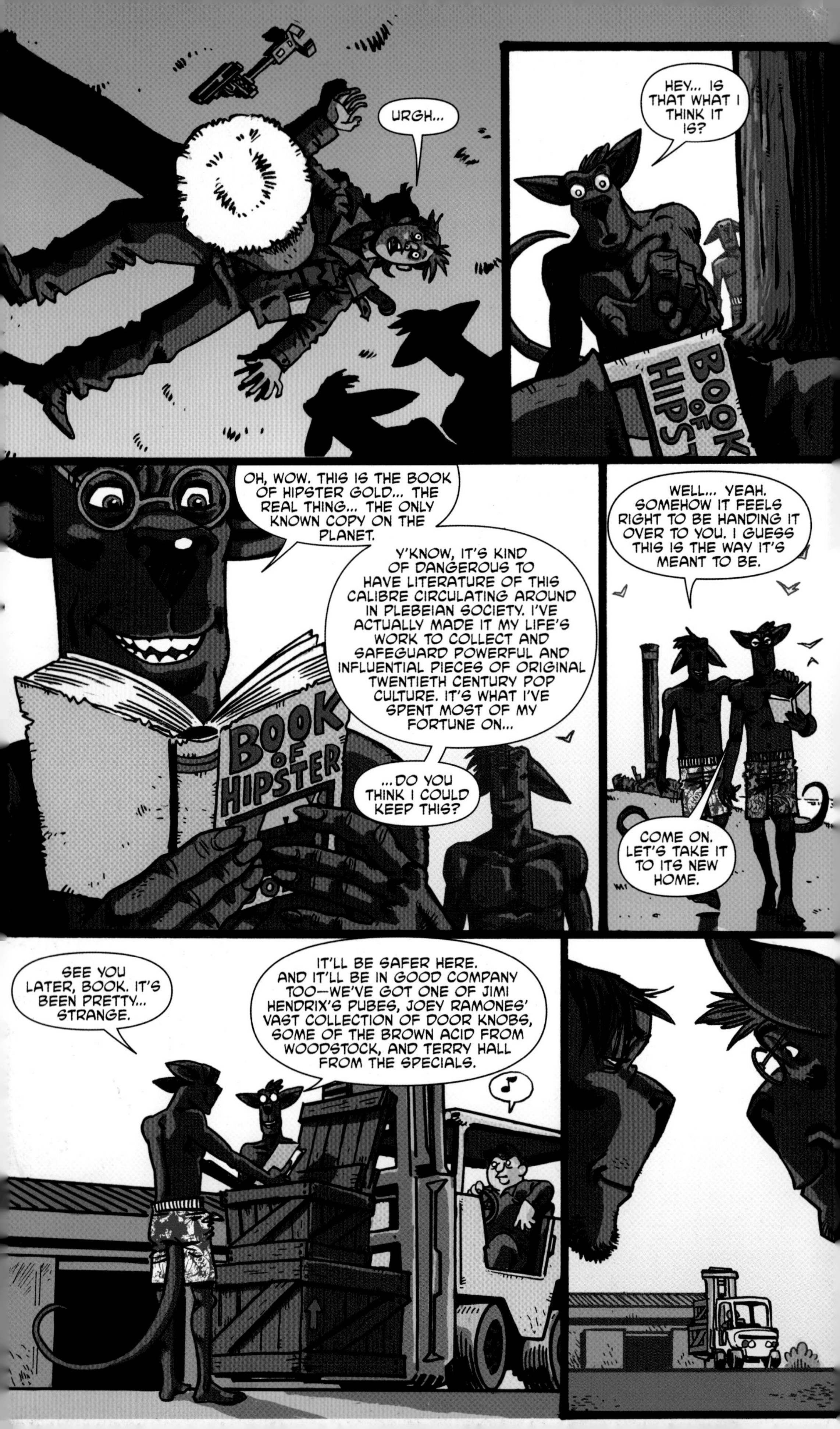
URGH...
HEY... IS THAT WHAT I THINK IT IS?
BOOK OF HIPSTER
OH, WOW. THIS IS THE BOOK OF HIPSTER GOLD... THE REAL THING... THE ONLY KNOWN COPY ON THE PLANET.
Y'KNOW, IT'S KIND OF DANGEROUS TO HAVE LITERATURE OF THIS CALIBRE CIRCULATING AROUND IN PLEBEIAN SOCIETY. I'VE ACTUALLY MADE IT MY LIFE'S WORK TO COLLECT AND SAFEGUARD POWERFUL AND INFLUENTIAL PIECES OF ORIGINAL TWENTIETH CENTURY POP CULTURE. IT'S WHAT I'VE SPENT MOST OF MY FORTUNE ON...
...DO YOU THINK I COULD KEEP THIS?
BOOK OF HIPSTER
WELL... YEAH. SOMEHOW IT FEELS RIGHT TO BE HANDING IT OVER TO YOU. I GUESS THIS IS THE WAY IT'S MEANT TO BE.
COME ON. LET'S TAKE IT TO ITS NEW HOME.
SEE YOU LATER, BOOK. IT'S BEEN PRETTY... STRANGE.
IT'LL BE SAFER HERE. AND IT'LL BE IN GOOD COMPANY TOO—WE'VE GOT ONE OF JIMI HENDRIX'S PUBES, JOEY RAMONES' VAST COLLECTION OF DOOR KNOBS, SOME OF THE BROWN ACID FROM WOODSTOCK, AND TERRY HALL FROM THE SPECIALS.
♪

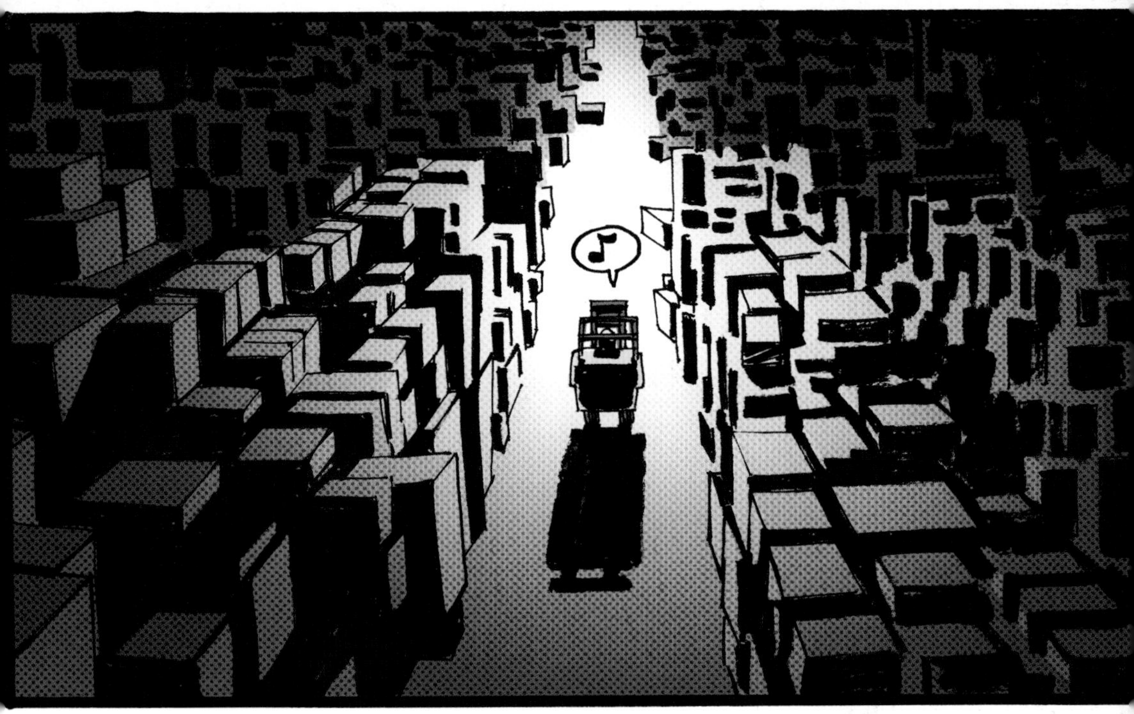

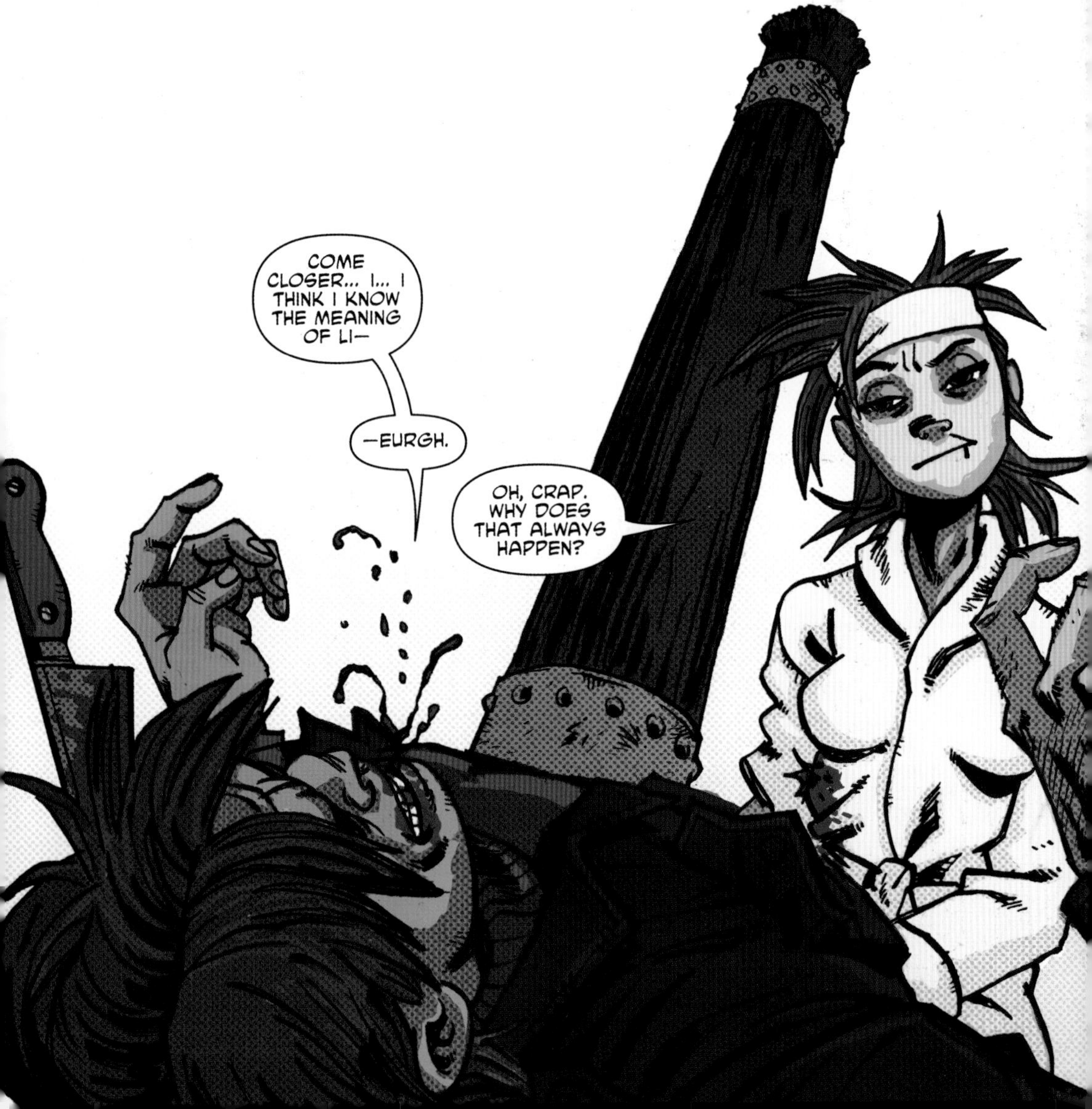
COME CLOSER... I... I THINK I KNOW THE MEANING OF LI—
—EURGH.
OH, CRAP. WHY DOES THAT ALWAYS HAPPEN?

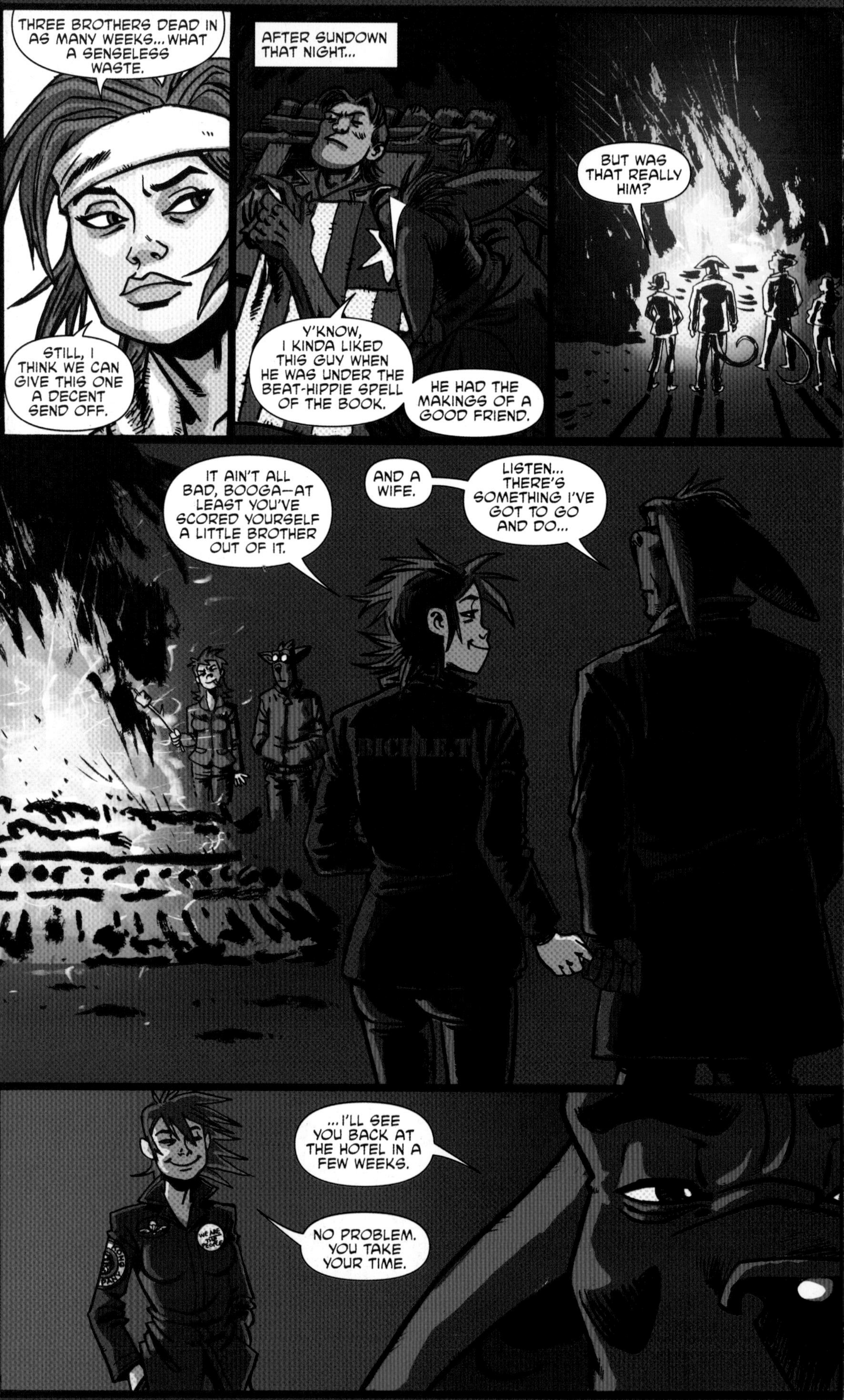
THREE BROTHERS DEAD IN AS MANY WEEKS... WHAT A SENSELESS WASTE.
STILL, I THINK WE CAN GIVE THIS ONE A DECENT SEND OFF.
AFTER SUNDOWN THAT NIGHT...
Y'KNOW, I KINDA LIKED THIS GUY WHEN HE WAS UNDER THE BEAT-HIPPIE SPELL OF THE BOOK.
HE HAD THE MAKINGS OF A GOOD FRIEND.
BUT WAS THAT REALLY HIM?
IT AIN'T ALL BAD, BOOGA—AT LEAST YOU'VE SCORED YOURSELF A LITTLE BROTHER OUT OF IT.
AND A WIFE.
LISTEN... THERE'S SOMETHING I'VE GOT TO GO AND DO...
...I'LL SEE YOU BACK AT THE HOTEL IN A FEW WEEKS.
NO PROBLEM. YOU TAKE YOUR TIME.
WE ARE THE PEOPLE

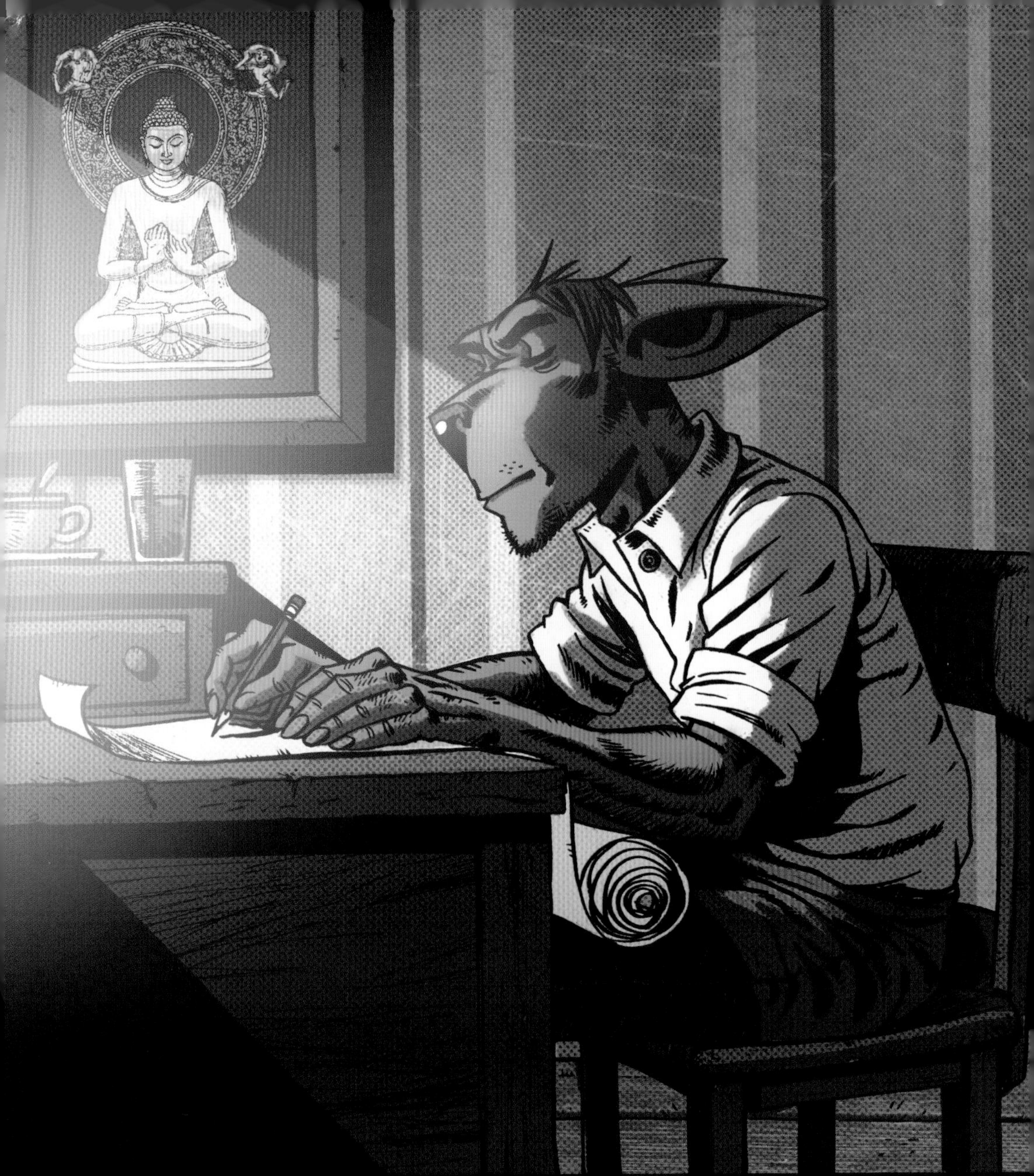

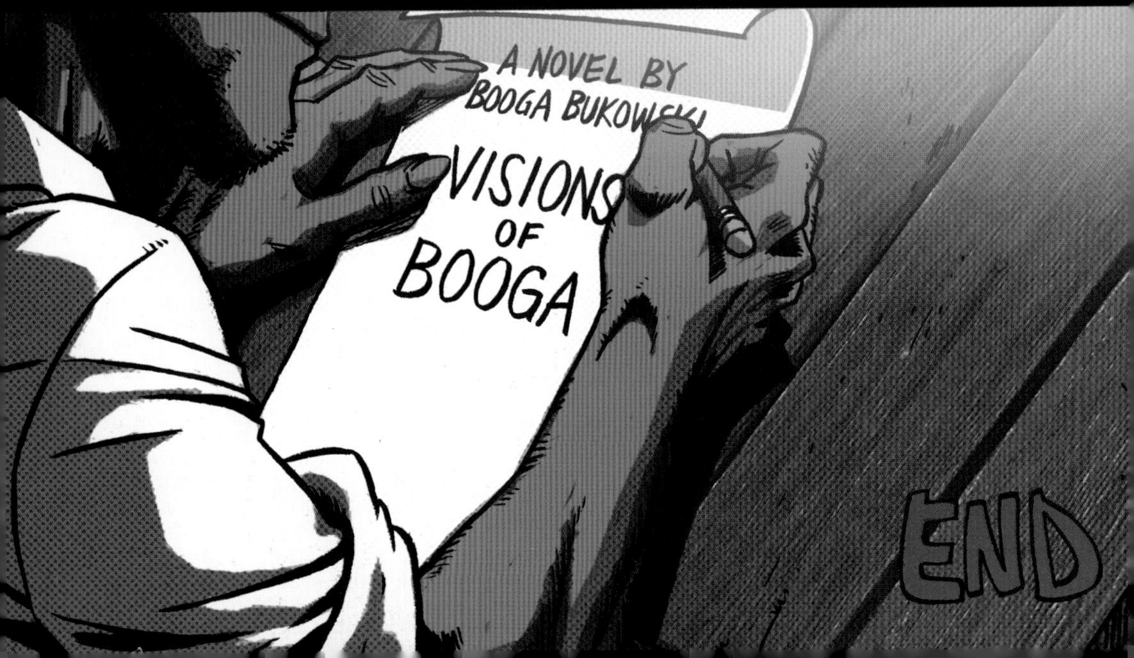
A NOVEL BY
BOOGA BUKOWSKI
VISIONS OF BOOGA
END

ADVERTISMINT

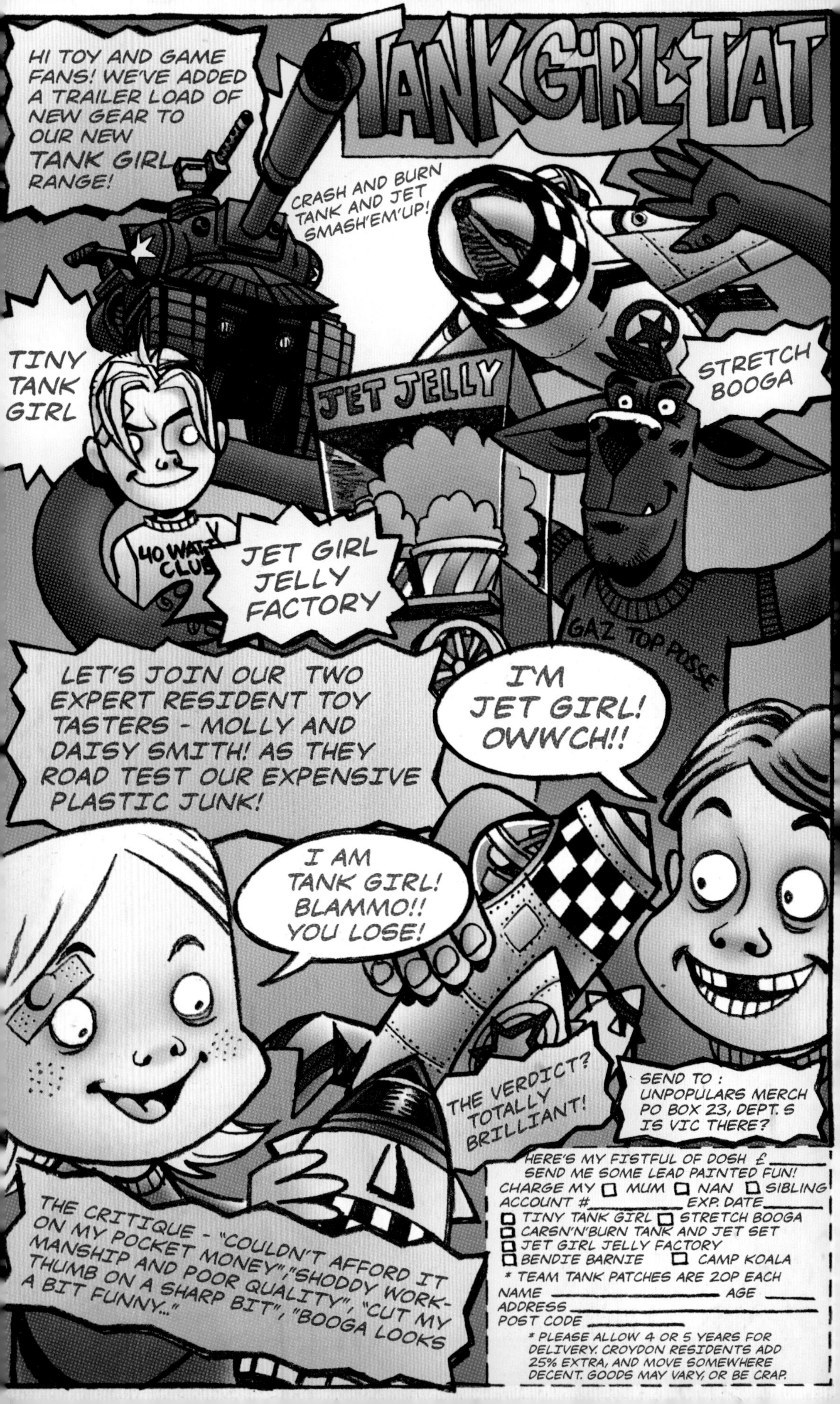
TANK GIRL TAT
HI TOY AND GAME FANS! WE'VE ADDED A TRAILER LOAD OF NEW GEAR TO OUR NEW TANK GIRL RANGE!
CRASH AND BURN TANK AND JET SMASH'EM'UP!
TINY TANK GIRL
JET JELLY
STRETCH BOOGA
40 WATT CLUB
JET GIRL JELLY FACTORY
GAZ TOP POSSE
LET'S JOIN OUR TWO EXPERT RESIDENT TOY TASTERS - MOLLY AND DAISY SMITH! AS THEY ROAD TEST OUR EXPENSIVE PLASTIC JUNK!
I'M JET GIRL! OWWCH!!
I AM TANK GIRL! BLAMMO!! YOU LOSE!
THE VERDICT? TOTALLY BRILLIANT!
SEND TO : UNPOPULARS MERCH PO BOX 23, DEPT. 6 IS VIC THERE?
THE CRITIQUE - "COULDN'T AFFORD IT ON MY POCKET MONEY","SHODDY WORKMANSHIP AND POOR QUALITY", "CUT MY THUMB ON A SHARP BIT", "BOOGA LOOKS A BIT FUNNY..."
HERE'S MY FISTFUL OF DOSH £
SEND ME SOME LEAD PAINTED FUN!
CHARGE MY ☐ MUM ☐ NAN ☐ SIBLING
ACCOUNT # EXP. DATE
☐ TINY TANK GIRL ☐ STRETCH BOOGA
☐ CARSN'N'BURN TANK AND JET SET
☐ JET GIRL JELLY FACTORY
☐ BENDIE BARNIE ☐ CAMP KOALA
* TEAM TANK PATCHES ARE 20P EACH
NAME AGE
ADDRESS
POST CODE
* PLEASE ALLOW 4 OR 5 YEARS FOR DELIVERY. CROYDON RESIDENTS ADD 25% EXTRA, AND MOVE SOMEWHERE DECENT. GOODS MAY VARY, OR BE CRAP.

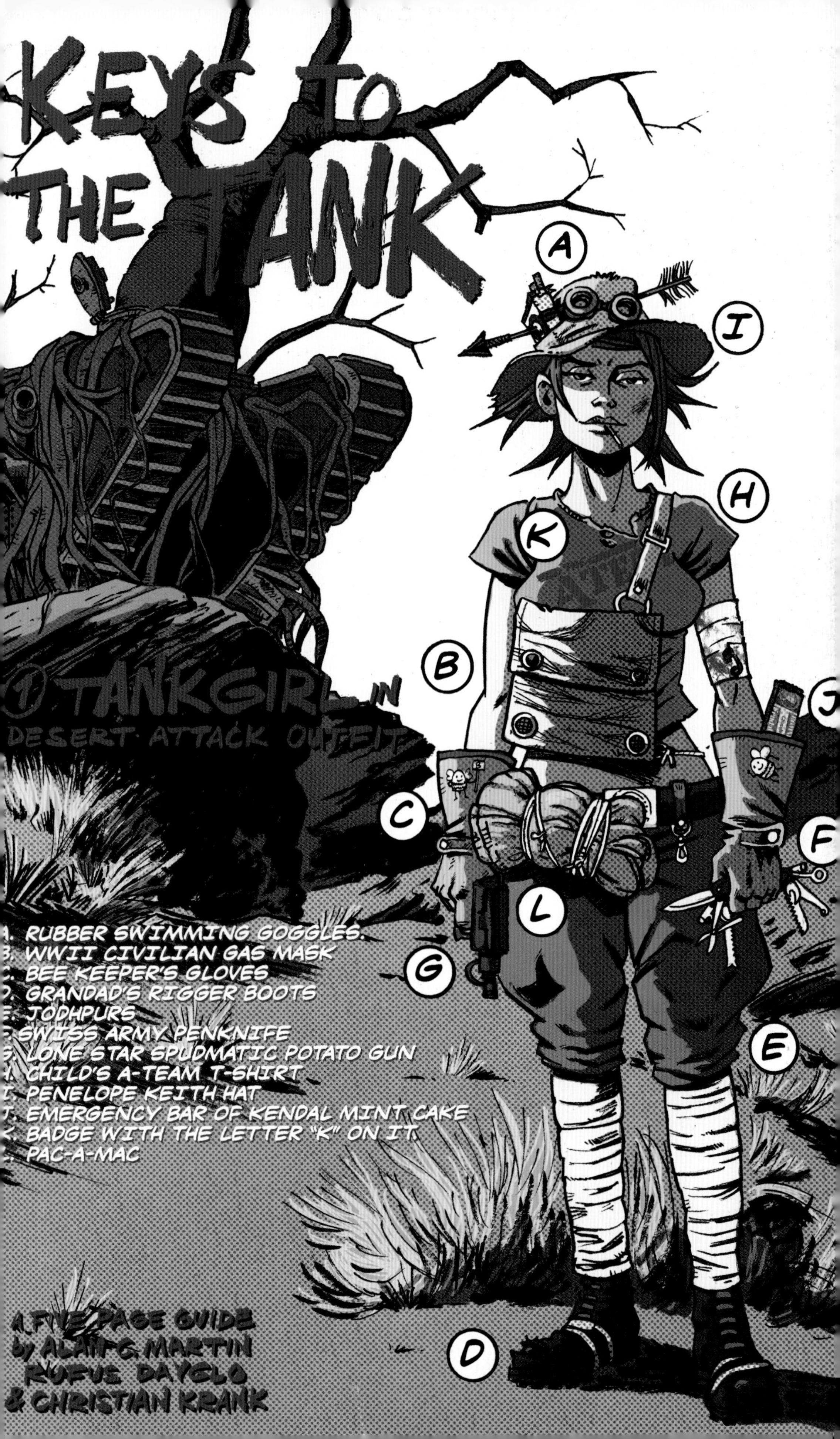
KEYS TO THE TANK
A
I
H
K
1 TANKGIRL IN DESERT ATTACK OUTFIT
B
J
C
F
L
G
E
D
RUBBER SWIMMING GOGGLES.
WWII CIVILIAN GAS MASK
BEE KEEPER'S GLOVES
GRANDAD'S RIGGER BOOTS
JODHPURS
SWISS ARMY PENKNIFE
LONE STAR SPUDMATIC POTATO GUN
CHILD'S A-TEAM T-SHIRT
PENELOPE KEITH HAT
EMERGENCY BAR OF KENDAL MINT CAKE
BADGE WITH THE LETTER "K" ON IT.
PAC-A-MAC
A FIVE PAGE GUIDE
by ALAN C. MARTIN
RUFUS DAYGLO
& CHRISTIAN KRANK

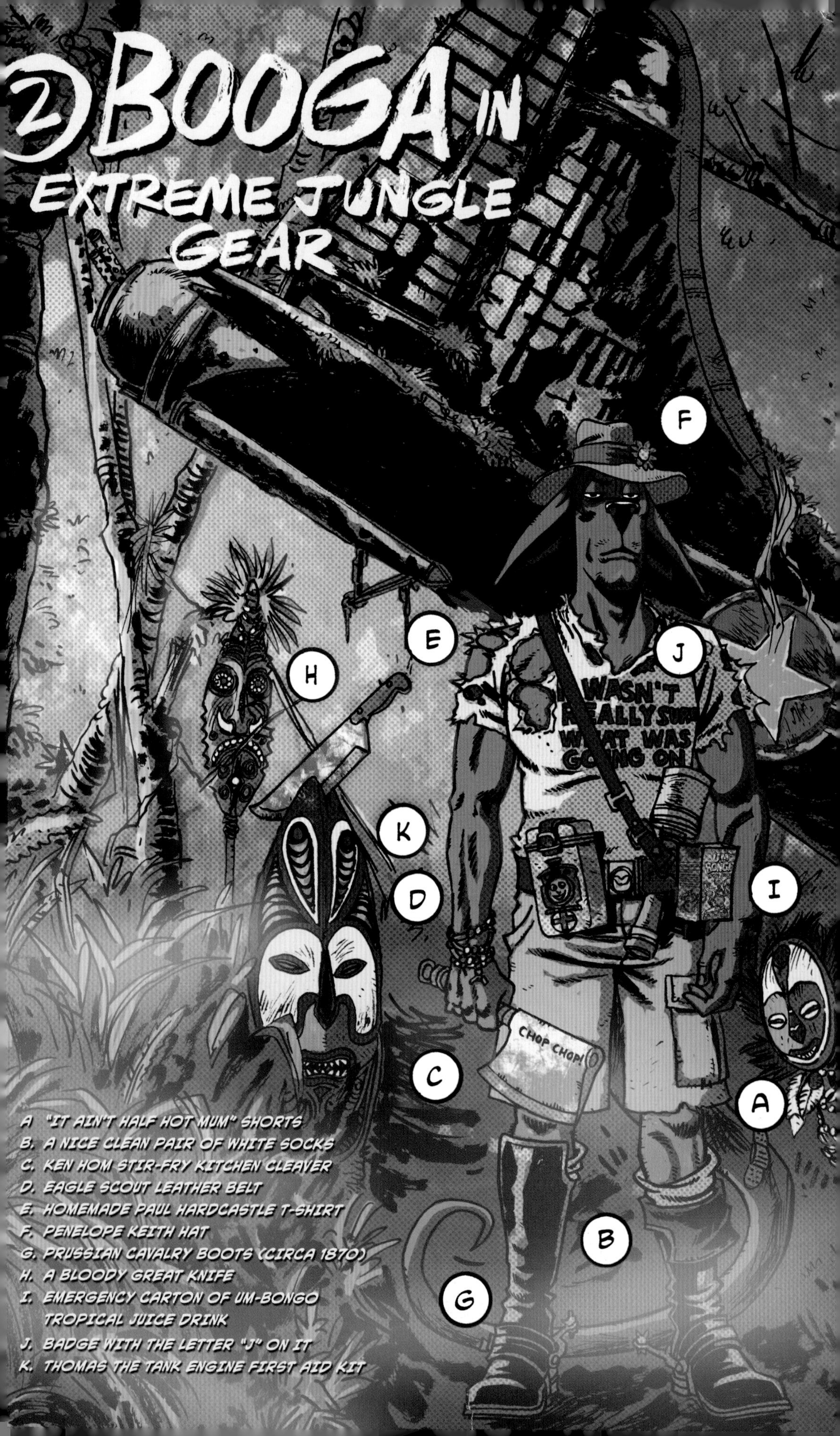

2 BOOGA IN EXTREME JUNGLE GEAR
F
E
J
H
K
D
I
CHOP CHOP!
C
A
B
G
A "IT AIN'T HALF HOT MUM" SHORTS
B. A NICE CLEAN PAIR OF WHITE SOCKS
C. KEN HOM STIR-FRY KITCHEN CLEAVER
D. EAGLE SCOUT LEATHER BELT
E. HOMEMADE PAUL HARDCASTLE T-SHIRT
F. PENELOPE KEITH HAT
G. PRUSSIAN CAVALRY BOOTS (CIRCA 1870)
H. A BLOODY GREAT KNIFE
I. EMERGENCY CARTON OF UM-BONGO TROPICAL JUICE DRINK
J. BADGE WITH THE LETTER "J" ON IT
K. THOMAS THE TANK ENGINE FIRST AID KIT

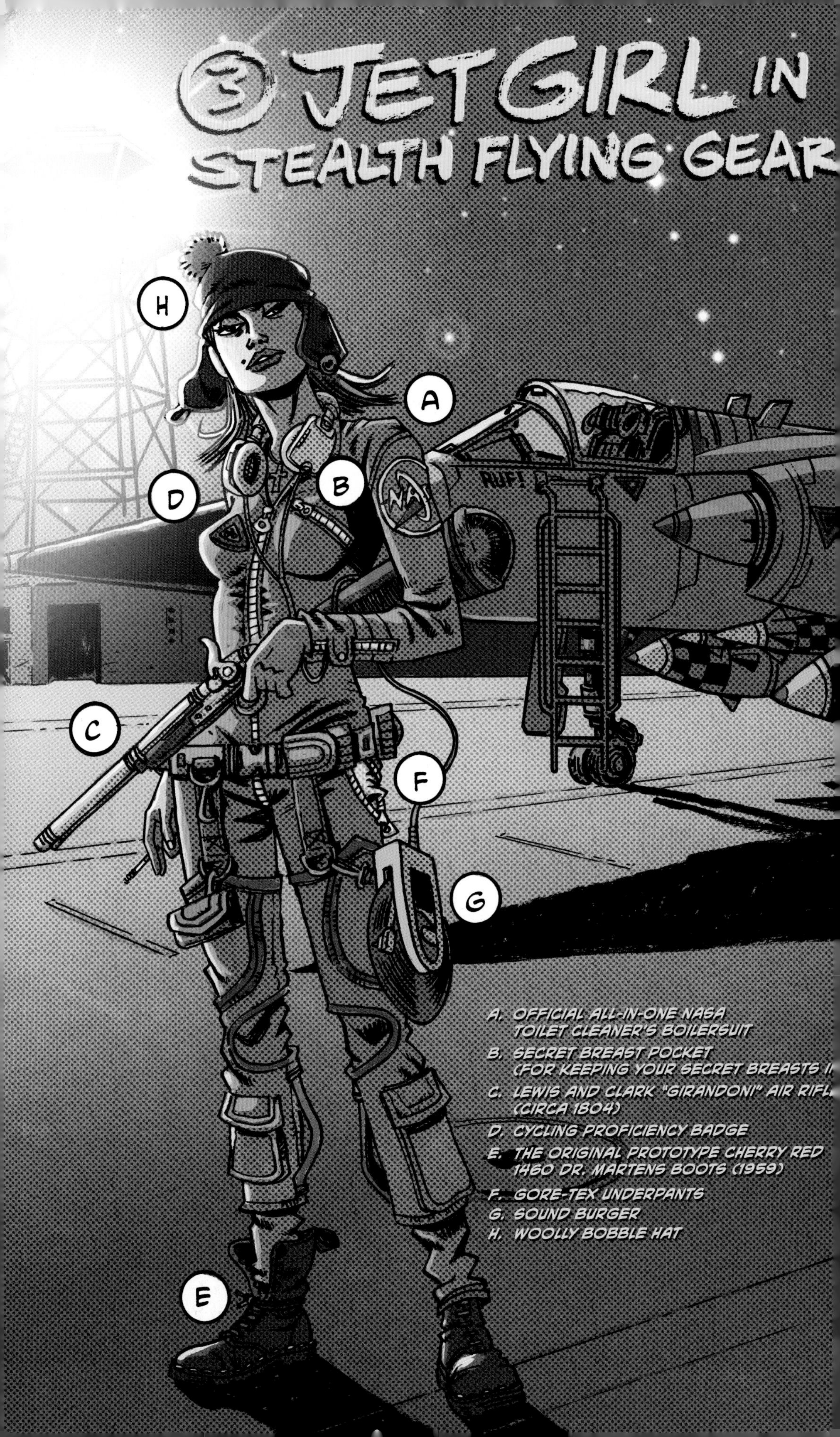
③ JET GIRL IN
STEALTH FLYING GEAR
H
A
B
D
RUF!
C
F
G
E
A. OFFICIAL ALL-IN-ONE NASA
TOILET CLEANER'S BOILERSUIT
B. SECRET BREAST POCKET
(FOR KEEPING YOUR SECRET BREASTS I
C. LEWIS AND CLARK "GIRANDONI" AIR RIFL
(CIRCA 1804)
D. CYCLING PROFICIENCY BADGE
E. THE ORIGINAL PROTOTYPE CHERRY RED
1460 DR. MARTENS BOOTS (1959)
F. GORE-TEX UNDERPANTS
G. SOUND BURGER
H. WOOLLY BOBBLE HAT

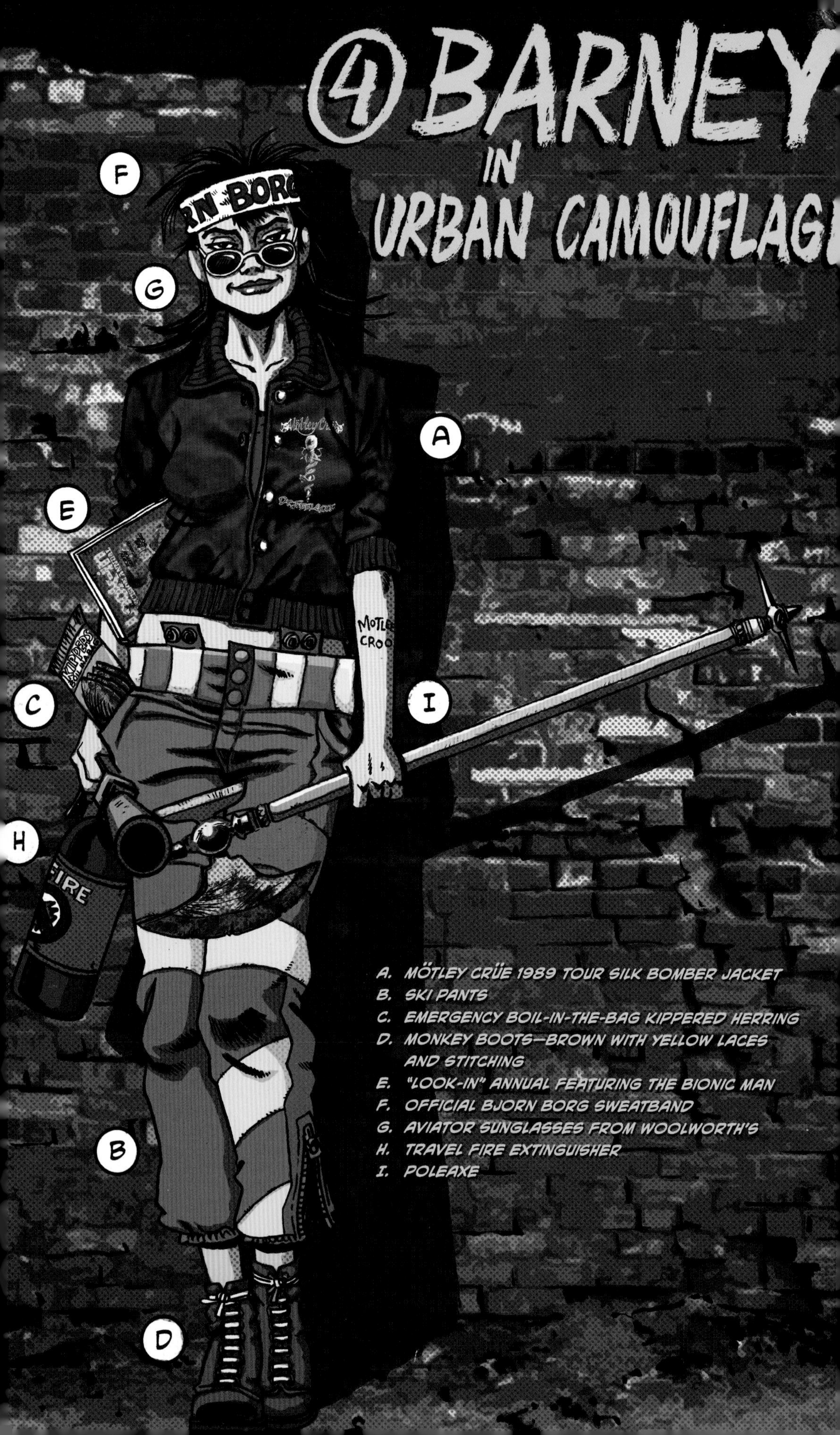
④ BARNEY
IN
URBAN CAMOUFLAGE
F
G
A
E
C
I
H
B
D
MOTLEE CROO
KIPPERS
FIRE
A. MÖTLEY CRÜE 1989 TOUR SILK BOMBER JACKET
B. SKI PANTS
C. EMERGENCY BOIL-IN-THE-BAG KIPPERED HERRING
D. MONKEY BOOTS—BROWN WITH YELLOW LACES AND STITCHING
E. "LOOK-IN" ANNUAL FEATURING THE BIONIC MAN
F. OFFICIAL BJORN BORG SWEATBAND
G. AVIATOR SUNGLASSES FROM WOOLWORTH'S
H. TRAVEL FIRE EXTINGUISHER
I. POLEAXE

5) CRUISER TANK IN FULL RACING LIVERY

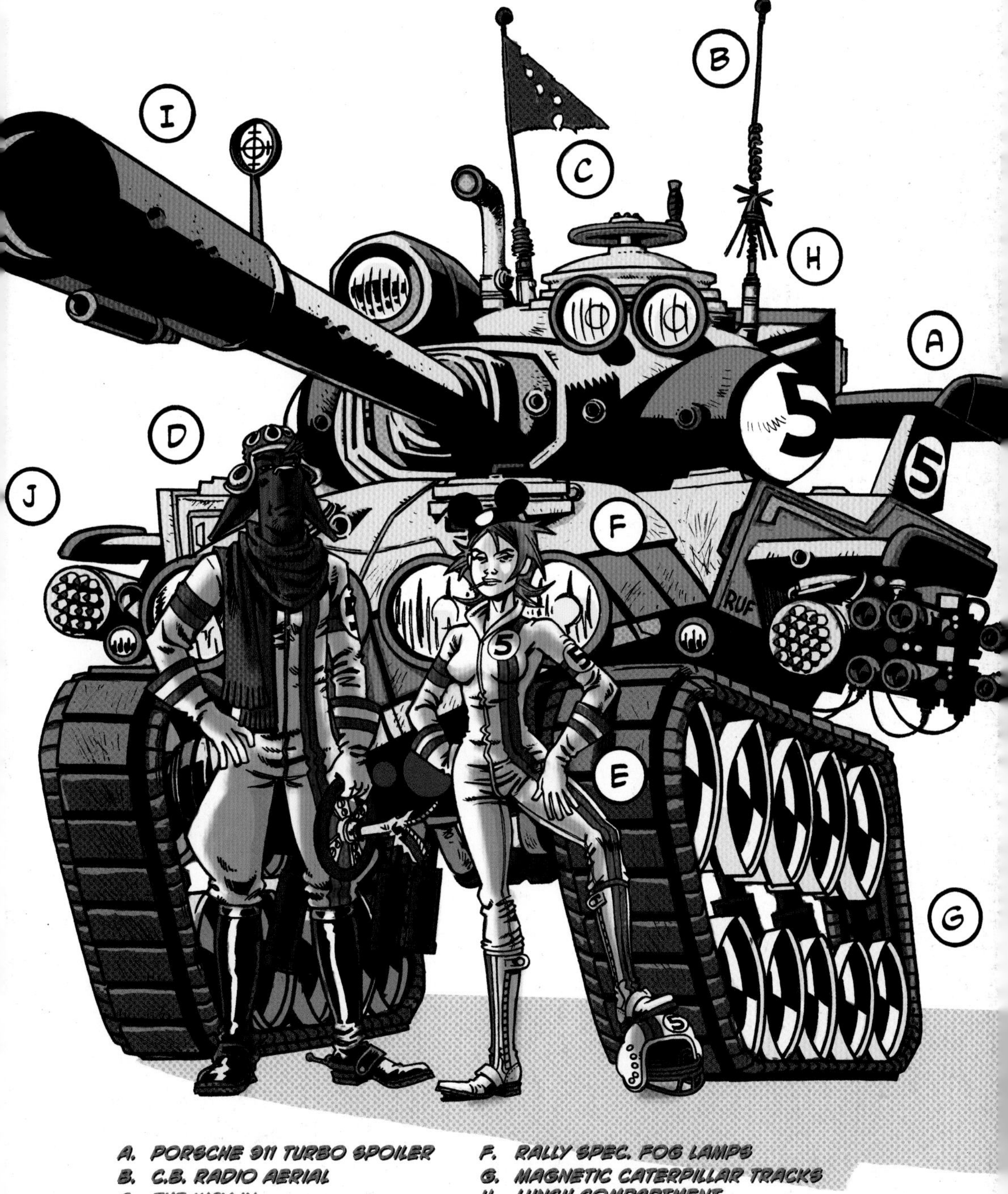

B
I
C
H
A
5
D
J
F
RUF
E
G

A. PORSCHE 911 TURBO SPOILER
B. C.B. RADIO AERIAL
C. THE WAY IN
D. TANK DRIVER
E. NAVIGATOR/MECHANIC
F. RALLY SPEC. FOG LAMPS
G. MAGNETIC CATERPILLAR TRACKS
H. LUNCH COMPARTMENT
I. RE-MODELED 8.8 CM KAMPFWAGENKANONE 36 L/56 CANNON FROM A TIGER1 TANK
J. FIZZBOMBS

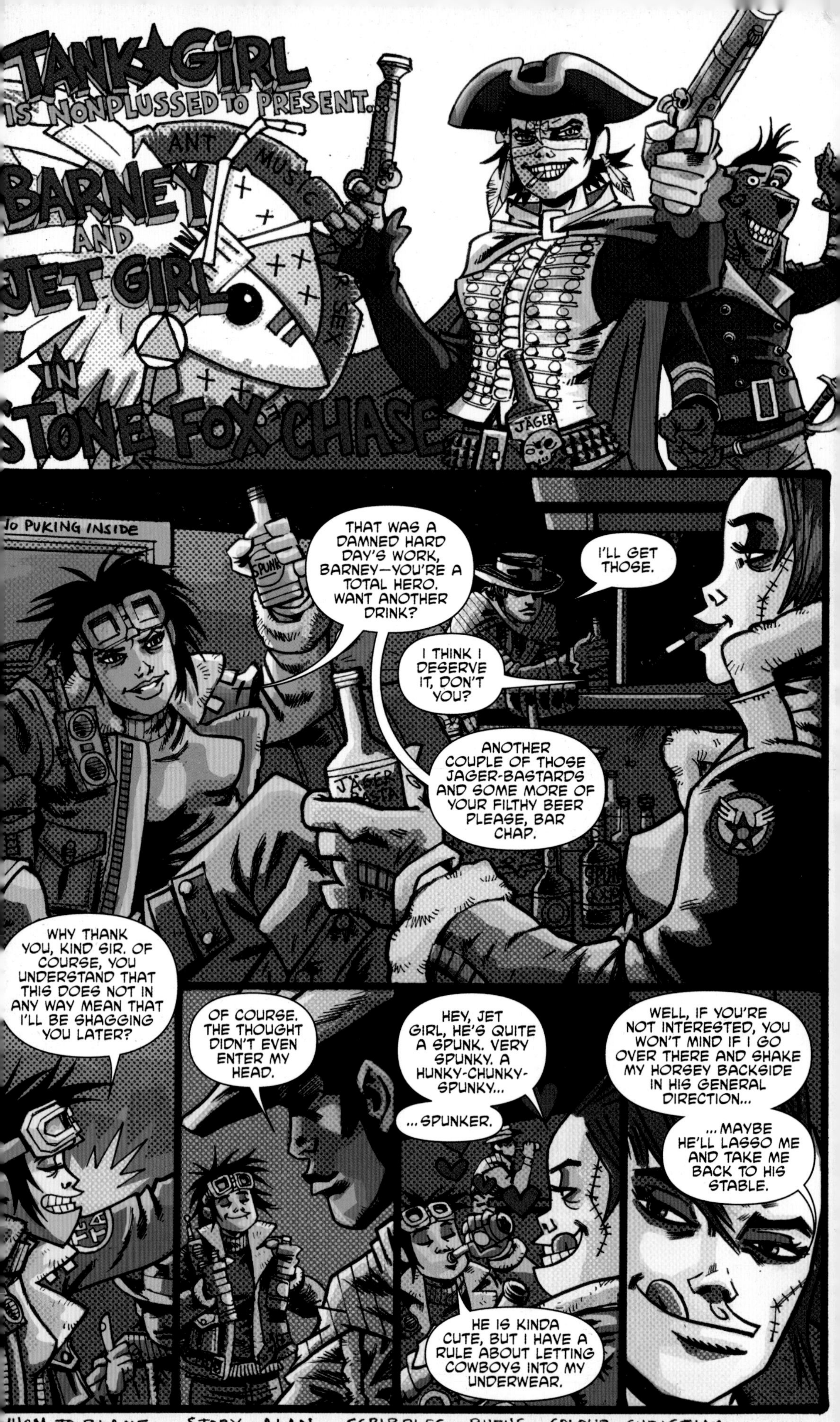
TANK GIRL
IS NONPLUSSED TO PRESENT...
BARNEY AND JET GIRL IN
STONE FOX CHASE
ANT MUSIC
SEX
JÄGER
NO PUKING INSIDE
SPUNK
THAT WAS A DAMNED HARD DAY'S WORK, BARNEY—YOU'RE A TOTAL HERO. WANT ANOTHER DRINK?
I'LL GET THOSE.
I THINK I DESERVE IT, DON'T YOU?
ANOTHER COUPLE OF THOSE JAGER-BASTARDS AND SOME MORE OF YOUR FILTHY BEER PLEASE, BAR CHAP.
WHY THANK YOU, KIND SIR. OF COURSE, YOU UNDERSTAND THAT THIS DOES NOT IN ANY WAY MEAN THAT I'LL BE SHAGGING YOU LATER?
OF COURSE. THE THOUGHT DIDN'T EVEN ENTER MY HEAD.
HEY, JET GIRL, HE'S QUITE A SPUNK. VERY SPUNKY. A HUNKY-CHUNKY-SPUNKY...
...SPUNKER.
HE IS KINDA CUTE, BUT I HAVE A RULE ABOUT LETTING COWBOYS INTO MY UNDERWEAR.
WELL, IF YOU'RE NOT INTERESTED, YOU WON'T MIND IF I GO OVER THERE AND SHAKE MY HORSEY BACKSIDE IN HIS GENERAL DIRECTION...
...MAYBE HE'LL LASSO ME AND TAKE ME BACK TO HIS STABLE.

WHOM TO BLAME... STORY - ALAN SCRIBBLES - RUFUS COLOUR - CHRISTIAN

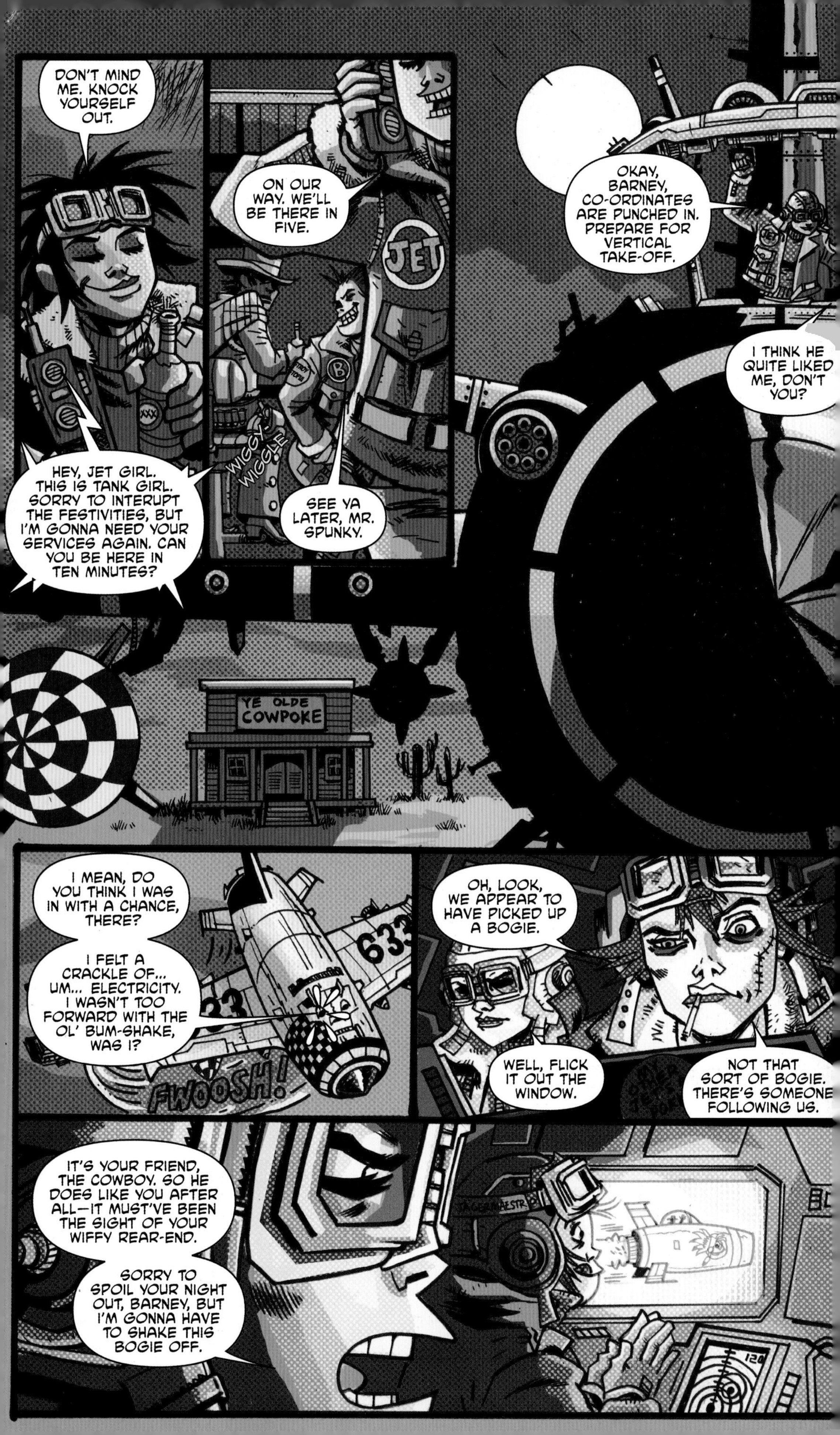
DON'T MIND ME. KNOCK YOURSELF OUT.
HEY, JET GIRL. THIS IS TANK GIRL. SORRY TO INTERUPT THE FESTIVITIES, BUT I'M GONNA NEED YOUR SERVICES AGAIN. CAN YOU BE HERE IN TEN MINUTES?
ON OUR WAY. WE'LL BE THERE IN FIVE.
JET
WIGGY WIGGLE
SEE YA LATER, MR. SPUNKY.
OKAY, BARNEY, CO-ORDINATES ARE PUNCHED IN. PREPARE FOR VERTICAL TAKE-OFF.
I THINK HE QUITE LIKED ME, DON'T YOU?
YE OLDE COWPOKE
I MEAN, DO YOU THINK I WAS IN WITH A CHANCE, THERE?
I FELT A CRACKLE OF... UM... ELECTRICITY. I WASN'T TOO FORWARD WITH THE OL' BUM-SHAKE, WAS I?
633
FWOOSH!
OH, LOOK, WE APPEAR TO HAVE PICKED UP A BOGIE.
WELL, FLICK IT OUT THE WINDOW.
NOT THAT SORT OF BOGIE. THERE'S SOMEONE FOLLOWING US.
IT'S YOUR FRIEND, THE COWBOY. SO HE DOES LIKE YOU AFTER ALL—IT MUST'VE BEEN THE SIGHT OF YOUR WIFFY REAR-END.
SORRY TO SPOIL YOUR NIGHT OUT, BARNEY, BUT I'M GONNA HAVE TO SHAKE THIS BOGIE OFF.

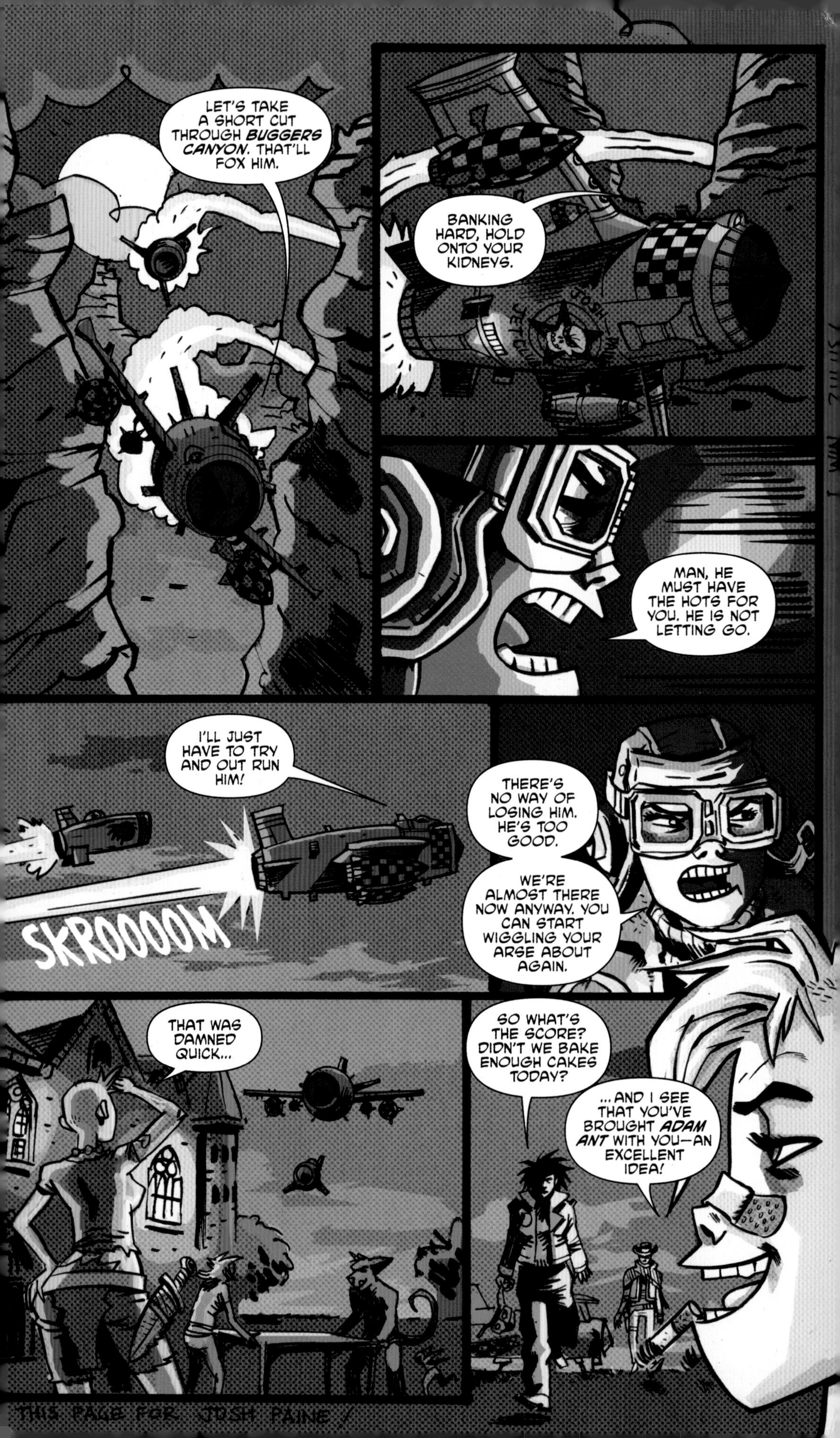

LET'S TAKE A SHORT CUT THROUGH *BUGGERS CANYON*. THAT'LL FOX HIM.
BANKING HARD, HOLD ONTO YOUR KIDNEYS.
MAN, HE MUST HAVE THE HOTS FOR YOU. HE IS NOT LETTING GO.
I'LL JUST HAVE TO TRY AND OUT RUN HIM!
SKROOOOOM
THERE'S NO WAY OF LOSING HIM. HE'S TOO GOOD.
WE'RE ALMOST THERE NOW ANYWAY. YOU CAN START WIGGLING YOUR ARSE ABOUT AGAIN.
THAT WAS DAMNED QUICK...
SO WHAT'S THE SCORE? DIDN'T WE BAKE ENOUGH CAKES TODAY?
...AND I SEE THAT YOU'VE BROUGHT *ADAM ANT* WITH YOU—AN EXCELLENT IDEA!
THIS PAGE FOR JOSH PAINE!

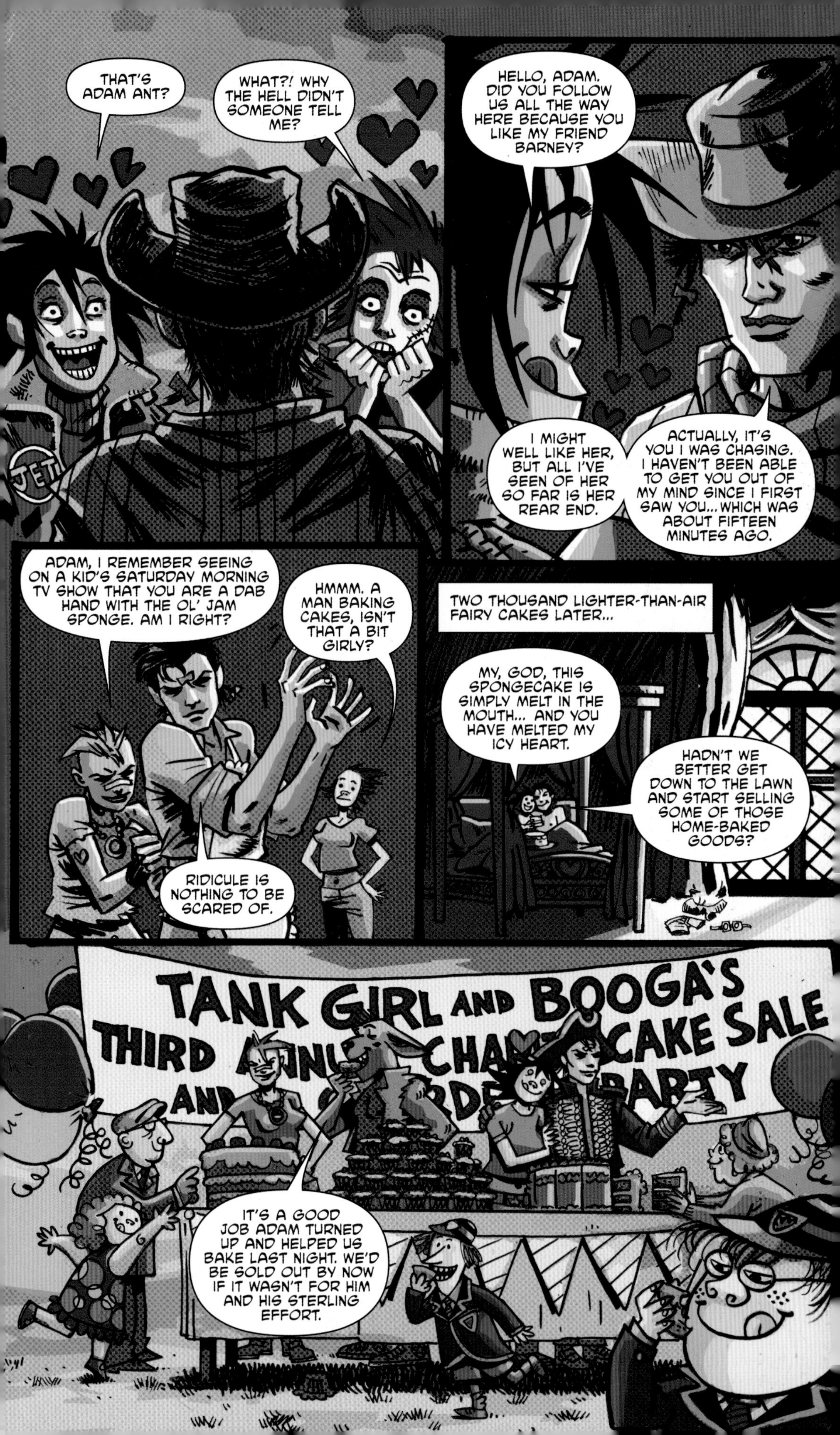
THAT'S ADAM ANT?
WHAT?! WHY THE HELL DIDN'T SOMEONE TELL ME?
HELLO, ADAM. DID YOU FOLLOW US ALL THE WAY HERE BECAUSE YOU LIKE MY FRIEND BARNEY?
I MIGHT WELL LIKE HER, BUT ALL I'VE SEEN OF HER SO FAR IS HER REAR END.
ACTUALLY, IT'S YOU I WAS CHASING. I HAVEN'T BEEN ABLE TO GET YOU OUT OF MY MIND SINCE I FIRST SAW YOU...WHICH WAS ABOUT FIFTEEN MINUTES AGO.
JET
ADAM, I REMEMBER SEEING ON A KID'S SATURDAY MORNING TV SHOW THAT YOU ARE A DAB HAND WITH THE OL' JAM SPONGE. AM I RIGHT?
HMMM. A MAN BAKING CAKES, ISN'T THAT A BIT GIRLY?
RIDICULE IS NOTHING TO BE SCARED OF.
TWO THOUSAND LIGHTER-THAN-AIR FAIRY CAKES LATER...
MY, GOD, THIS SPONGECAKE IS SIMPLY MELT IN THE MOUTH... AND YOU HAVE MELTED MY ICY HEART.
HADN'T WE BETTER GET DOWN TO THE LAWN AND START SELLING SOME OF THOSE HOME-BAKED GOODS?
TANK GIRL AND BOOGA'S
IT'S A GOOD JOB ADAM TURNED UP AND HELPED US BAKE LAST NIGHT. WE'D BE SOLD OUT BY NOW IF IT WASN'T FOR HIM AND HIS STERLING EFFORT.

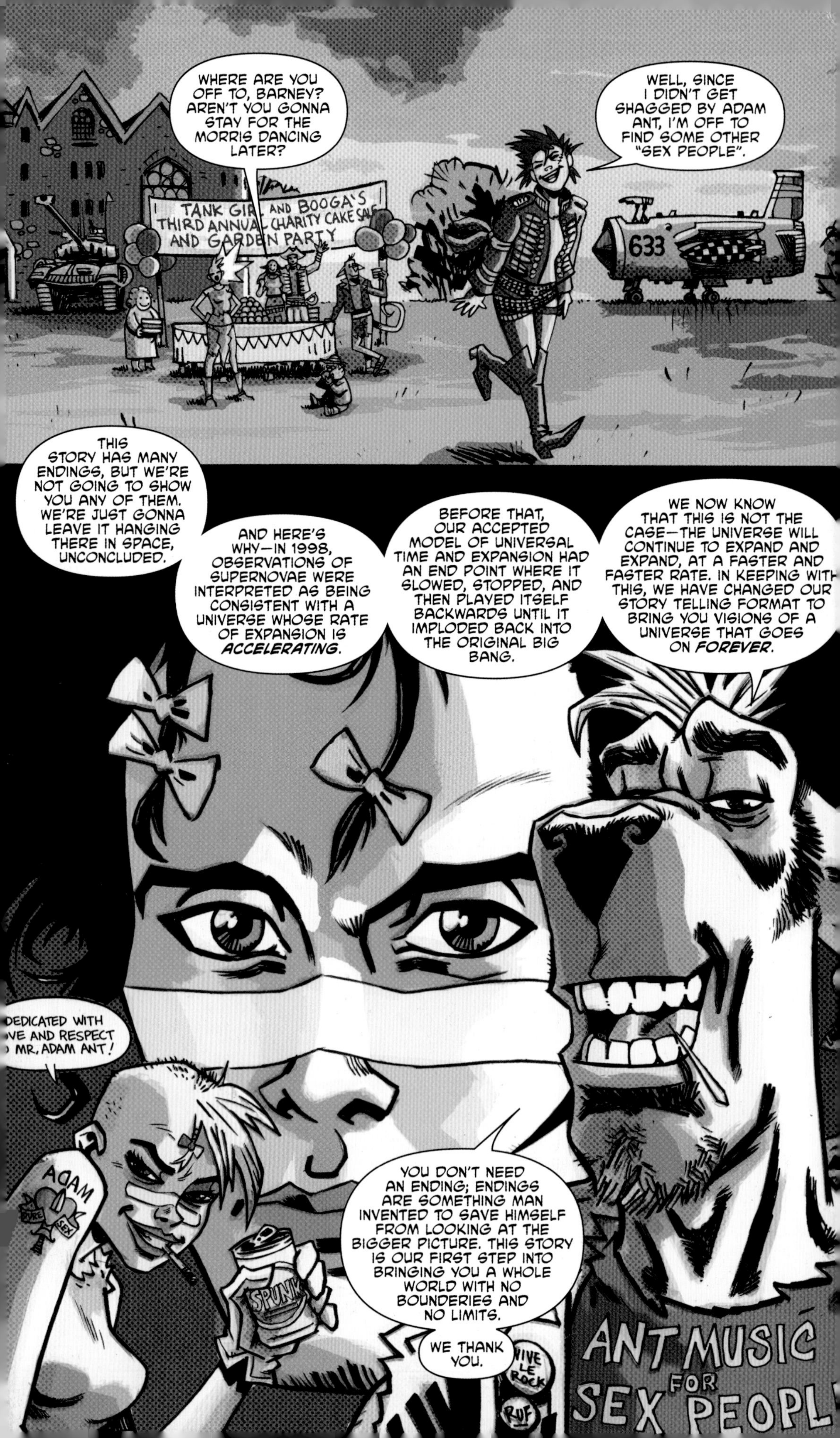
WHERE ARE YOU OFF TO, BARNEY? AREN'T YOU GONNA STAY FOR THE MORRIS DANCING LATER?
WELL, SINCE I DIDN'T GET SHAGGED BY ADAM ANT, I'M OFF TO FIND SOME OTHER "SEX PEOPLE".
TANK GIRL AND BOOGA'S THIRD ANNUAL CHARITY CAKE SALE AND GARDEN PARTY
633
THIS STORY HAS MANY ENDINGS, BUT WE'RE NOT GOING TO SHOW YOU ANY OF THEM. WE'RE JUST GONNA LEAVE IT HANGING THERE IN SPACE, UNCONCLUDED.
AND HERE'S WHY—IN 1998, OBSERVATIONS OF SUPERNOVAE WERE INTERPRETED AS BEING CONSISTENT WITH A UNIVERSE WHOSE RATE OF EXPANSION IS *ACCELERATING*.
BEFORE THAT, OUR ACCEPTED MODEL OF UNIVERSAL TIME AND EXPANSION HAD AN END POINT WHERE IT SLOWED, STOPPED, AND THEN PLAYED ITSELF BACKWARDS UNTIL IT IMPLODED BACK INTO THE ORIGINAL BIG BANG.
WE NOW KNOW THAT THIS IS NOT THE CASE—THE UNIVERSE WILL CONTINUE TO EXPAND AND EXPAND, AT A FASTER AND FASTER RATE. IN KEEPING WITH THIS, WE HAVE CHANGED OUR STORY TELLING FORMAT TO BRING YOU VISIONS OF A UNIVERSE THAT GOES ON *FOREVER*.
DEDICATED WITH VE AND RESPECT MR. ADAM ANT!
ADAM
YOU DON'T NEED AN ENDING; ENDINGS ARE SOMETHING MAN INVENTED TO SAVE HIMSELF FROM LOOKING AT THE BIGGER PICTURE. THIS STORY IS OUR FIRST STEP INTO BRINGING YOU A WHOLE WORLD WITH NO BOUNDERIES AND NO LIMITS.
WE THANK YOU.
SPUNK
VIVE LE ROCK
RUF
ANT MUSIC FOR SEX PEOPL

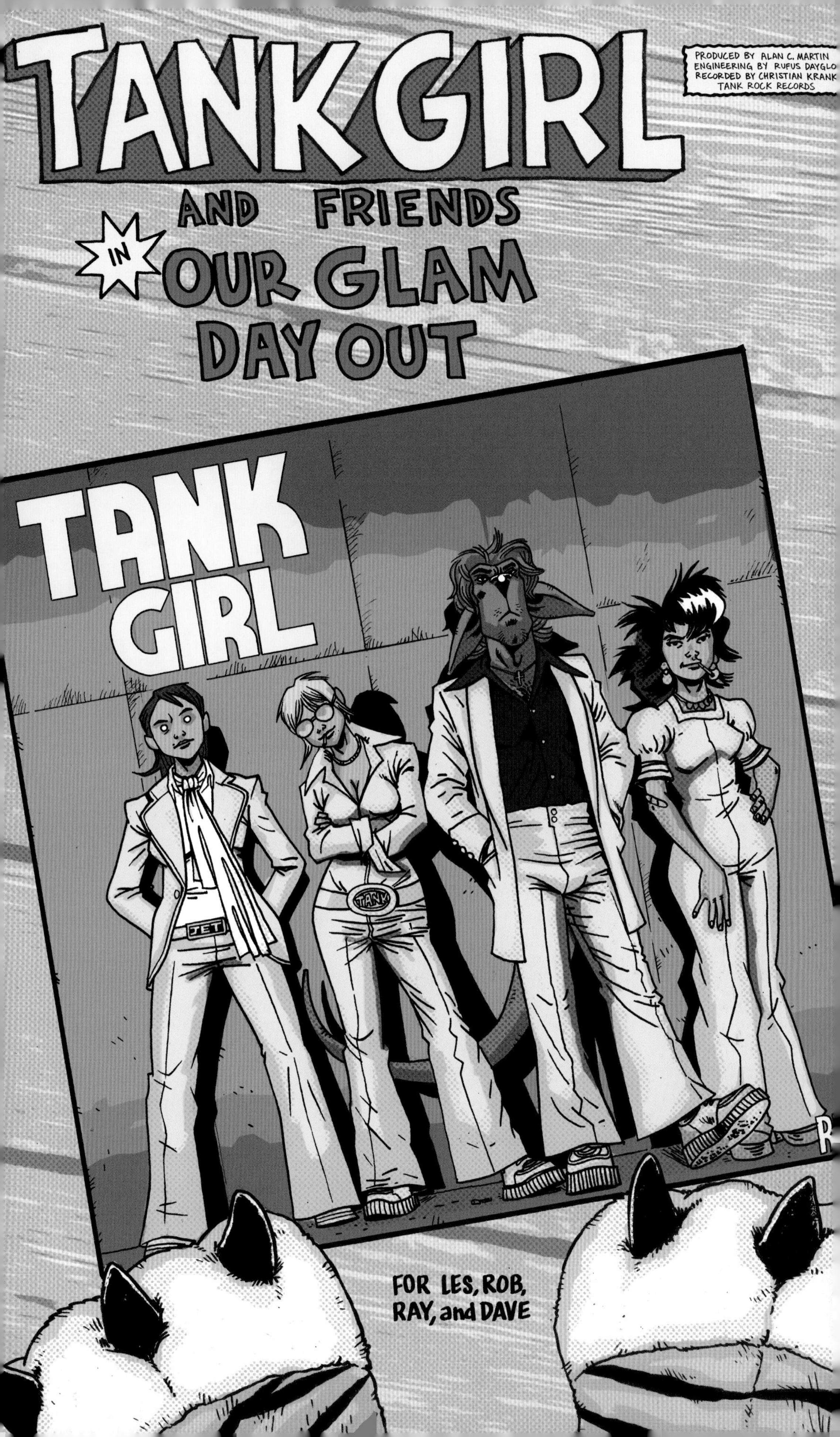
TANK GIRL
PRODUCED BY ALAN C. MARTIN
ENGINEERING BY RUFUS DAYGLO
RECORDED BY CHRISTIAN KRANK
TANK ROCK RECORDS
AND FRIENDS
IN
OUR GLAM
DAY OUT
TANK
GIRL
JET
TANK
FOR LES, ROB,
RAY, and DAVE

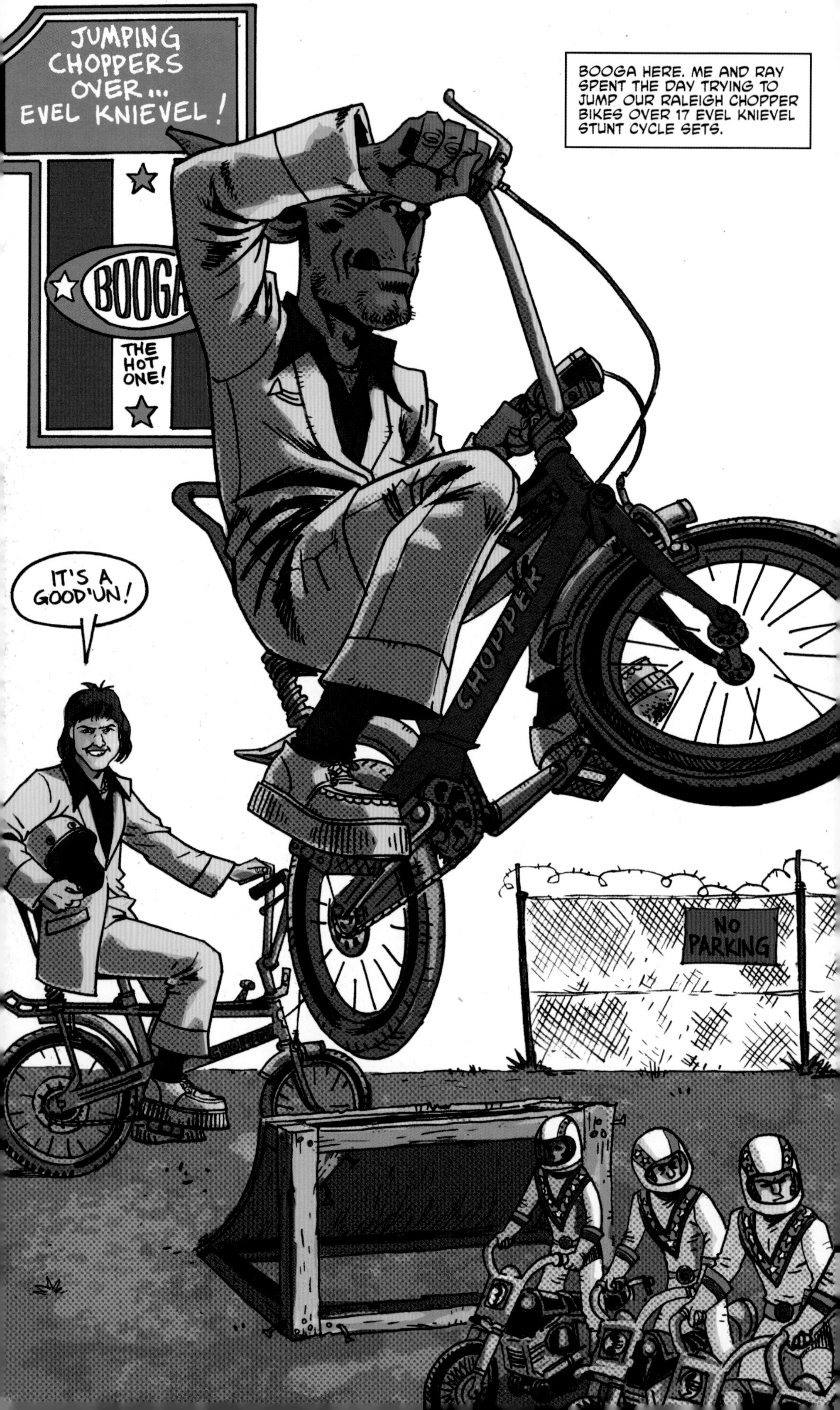
JUMPING CHOPPERS OVER... EVEL KNIEVEL!
BOOGA HERE. ME AND RAY SPENT THE DAY TRYING TO JUMP OUR RALEIGH CHOPPER BIKES OVER 17 EVEL KNIEVEL STUNT CYCLE SETS.
BOOGA
THE HOT ONE!
IT'S A GOOD'UN!
CHOPPER
NO PARKING

PUB LUNCH

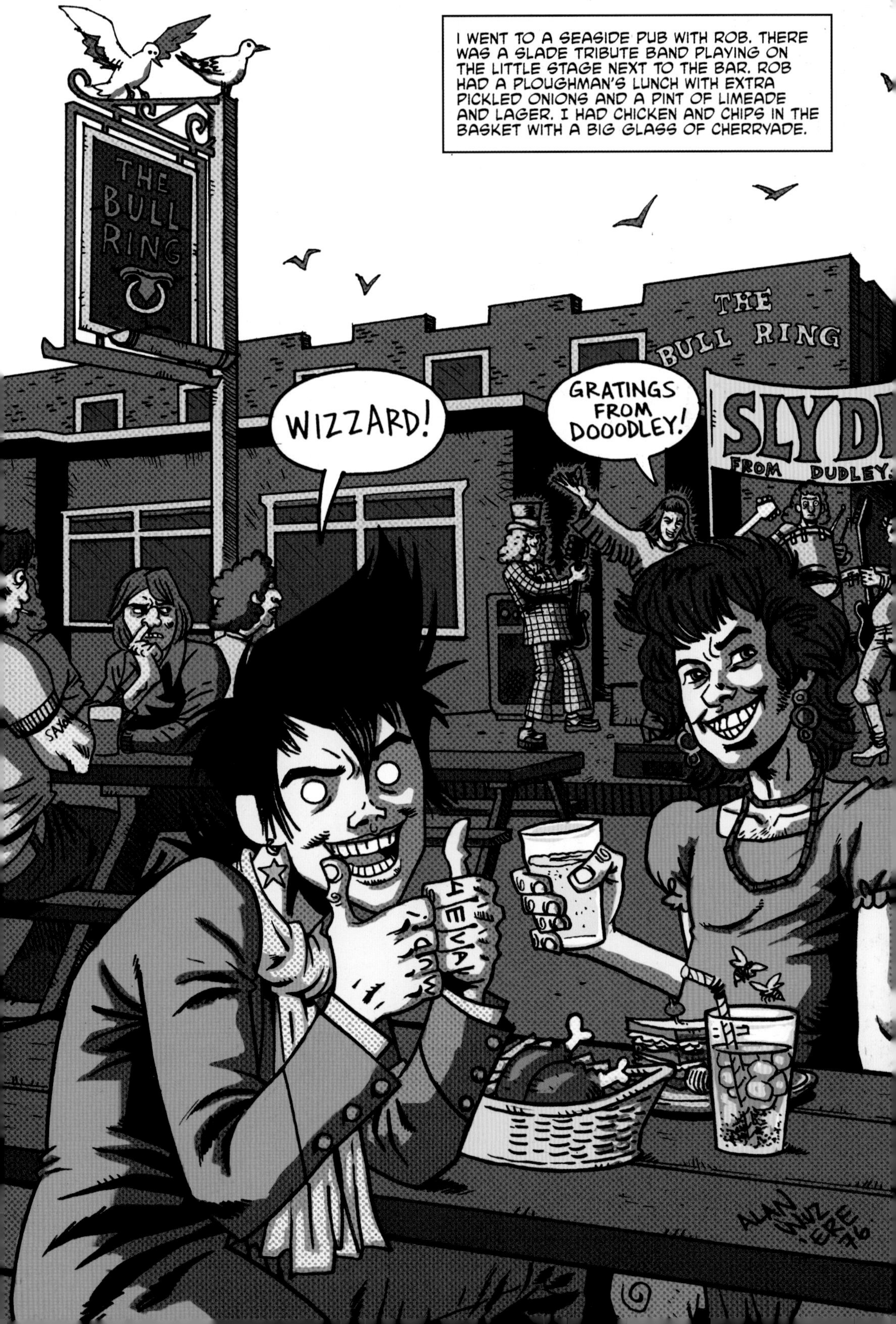
I WENT TO A SEASIDE PUB WITH ROB. THERE WAS A SLADE TRIBUTE BAND PLAYING ON THE LITTLE STAGE NEXT TO THE BAR. ROB HAD A PLOUGHMAN'S LUNCH WITH EXTRA PICKLED ONIONS AND A PINT OF LIMEADE AND LAGER. I HAD CHICKEN AND CHIPS IN THE BASKET WITH A BIG GLASS OF CHERRYADE.
THE BULL RING
THE BULL RING
SLYD
FROM DUDLEY
WIZZARD!
GRATINGS FROM DOOODLEY!

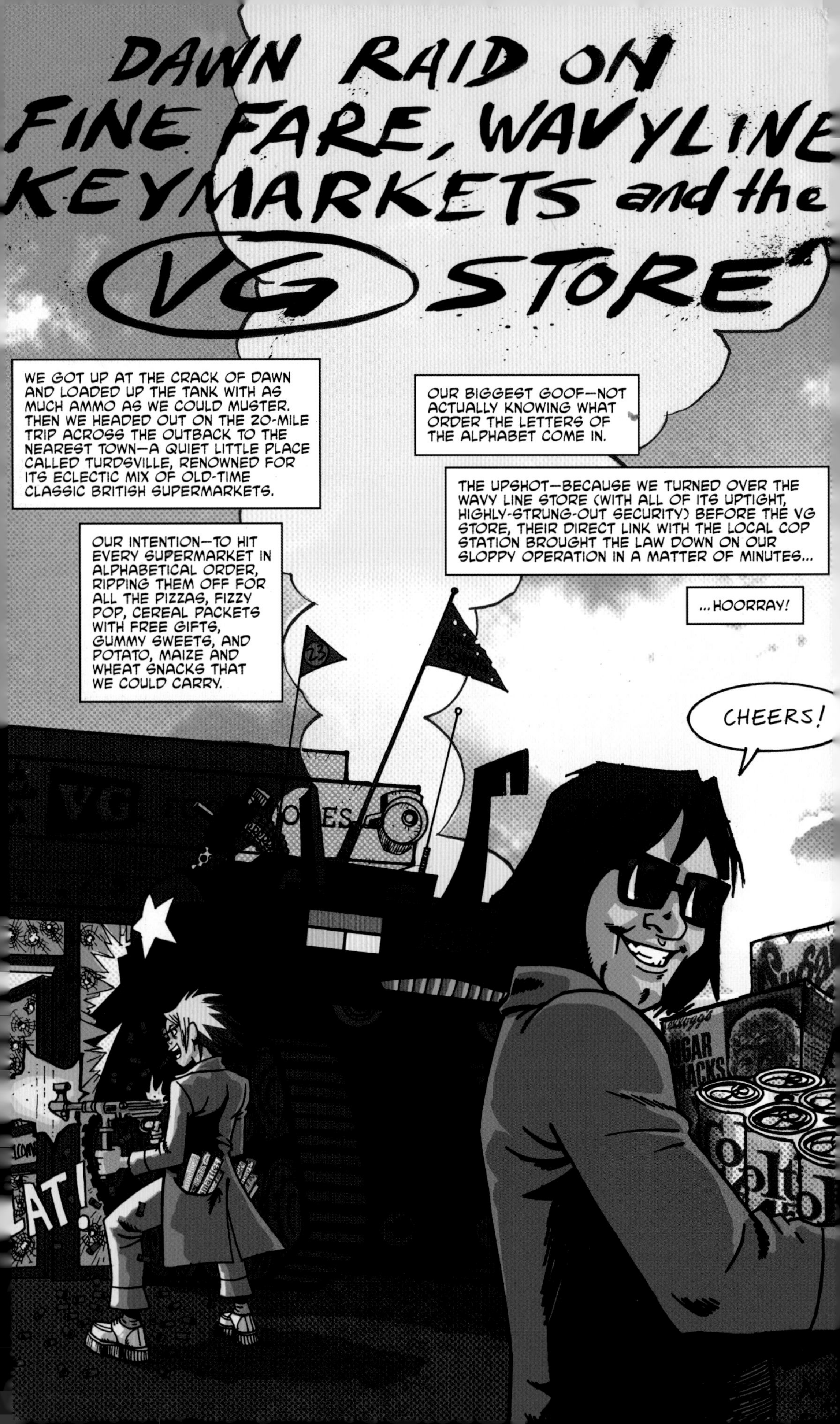
DAWN RAID ON FINE FARE, WAVYLINE KEYMARKETS and the VG STORE
WE GOT UP AT THE CRACK OF DAWN AND LOADED UP THE TANK WITH AS MUCH AMMO AS WE COULD MUSTER. THEN WE HEADED OUT ON THE 20-MILE TRIP ACROSS THE OUTBACK TO THE NEAREST TOWN—A QUIET LITTLE PLACE CALLED TURDSVILLE, RENOWNED FOR ITS ECLECTIC MIX OF OLD-TIME CLASSIC BRITISH SUPERMARKETS.
OUR INTENTION—TO HIT EVERY SUPERMARKET IN ALPHABETICAL ORDER, RIPPING THEM OFF FOR ALL THE PIZZAS, FIZZY POP, CEREAL PACKETS WITH FREE GIFTS, GUMMY SWEETS, AND POTATO, MAIZE AND WHEAT SNACKS THAT WE COULD CARRY.
OUR BIGGEST GOOF—NOT ACTUALLY KNOWING WHAT ORDER THE LETTERS OF THE ALPHABET COME IN.
THE UPSHOT—BECAUSE WE TURNED OVER THE WAVY LINE STORE (WITH ALL OF ITS UPTIGHT, HIGHLY-STRUNG-OUT SECURITY) BEFORE THE VG STORE, THEIR DIRECT LINK WITH THE LOCAL COP STATION BROUGHT THE LAW DOWN ON OUR SLOPPY OPERATION IN A MATTER OF MINUTES...
...HOORRAY!
CHEERS!
VG

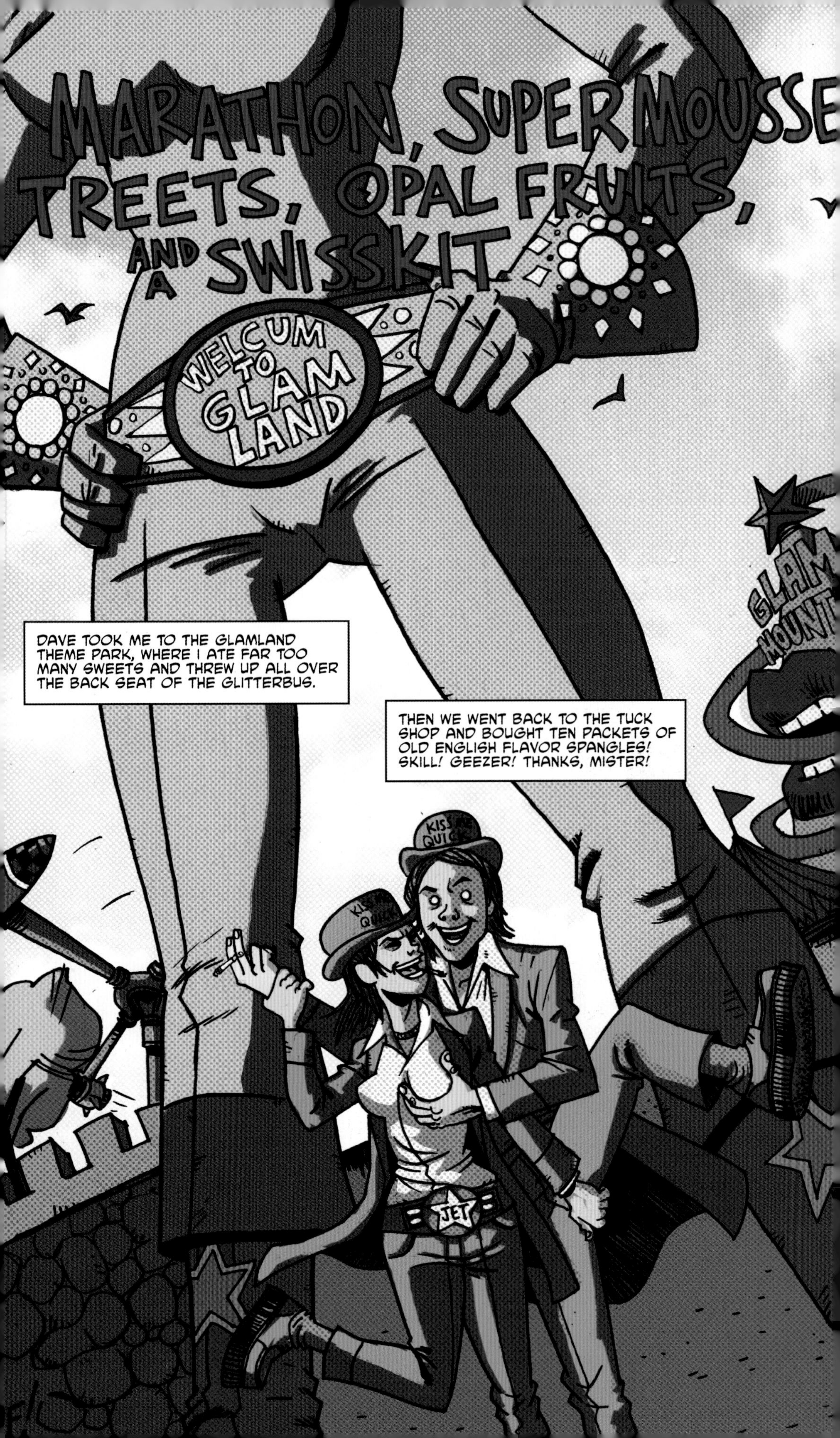
MARATHON, SUPERMOUSSE
TREETS, OPAL FRUITS,
AND A SWISSKIT.
WELCUM TO GLAM LAND
GLAM
DAVE TOOK ME TO THE GLAMLAND THEME PARK, WHERE I ATE FAR TOO MANY SWEETS AND THREW UP ALL OVER THE BACK SEAT OF THE GLITTERBUS.
THEN WE WENT BACK TO THE TUCK SHOP AND BOUGHT TEN PACKETS OF OLD ENGLISH FLAVOR SPANGLES! SKILL! GEEZER! THANKS, MISTER!
JET

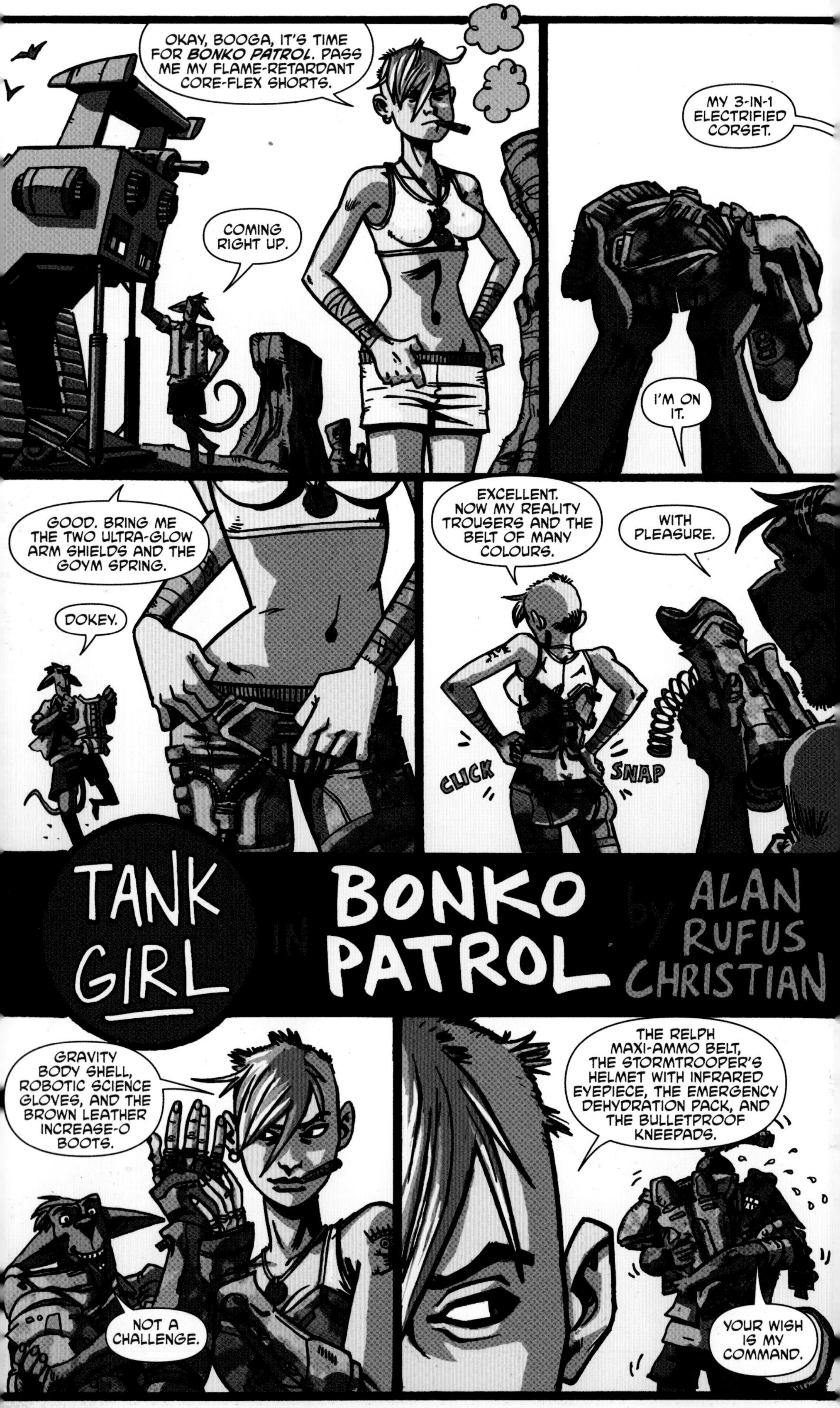
OKAY, BOOGA, IT'S TIME FOR BONKO PATROL. PASS ME MY FLAME-RETARDANT CORE-FLEX SHORTS.
COMING RIGHT UP.
MY 3-IN-1 ELECTRIFIED CORSET.
I'M ON IT.
GOOD. BRING ME THE TWO ULTRA-GLOW ARM SHIELDS AND THE GOYM SPRING.
DOKEY.
EXCELLENT. NOW MY REALITY TROUSERS AND THE BELT OF MANY COLOURS.
WITH PLEASURE.
CLICK
SNAP
TANK GIRL IN BONKO PATROL BY ALAN RUFUS CHRISTIAN
GRAVITY BODY SHELL, ROBOTIC SCIENCE GLOVES, AND THE BROWN LEATHER INCREASE-O BOOTS.
NOT A CHALLENGE.
THE RELPH MAXI-AMMO BELT, THE STORMTROOPER'S HELMET WITH INFRARED EYEPIECE, THE EMERGENCY DEHYDRATION PACK, AND THE BULLETPROOF KNEEPADS.
YOUR WISH IS MY COMMAND.

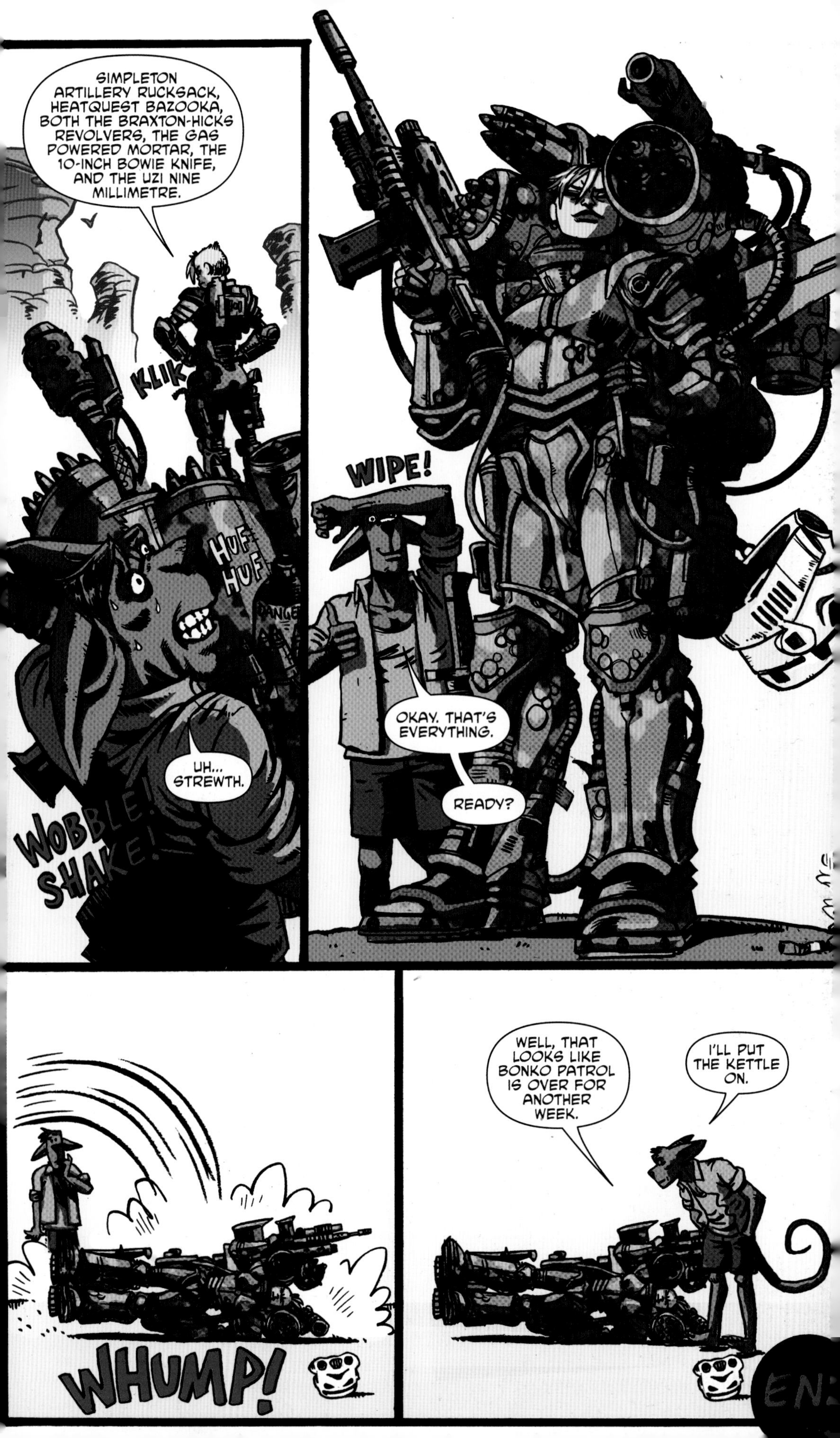
SIMPLETON ARTILLERY RUCKSACK, HEATQUEST BAZOOKA, BOTH THE BRAXTON-HICKS REVOLVERS, THE GAS POWERED MORTAR, THE 10-INCH BOWIE KNIFE, AND THE UZI NINE MILLIMETRE.
KLIK
HUF HUF
UH... STREWTH.
WOBBLE! SHAKE!
WIPE!
OKAY. THAT'S EVERYTHING.
READY?
WHUMP!
WELL, THAT LOOKS LIKE BONKO PATROL IS OVER FOR ANOTHER WEEK.
I'LL PUT THE KETTLE ON.

DIGGING THE LONELY ETERNITY

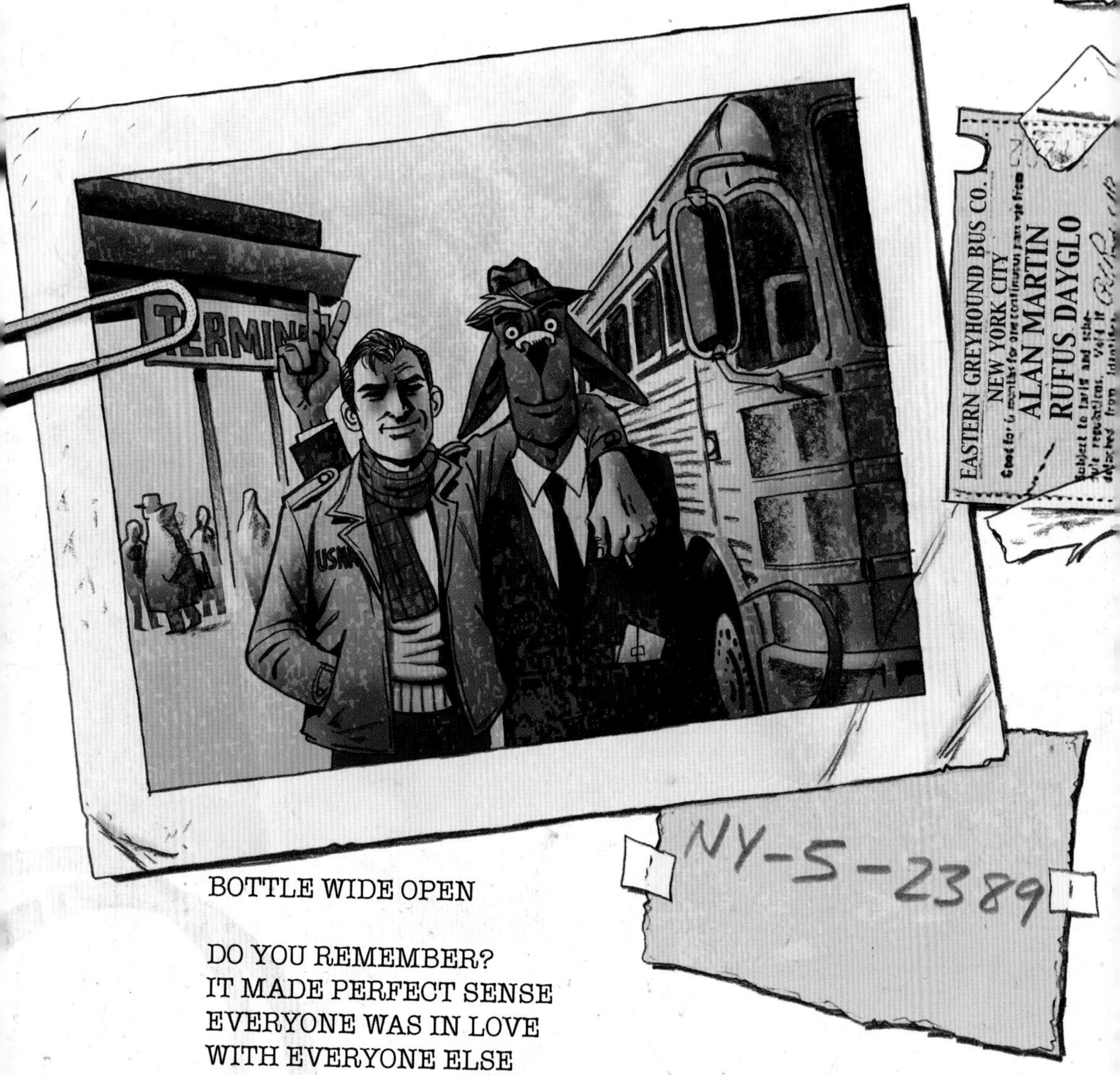
EASTERN GREYHOUND BUS CO.
NEW YORK CITY
ALAN MARTIN
RUFUS DAYGLO
NY-5-2389

BOTTLE WIDE OPEN

DO YOU REMEMBER?
IT MADE PERFECT SENSE
EVERYONE WAS IN LOVE
WITH EVERYONE ELSE
THE LIGHT SHONE DOWN
FROM THE EGG YOLK SUN
ONTO OUR STICKY BODIES
WE KISSED
AND PERSPIRED
ALL FOR ONE
AND ONE FOR ALL

HERE IT COMES AGAIN
I'VE CAPTURED IT IN A JAR
LIKE DUCHAMP'S BOTTLE OF PARIS AIR
I INTEND TO PULL OFF THE LID
AND FILL THE WORLD
WITH THE BEAUTY OF OUR HAPPY STENCH

STRAIGHT FROM THE BALLS

I'VE BEEN PUSHED
I'VE BEEN SHOVED
I'VE BEEN SHAT ON FROM ABOVE

I'VE BEEN BROKEN
LIKE A TOKEN
OF A LOVE THAT GOES UNSPOKEN

I'VE BEEN FOOLED
I'VE BEEN SWINDLED
MY POWER-PACK HAS DWINDLED

TRIED ESCAPE
FROM THIS SCHOOL
BASHED MY HEAD AGAINST THE WALL

I'M GIVING THIS TO YOU NOW

STRAIGHT FROM THE BALLS

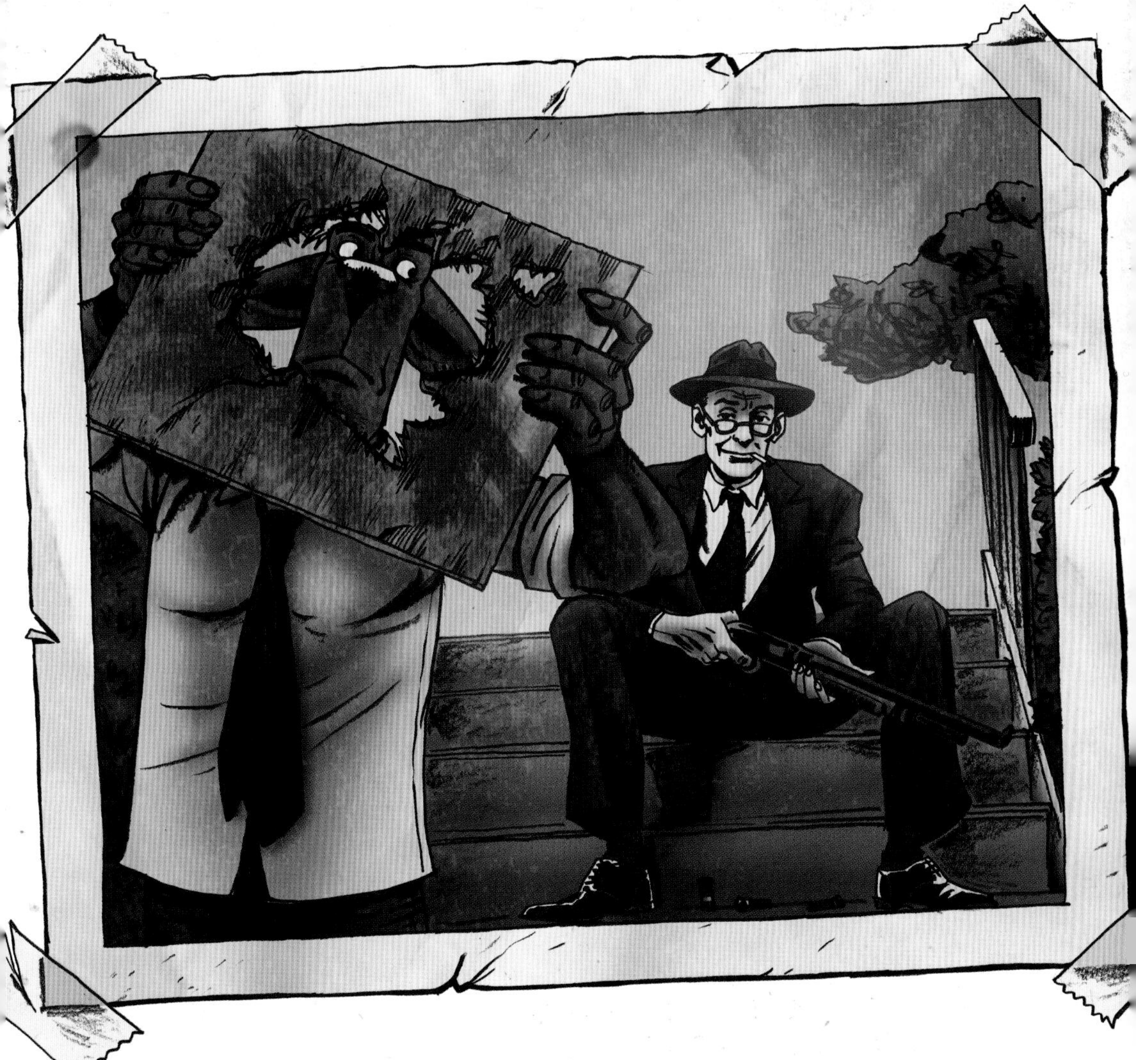

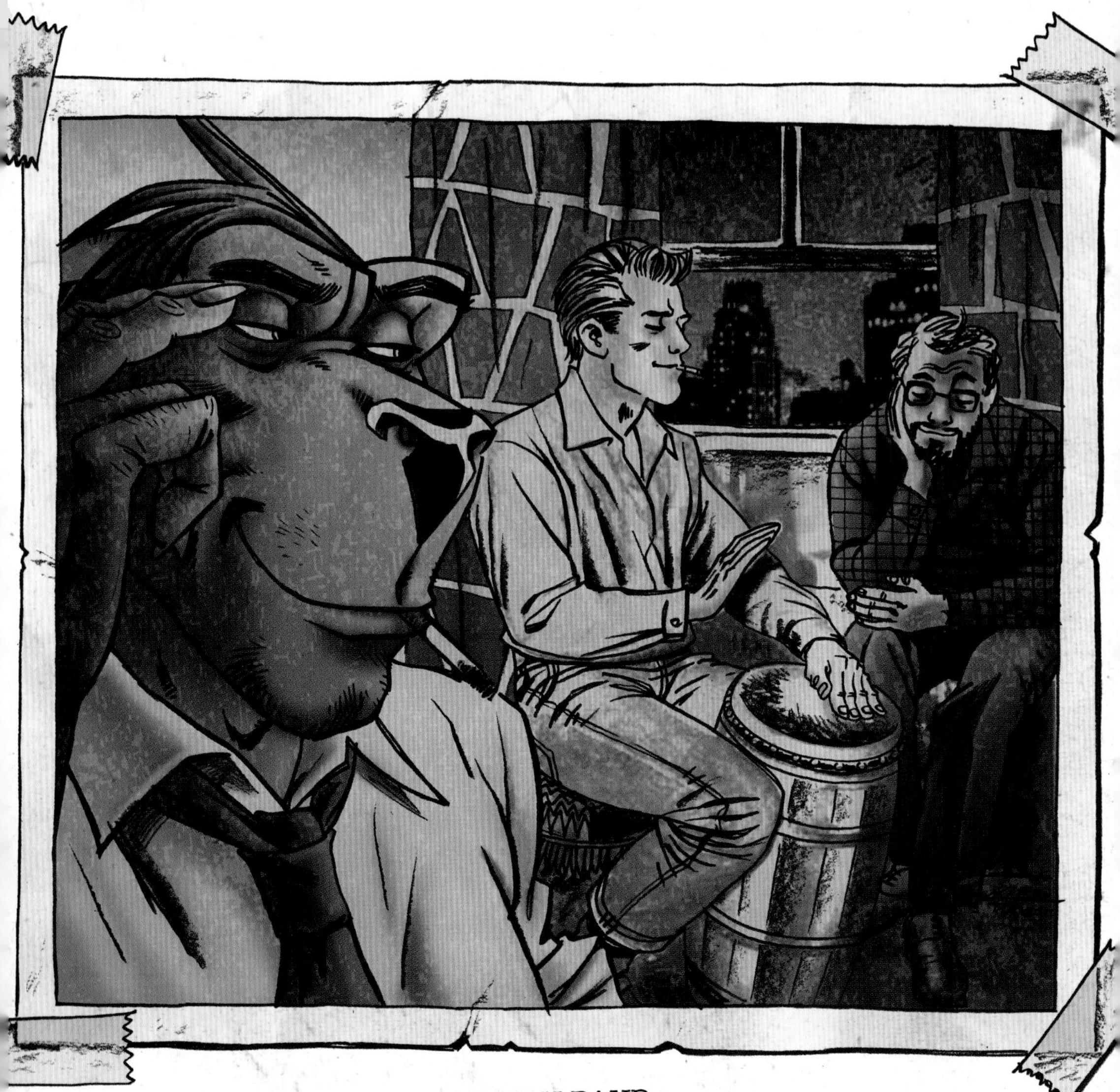

SUMMER IS A ONE-MAN-BAND

YOU'LL NEVER TRULY FIND YOURSELF
UNTIL YOU THE DAY YOU LOSE YOURSELF
ON A STREET WHERE YOU'VE NEVER BEEN
LEAVING YOUR SHOES ROUND SOMEONE'S HOUSE
SUCH A BLOODY HOT DAY
THE THIRST IN YOUR THROAT
CAN ONLY BE SATED
BY THE WORLD'S COLDEST BEER
IN THE WORLDS TALLEST GLASS
SERVED BY THE WORLD'S SWEETEST BARMAID
THE TWINKLE IN HER EYE
THE BRIGHTEST STAR IN THE SKY
ALPHA CENTAURI
JEANS COLLAPSE AROUND YOUR LEGS
FRAYING UNTO THE WIND
CRACKS APPEAR
IN THE DRY, DRY GROUND
YOUR ONE AND ONLY FRIEND

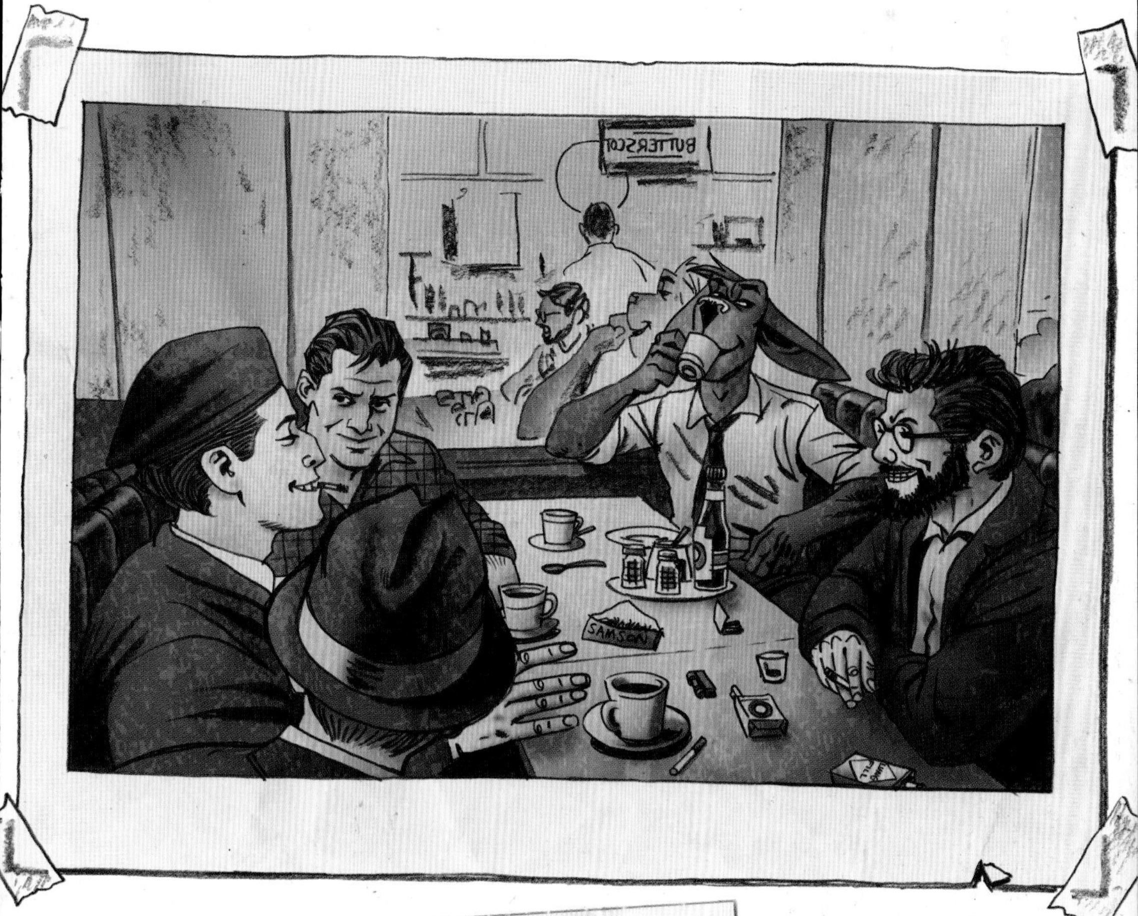
SAMSON

YOUR ORDER NUMBER
69

THE DEVIL AND THE DINOSAUR

THE DEVIL AND THE DINOSAUR
WERE OUT WALKING ON THE ROAD
SAID THE DEVIL TO THE DINOSAUR
"I'M GOING TO EXPLODE"

"NO PROBLEM" REPLIED THE DINOSAUR
"GO AHEAD AND BLOW UP RIGHT BY ME –
I'LL EXTINGUISH YOU IN AN INSTANT,
WITH A GIANT PREHISTORIC WEE"

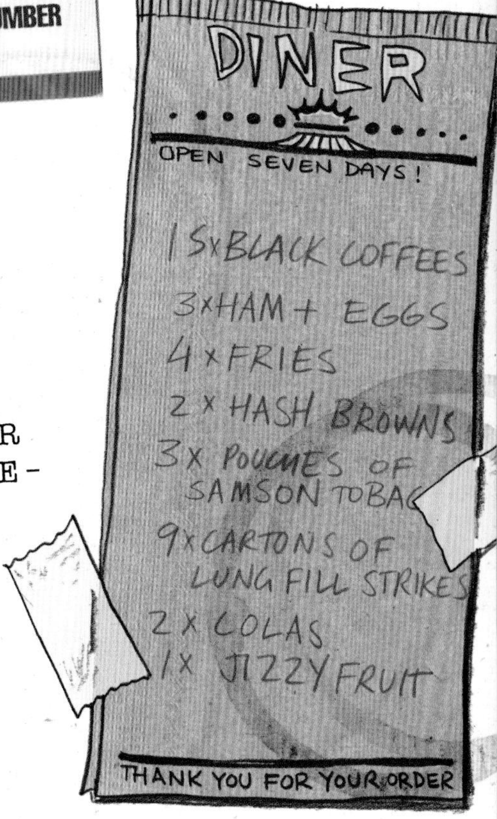
DINER
OPEN SEVEN DAYS!
15 x BLACK COFFEES
3 x HAM + EGGS
4 x FRIES
2 x HASH BROWNS
3 x POUCHES OF SAMSON TOBAC
9 x CARTONS OF LUNG FILL STRIKES
2 x COLAS
1 x JIZZY FRUIT
THANK YOU FOR YOUR ORDER

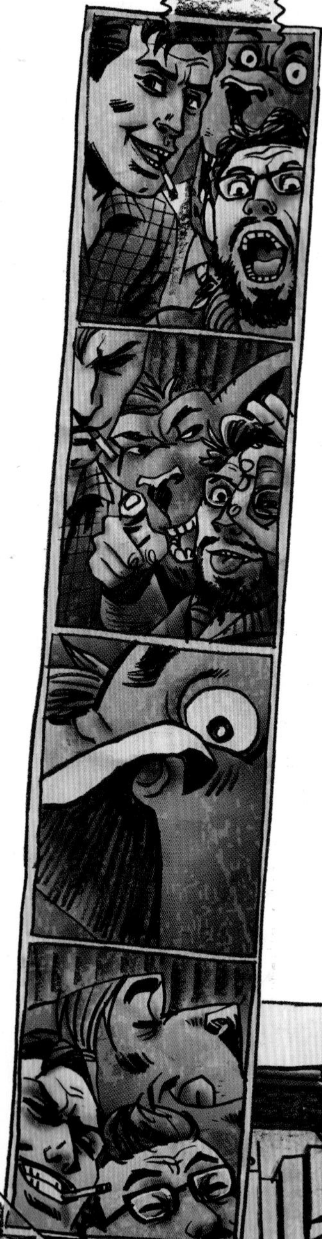

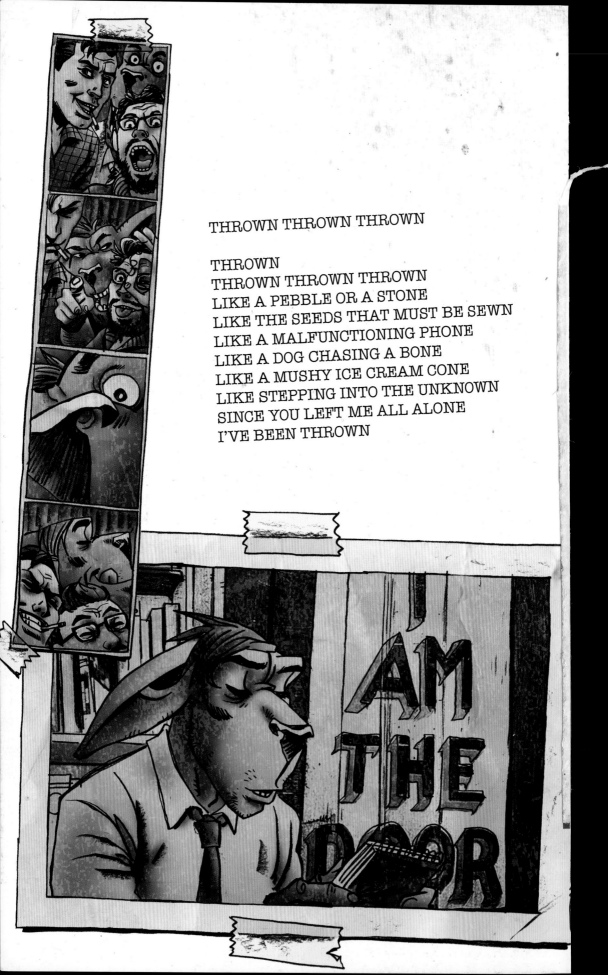

THROWN THROWN THROWN

THROWN
THROWN THROWN THROWN
LIKE A PEBBLE OR A STONE
LIKE THE SEEDS THAT MUST BE SEWN
LIKE A MALFUNCTIONING PHONE
LIKE A DOG CHASING A BONE
LIKE A MUSHY ICE CREAM CONE
LIKE STEPPING INTO THE UNKNOWN
SINCE YOU LEFT ME ALL ALONE
I'VE BEEN THROWN

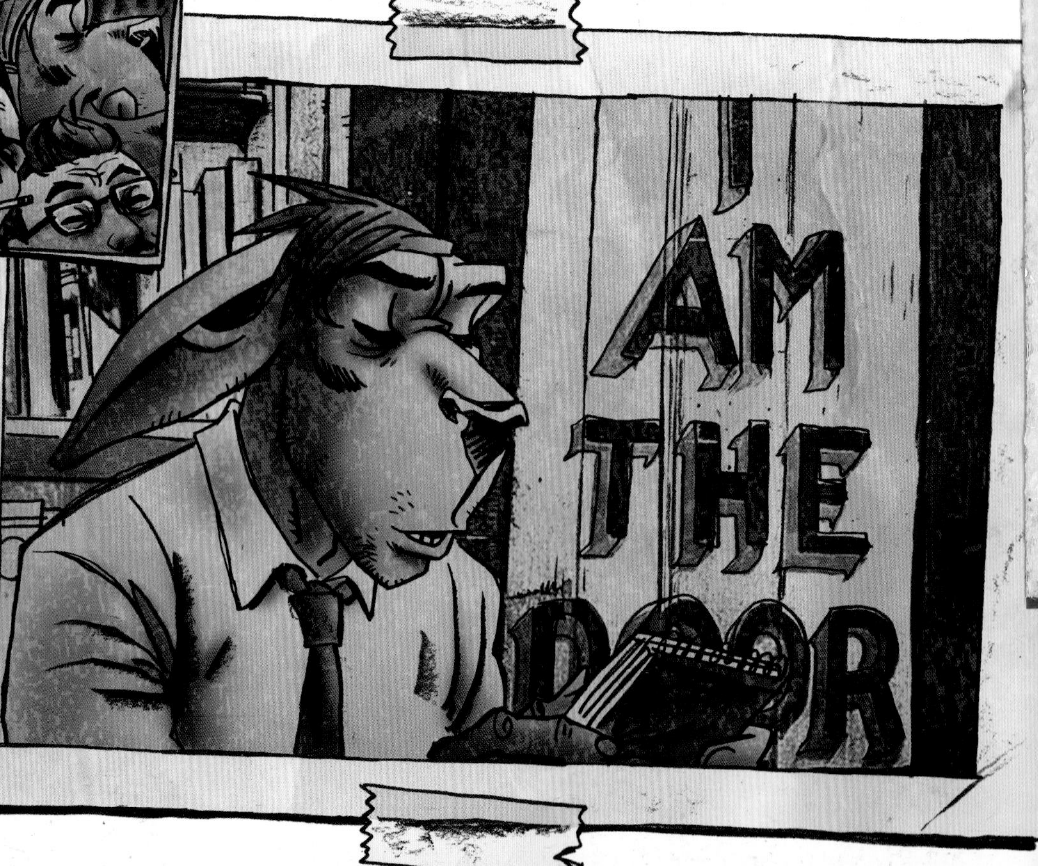
I AM THE DOOR

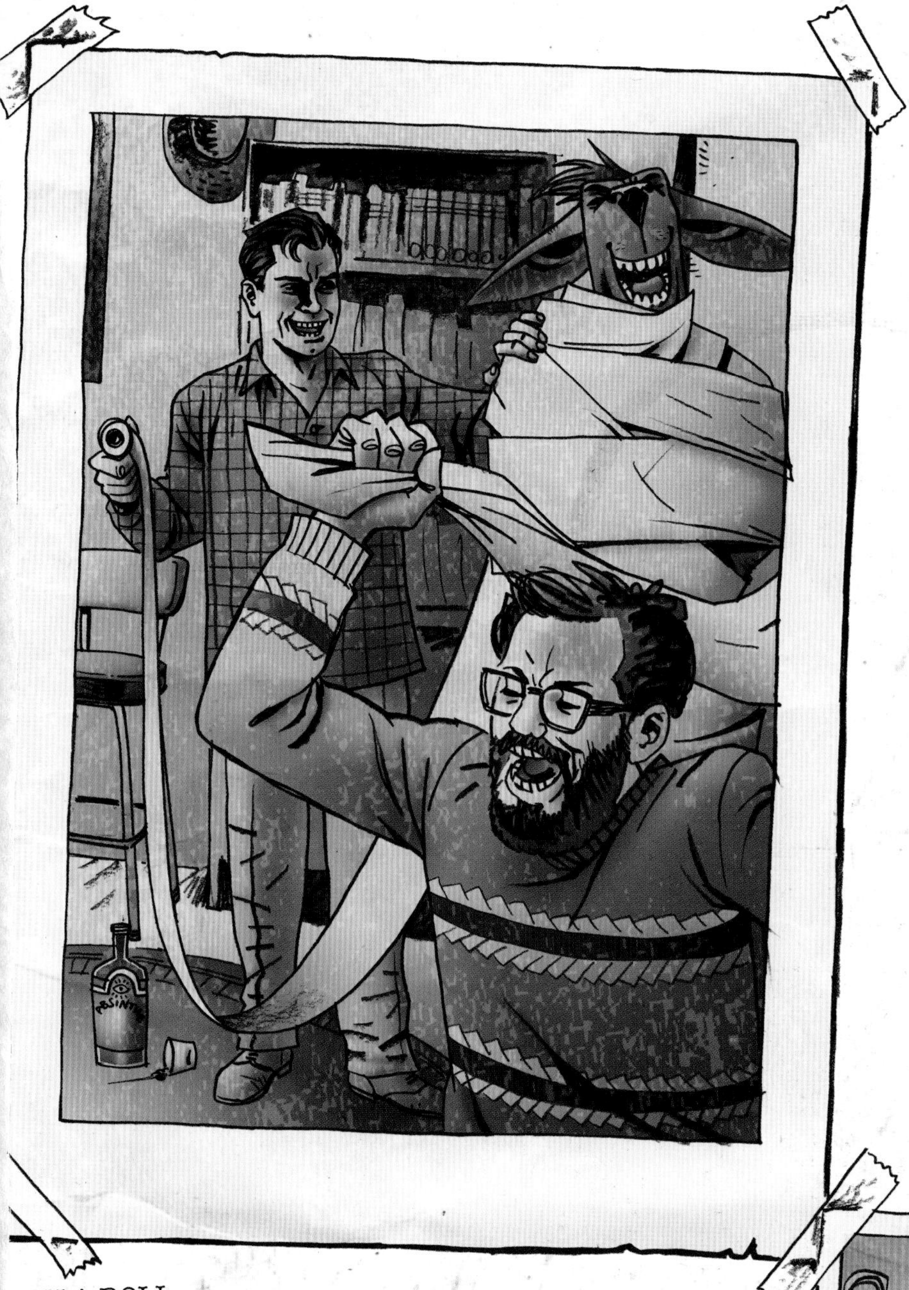

ON A ROLL

I USED A CONTINUOUS ROLL OF PAPER
TO GET MY IDEAS DOWN
TWELVE INCHES WIDE AND THIRTY FOOT LONG
TEN THOUSAND ADJECTIVES, VERBS AND NOUNS

I USED A TYPEWRITER AND A PENCIL
TO CONVERT MY SOUL INTO TEXT
IT DRIPPED FROM MY CHIN AND SEEPED OUT MY SKIN
THROUGH THE HOLES IN MY STRING VEST

I USED A ROLL OF TOILET PAPER
TO FINISH WHAT I HAD TO SAY
YOU READ IT IN ONE AND THEN WIPED YOUR BUM
AND YOU FLUSHED MY MEMORIES AWAY

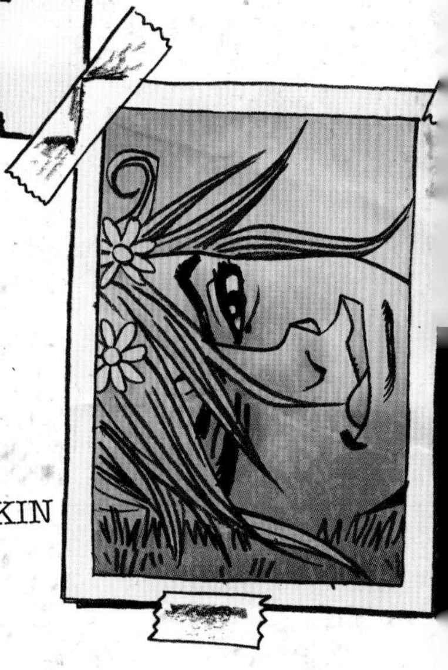

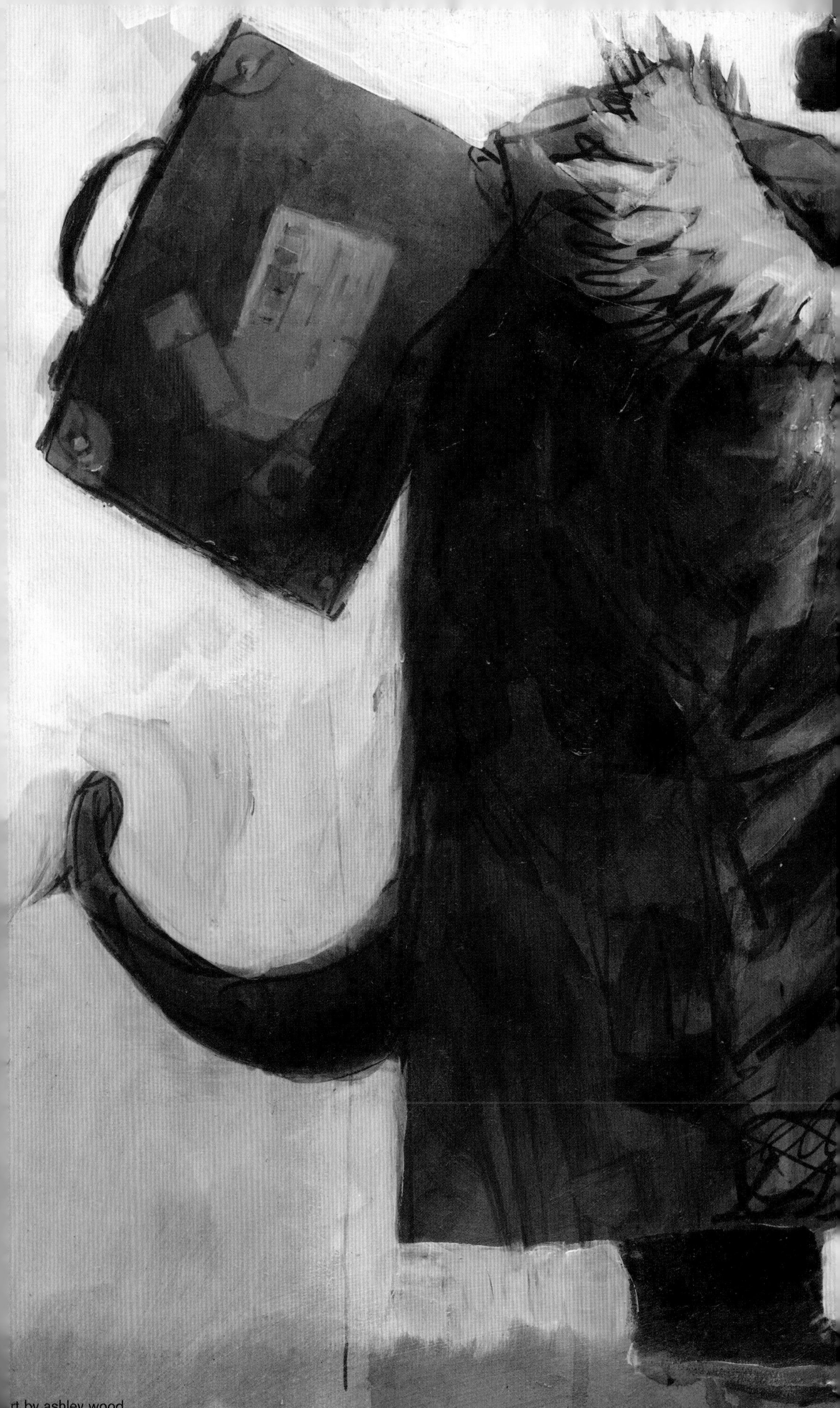

art by ashley wood

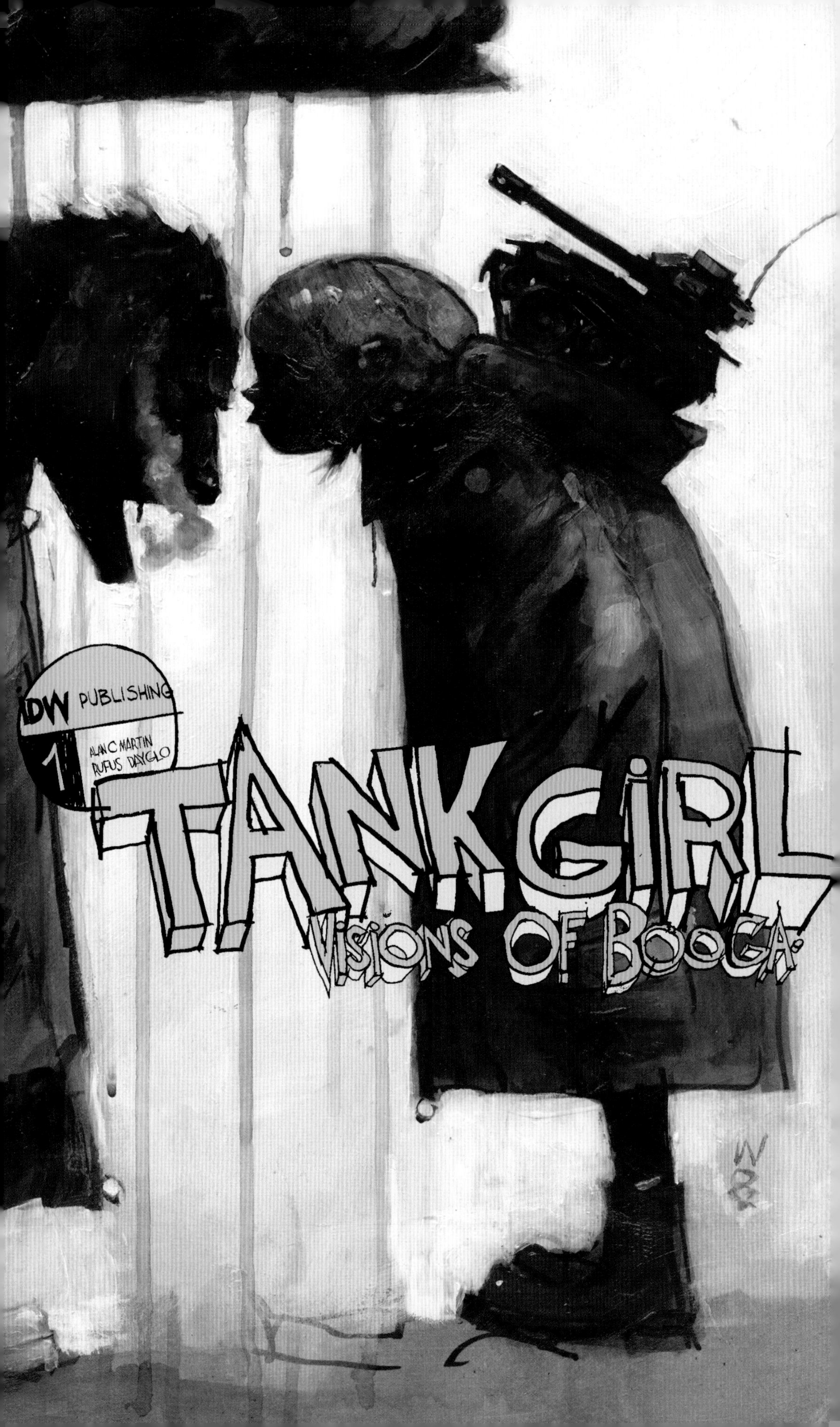
IDW PUBLISHING
1
ALAN C MARTIN
RUFUS DAYGLO
TANK GIRL
VISIONS OF BOOGA

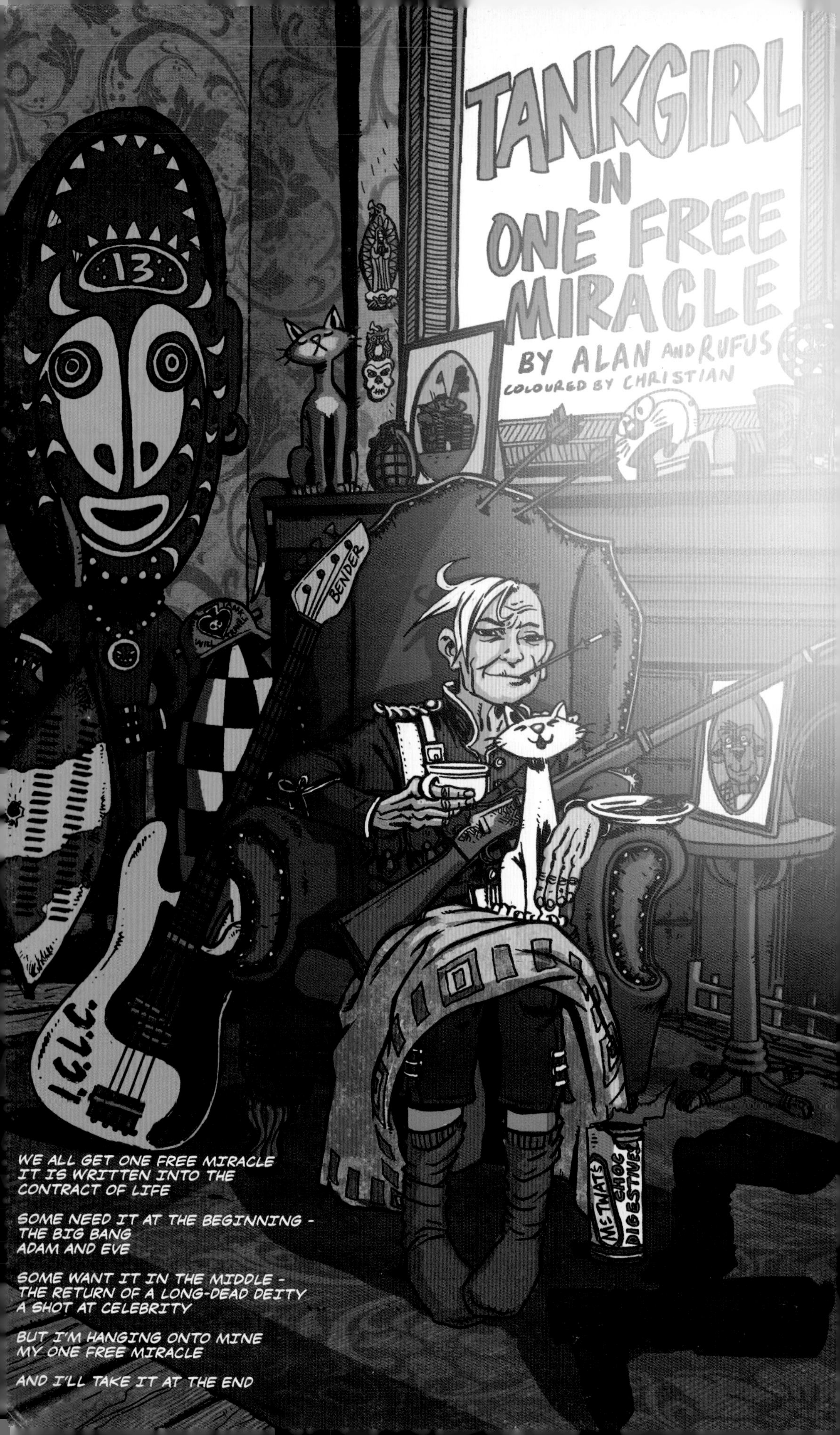
TANKGIRL
IN
ONE FREE
MIRACLE
BY ALAN AND RUFUS
COLOURED BY CHRISTIAN
13
BENDER
I.C.L.C.
McTWATS
CHOC
DIGESTIVES
WE ALL GET ONE FREE MIRACLE
IT IS WRITTEN INTO THE
CONTRACT OF LIFE

SOME NEED IT AT THE BEGINNING -
THE BIG BANG
ADAM AND EVE

SOME WANT IT IN THE MIDDLE -
THE RETURN OF A LONG-DEAD DEITY
A SHOT AT CELEBRITY

BUT I'M HANGING ONTO MINE
MY ONE FREE MIRACLE

AND I'LL TAKE IT AT THE END